D1615182

# ALL STRANGERS HERE

*100 Years of Personal Writing from the Irish Foreign Service*

**An Roinn Gnóthaí Eachtracha**
Department of Foreign Affairs

Angela Byrne
Ragnar Deeney Almqvist
Helena Nolan
*Editors*

# ALL STRANGERS HERE

*100 Years of Personal Writing from the Irish Foreign Service*

ARLEN
HOUSE

ALL STRANGERS HERE:
*100 Years of Personal Writing from the Irish Foreign Service*

is published in 2021 by
ARLEN HOUSE
42 Grange Abbey Road
Baldoyle, Dublin 13, Ireland
Phone: 00 353 86 8360236
www.arlenhouse.ie

978–1–85132–248–0

Distributed internationally by
SYRACUSE UNIVERSITY PRESS
621 Skytop Road, Suite 110
Syracuse, NY 13244–5290
Phone: 315–443–5534 supress@syr.edu
syracuseuniversitypress.syr.edu

Cover illustration by Paula McGloin

# CONTENTS

This book is dedicated to
Kate Slattery and Eavan Boland,
gone too soon,
and to all those who before,
now, and in the future

*'each day, pitch camp farther from their birthplace,
those who, each day, hail in their boat on other banks'*

– Denis Devlin

Wanderlust infected me, as it had the medieval monks I read about – like them, I longed to get out of Ireland and see the world, to live in some other country, although not for the same reasons.

– Éilís Ní Dhuibhne,
*Twelve Thousand Days: A Memoir of Love and Loss*
(Blackstaff Press, 2018), p. 11.

# ACKNOWLEDGEMENTS

This project enjoyed the support of colleagues in the Department of Foreign Affairs, particularly Secretary General Niall Burgess, who had the original vision for the book. The co-editors and reference group had expert input from DFA colleagues Gerard Keown, Eugene Downes, and Ciarán Kelleher Byrne, and the administrative support of Jill Corish and Emma McLoughlin. Éilís Ní Dhuibhne gave generously of her time, including to advise on Irish-language texts.

Thanks to Frank Callanan SC for sharing his knowledge of Conor Cruise O'Brien's publications, and to Maureen Kennelly and Michael Kennedy for advice and support in the early stages of the project. Thanks also to those colleagues, friends and family members of authors who helped to source and track down material.

Finally, we are grateful to the authors, estates, publishers and rights holders who granted permission for the republication of the pieces collected in this volume. Every effort was made to trace the correct rights holder for each piece, but we will be glad to be informed of any errors or omissions by contacting Culture Unit, Department of Foreign Affairs, 79–80 St Stephen's Green South, Dublin 2, Ireland.

## Niall Burgess
*Secretary General, Department of Foreign Affairs*

Throughout its first century, the Irish Civil Service has sheltered many fine writers. For some, it provided a reliable income and whiled away the hours between bursts of creativity. For others, their official and personal writing lives were inseparable – though it would be hard to surpass the pride in his profession proclaimed by the British poet CH Sisson who described himself as 'primarily a civil servant – like Chaucer'.

During the decade from 1960, Thomas Kinsella worked at the Department of Finance, Máirtín Ó Direáin at the Department of Education, Dennis O'Driscoll at the Revenue Commissioners and Máire Mhac an tSaoi, Conor Cruise O'Brien and Valentin Iremonger at the Department of External Affairs. Over at the Department of Local Government Richard Power worked at a desk previously occupied by Brian O'Nolan, prompting his wife Ann to remark that the Civil Service 'must have been the biggest patron of the arts since the Medici'.

Sometimes, personal poetic rivalries amplified deeper departmental rivalries. The wrong-headed and time-honoured view of the Diplomatic Service from within the Department of Finance – that we are more style than substance – found its literary expression in Thomas Kinsella's description of Valentin Iremonger:

> You were raven-quiffed and tall
> and smiling above us in public,
> formal and at ease. Established.
> Introducing I have forgotten what.

Some of the most important and influential texts crafted in the Department of Foreign Affairs are not in this anthology. The foundational texts of the Irish peace process – the Anglo-Irish Agreement, Downing Street Declaration and Good Friday Agreement – are more than diplomatic and legal texts. They are exercises in the precise and imaginative use of language to span a difference, reveal something shared or even to inspire. The same could be said of the 'Irish Resolutions' at the United Nations, which led to the Treaty on the Non-Proliferation of Nuclear Weapons – still the cornerstone of the nuclear non-proliferation regime.

To a great extent the official documents so superbly collected and edited by the Royal Irish Academy are also absent. If the Academy's *Documents on Irish Foreign Policy* are unlikely page-turners, that is due in large part to the quality of the writing, often vivid and compelling.

What this volume *does* reveal, for the first time in one place, is the rich hinterland of personal, creative and reflective writing that has nourished official word-craft at the Department of Foreign Affairs.

While some public servants bring their work home, those who serve overseas reverse that process and bring their families to work. That life was a formative influence on writers from Maeve Brennan to Eavan Boland and it seems appropriate to reflect this dimension in the writing selected here.

The idea for this anthology was born on a winter's night in a Dublin pub. That it progressed so far is due mainly to those who walked out into that night with a clear belief in its value and a dogged determination to make it happen. The editors won't thank themselves but I do.

For as diplomacy evolves new forms, digital and technological, words will always be its very fabric.

# RÉAMHRÁ

## Niall Burgess
### *Ard-Rúnaí, An Roinn Gnóthaí Eachtracha*

Ó bunaíodh é, le céad bliain anuas thug Státseirbhís na hÉireann tearmann do mhórchuid scríbhneoirí fiúntacha. Do roinnt acu, seans gur thug an tSeirbhís teacht isteach rialta, agus caitheamh aimsire, mar a déarfá, idir babhtaí cruthaitheacha. Agus do dhaoine eile, ní raibh deighilt ar bith idir an saol pearsanta agus an dualgas oifigiúil. Bhfuil sárú ar an an ráiteas a thug an file Sasanach, CH Sisson, uaigh, a léiríonn chomh bródúil a bhí sé as a ghairm, chuir sé síos air féin mar 'primarily a civil servant – like Chaucer'.

Chaith Thomas Kinsella deich mbliana, ó 1960, ag obair sa Roinn Airgeadais. Bhí Máirtín Ó Direáin sa Roinn Oideachais, Dennis O'Driscoll leis na Coimisinéirí Ioncaim, agus Máire Mhac an tSaoi, Conor Cruise O'Brien, and Valentin Iremonger, sa Roinn Gnóthaí Eachtracha. Thall ins an Roinn Rialtais Áitiúil bhí Richard Power ag obair ag an deasc ina bhíodh Brian Ó Nualláin ag obair lá den tsaol, comhtharlú a spreag a bhean chéile, Ann, chun magadh gurbh é a bhí sa Státseirbhís ná 'the biggest patron of the arts since the Medici.'

Anois is arís baineadh úsáid as bua na filíochta chun faobhar a chur ar an iomaíocht a bhíonn ann idir ranna an stáit. Mar shampla, tá dearcadh seanbhunaithe sa Roinn Airgeadais go bhfuilimid, sa Roinn Gnóthaí Eachtracha, níos dírithe ar an deilbh seachas an damhna – rud nach bhfuil fírinne ar bith ag baint leis. Chuir Thomas Kinsella dreach liteartha ar an tuairim seo ina chur síos ar Valentin Iremonger:

You were raven-quiffed and tall
And smiling above us in public,

Formal and at ease. Established
Introducing I have forgotten what.

Mar a tharlaíonn, níl cuid de na téacsanna is tábhachtaí a scríobhadh sa Roinn Gnóthaí Eachtracha sa chnuasach seo. Mar ní foláir a lua nach cáipéisí dlíthiúla agus taidhleoireachta amháin atá i dtéacsanna bhunaidh phroiséas síochána na hÉireann An Comhaontú Angla-Éireannach, Dearbhú Shráid Downing, Comhaontú Aoine an Chéasta, ach scríbhinní galánta a bhaineann úsáid as stíl bheacht agus cruthaitheach d'aon ghnó chun teacht timpeall ar achrann, comhthuiscint a léiriú, nó fiú chun spreagadh a thabhairt. Litríocht atá sna téacsanna seo. Agus d'fhéadfaí an rud céanna a rá faoi 'Irish Resolutions' ag na Náisiúin Aontaithe, a spreag an Conradh Neamhiomadú Armán Núicléach – bunachar an fheachtais ar son neamhiomadú núicléach.

Den chuid is mó, níl na doiciméidí oifigiúla atá bailithe agus eagraithe ag Acadamh Ríoga na hÉireann ar fáil ins an chnuasach seo. Tá siadsan foilsithe i Documents on Irish Foreign Policy, agus más rud é nach ropleabhar atá san imleabhar áirithe sin, is ar ardchaighdeán na scríbhneoireachta atá an locht, bríomhar agus tarraingteach mar atá sé.

Ach séard a léiríonn an t-imleabhar seo ná an cúlra atá ag an scríbhneoireacht oifigiúil sin – stórchiste litríochta agus scríbhneoireachta pearsanta, cruthaitheach, agus athmhachnamhach, a chothaíonn an chruthaitheacht oifigiúil.

Tá sé de nós ag státseirbhísigh áirithe a gcuid oibre a thabhairt abhaile leo. Déanann oifigigh ár Roinne a mhalairt, agus tógann siad an teaghlach ar fad leo go dtí an t-ionad oibre thar lear. Mar sin, bhí tionchar nach beag ag saol an taidhleora ar leithéidí Maeve Brennan agus Eavan Boland, agus a lán eile a bhí i dteaghlach taidhleora – agus is cuí go bhfuil an ghné sin dár eispéireas speisialta á léiriú ins an bhailiúchán seo.

Tháinig an smaoineamh le haghaidh an chnuasaigh dos na heagarthóirí oíche áirithe gheimhridh i dteach tábhairne i mBaile Átha Cliath. Tá moladh tuillte acu toisc nár scaoileadar leis an smaoineamh maith sin ach gur leanadar leo go díograiseach go dtí go raibh an aisling curtha i gcrích. Dian-obair. Gabhaim buíochas leo aisti.

Tá an taidhleoireacht de shíor ag forbairt agus ag athrú, ag baint úsáid as modhanna nua digiteacha agus teicniúla. Ach beidh ár gceird i gcónaí bunaithe ar rud amháin: na focail.

# ALL STRANGERS HERE

*100 Years of Personal Writing from the Irish Foreign Service*

# Introduction

*Angela Byrne, Ragnar Deeney Almqvist,*
*Éilís Ní Dhuibhne, Helena Nolan*

Words matter. The astute use of language has always been vital for the conduct of relationships – business, personal, diplomatic – and the soft skills of communication, persuasion and negotiation are essential in the kit of all diplomats. In diplomacy, words are our raw materials, our tools and our end product; a negotiation can turn on the use of the indefinite article and a good sentence can save a life, or in the case of international peace agreements and disarmament treaties, many, many lives.

Diplomacy attracts writers. Until very recently, the entrance exam for Third Secretaries/Junior Diplomats in the Department of Foreign Affairs included a handwritten test, and a facility with language, including foreign languages, remains a key requirement when applying for the job. Small wonder, then, that so many of our diplomats have a flair for words and can deliver a pithy turn of phrase, as evidenced in the letters and reporting captured in the Royal Irish Academy's *Documents in Irish Foreign Policy* series.

This anthology is concerned with another type of writing, by officials of the Department and family members who have accompanied them on posting overseas. It is an attempt to showcase some of the more personal, imaginative and creative writing by these women and men, thereby opening a window on their interior life. We hope that this selection of work will take the reader behind the scenes and provide a glimpse between the lines of history, complementing the recent publication on the first 100 years of the Department – *Ireland: A Voice Among the Nations* (Royal Irish Academy, 2019) – and that it will contribute to the understanding of the role and the life of those who work in diplomacy and the critical importance of their words.

Since the birth of modern diplomacy in the eighteenth century, diplomats have been required to record their observations and experiences in official reports, usually not for sharing outside government circles. From the mid-nineteenth century, many began publishing their experiences and observations for a wider readership, tapping into the massive public appetite for first-hand accounts of exotic destinations and world-changing events. So, too, with Irish diplomats in the century since the establishment of our own foreign service. In the earliest days of Dáil Éireann's embryonic diplomatic corps (1919–22), writing skills were highly valued as representatives in Madrid, Paris and Berlin were charged with drumming up international support and recognition for the new Irish State through news bulletins. The trials and tribulations of the early decades of the Irish foreign service are illustrated in Gerard Keown and Niall Keogh's detailed accounts of day-to-day life and the challenges posed by early official events.

Over subsequent decades, Irish diplomats demonstrated how personal experiences inform and enrich understandings of international events and intercultural relations. Daniel Binchy drew on his formative experiences as a student in Germany when he was posted to Berlin. The depth of his knowledge of the country and its history shines through in his startlingly prescient observations on the rise of Adolf Hitler, published in 1933. More recently, Piaras Mac Éinrí's autobiographical reflections on British-Irish relations are a reminder of the enduring influences of early experiences – and even of early instilled prejudices – on interlocutors. First-hand experiences and personal reflections on events of international importance are a particular strength of the non-fiction pieces collected here. Robert Brennan's recollections of tensions between Ireland

and the USA during the Second World War are a reminder that when it came to patrolling Ireland's coastline in the early 1940s, Dublin's eyes were not only on Berlin, but also on London. Noel Dorr provides a behind-the-scenes look at the terrible events at Jadotville and the Congo in 1961, from the perspective of a young, trainee diplomat flung into the realities of Ireland's first participation in a UN peacekeeping mission. Joe Hayes's reflections on the Chernobyl disaster provide wry and poignant insights into the realities of diplomatic service and its potential impacts on personal safety and family life. More recently, Sinead Walsh's experience of on-the-ground crisis management during the West African Ebola outbreak of 2014 reflects Ireland's ongoing important role in development and aid work in the global south and resonates with our present pandemic experience.

As a whole, the non-fiction pieces collected in this volume are a reminder that diplomacy is, at its core, a set of relationships in which personal factors play a key role. In the writing of Eóin MacWhite, this takes the shape of a deep appreciation and knowledge of Irish and European history, literature, and archaeology that cast intercultural relations within their specific historical contexts. Dan Mulhall's account of the visit of Queen Victoria to Dublin in 1900 unveils the complexity of private views on an event of national political significance. In Bobby McDonagh's and Mary Whelan's essays, interpersonal relationships take centre stage and we are reminded of the human investment of personal reputations, energy, and emotional labour that lies behind every international treaty and campaign. But nowhere is the connection between the private and the public more unflinchingly expressed than in Máire Cruise O'Brien (Mhac an tSaoi)'s recollections of the beginning of her relationship with Conor Cruise O'Brien, which would proceed in the most public of circumstances, with his announcement of the end of his first marriage at a press conference while he was representative of the UN Secretary General in Katanga.

In diplomacy, we have two constant friends, clarity and ambiguity. Clarity is essential for reporting and analysis, ambiguity for the art of negotiation and agreement. As diplomats, we construct our own ambiguity. What we say, and how, when, and to whom, has a deep significance. It is the same for the writer and most especially for the poet, where creative ambiguity is a defining feature. Diplomacy often takes place in sentences that reveal as much as they hide; the same is true of poetry. The same flexibility, agility and creativity with words that define the poet are equally valuable for the diplomat and can be seen in numerous agreements, speeches and treaty preambles. Poetry is the spine of this collection and runs all the way through it, like the writing in a stick of rock.

The tradition of the poet diplomat is a long one, in Ireland and internationally, and there are many fine examples, including Chaucer, Boccaccio, Wyatt, Neruda, Miłosz, Paz, Dag Hammarskjöld and Saint-John Perse. The latter was also translated by our own Denis Devlin. A little known fact is that eight poet diplomats have won the Nobel Peace Prize. Seamus Heaney might be added to that list, given how often his lines are quoted by Irish Ministers, Ambassadors and Presidents. Indeed, poetry itself can been seen as a necessary and never more essential form of diplomacy, one that can help generate and enhance empathy and understanding. Of the creative arts, poetry is probably the closest to the art of diplomacy. Both work and play with words, like the monastic scribe and his cat, Pangur Bán, 'tis a like task we are at' – the languages of diplomacy and poetry both have the capacity to clarify and obfuscate at the same time, so that each of the poets collected here manages simultaneously to reveal and hide themselves, generating, we hope, a deep and rewarding experience for the reader.

Not surprisingly, the poems in this rich harvest whisper to each other across time and location, with a natural focus on identity and place. They constantly question who, where, and why we are, testing the nature of our humanity and our relationships with the natural and the urban worlds and, above all, with one another and with ourselves. These questions – which cannot easily be answered – are always the most interesting ones. We have selected and gathered poems here from 21 poets – 14 male and seven female – dating from the 1940s to the present day, where thankfully we continue to find a rich seam of work to continue the tradition of Boland, Iremonger and Devlin. Eavan Boland's loss last year was deeply felt and we are delighted to be able to include here some of her finest work.

We wanted to share writing by family members as well as Departmental officers, in the interests of inclusivity and to ensure representation of a diverse range of voices and experiences. A career in foreign affairs is a choice, not just for the officer, but for the family too, so it is important to capture some of that wider experience, as in Eavan Boland's very evocative writing about living 'over the shop' at the Irish Embassy in London. It is important, too, to recognise the gender balance represented in this volume. The fledgling Dáil Éireann foreign service posted five women to delegations seeking international recognition for the Irish republic: Máire O'Brien (Madrid), Nancy Wyse Power (Berlin), and Annie Vivanti, Cáit Ó Ceallaigh and Mairéad Gavan Duffy (all in Paris).[1] Opportunities for women were limited in the Department from the late 1920s onward, not least by the infamous Civil Service 'marriage bar'; Anne Anderson's essay recounts her later, personal experiences of gender discrimination. In 1947, women were permitted to enter the diplomatic corps at Third Secretary grade, with three appointees: Máire Mhac an tSaoi, Róisín O'Doherty (later McDonagh), and

Mary Tinney. While professional opportunities for women remained limited until the 1970s, spouses played very important roles in the establishment and maintenance of chanceries and residences, and in performing social and public functions. We are therefore delighted to count a number of spouses and children of diplomats among the contributors to this book.

I measc na scríbhneoirí a bhí gníomhach agus iad ag obair ar son an Stáit mar thaidhleoirí nó mar chuid de theaghlaigh taidhleora, tá roinnt a shaothraigh trí mheán na Gaeilge. Ina measc siúd, tarlaíonn sé go bhfuil beirt de mhórfhilí ár linne, Máire Mhac an tSaoi, agus Biddy Jenkinson. Den chuid is mó, roghnaíomar dánta leo siúd a spreagadh ag saol an taidhleora. Ach rud amháin a chuireann na dánta seo in iúl ná an tsaoirse a bhaineann le bheith ag scríobh i nGaeilge – tá dánta Mháire Mhac an tSaoi ar uairibh chomh réabhlóideach maidir le cur síos ar mhothúcháin agus gnéasúlacht na mban agus atá ficsean Edna O'Brien cuir i gcás. Is féidir le Biddy Jenkinson a hacmhainn grinn agus a heasurraim a léiriú go híorónta, gan bac ó na srianta a bheadh i gceist dá mba i mBéarla a bheadh sí ag scríobh.

Ní foláir smaoineamh go mbíonn tionchar ag saol an taidhleora ar an-chuid daoine seachas an t-oifigeach féin – ar a céile nó páirtí, a gaolta sa bhaile agus thar lear, agus, ach go háirithe, a páistí. Leabhar a thugann léargas den scoth ar an ngné seo de ghnóthaí eachtracha ná úrscéal do dhaoine óga, *Maidhc sa Danmhairg*, le P.D. Linín – níl mórán tráchta ar leabhair P.D. Linín na laethanta seo, ach b'fhiú an ceann seo ach go háirithe a chur i gcló arís.

Tá dúshlán nach beag ag baint le bheith i do chónaí thar lear, i dtíortha éagsúla, ar feadh do shaoil. Ach gan amhras tá buntáistí móra leis freisin, agus orthu siúd an seans a fhaigheann tú eolas a chur ar litríochtaí agus cultúir, agus teangacha nua. Címid torthaí na foghlama sin i saothair Irene Duffy Lynch agus Sheosaimhín Bean Mhic Néill, a bhain úsáid as an am a chaith siad i gcéin chun ficsean agus scéalta a aistriú go Gaeilge.

Women are also very well represented in the English-language fiction collected here. Annie Vivanti and Maeve Brennan are remarkable writers by any standard and, following the reappraisal of Brennan's work precipitated by Angela Bourke, enjoy deserved international recognition. Kate Cruise O'Brien and Kate Slattery's classically exact, realist short stories carry an equal emotional heft. The fiction of Sinéad Nic Coitir and Denyse Woods is more experimental in style, but reflects similar thematic concerns – notably, the divide between our internal and external selves and the restrictions society and family impose on women. Brennan, Cruise O'Brien and Woods are all diplomats' daughters and their writing, in different ways, appears shaped by that nomadic experience – a life of privilege, certainly, but also one of continual dislocation, oscillating between Irish and international society, at once part of both and neither. In 'A Daydream', one of her final pieces as *The New Yorker's* 'Long Winded Lady', Brennan reflects that her homesickness for East Hampton is mild, only 'because there are a number of places I am homesick for' – indeed, homesickness is such a feature of her life and work as to provide the subtitle for Bourke's biography, *Homesick at the New Yorker*. Kate Cruise O'Brien's 'A Sunday Walk' depicts the confusion of a girl coming to terms with her parents' separation – statistically, a more common occurrence in diplomatic households than in other professions. Her unhappiness is all the keener for being abroad – 'afraid of school … She didn't understand French anyway and … was always afraid they were laughing at her'.

Written in her first years as a diplomat, Kate Slattery's 'Moving' presents another family in the process of disintegration, this time as a result of domestic abuse. The protagonist here, the abused wife, is similarly alienated from the society around her but, on returning to Ireland, asserts her independence, to dramatic effect. In Sinéad Nic Coitir's 'Flick', a young pregnant woman watches images of suburbia race by, worrying at the prospect of life in an estate show house. A character in conflict with society or family, of course, is a mainstay in fiction, perhaps especially in the work of female writers. But there is still something notable in the dark thread running through so many of these stories – of intelligent women constrained by or alienated from the world around them. Although these constraints are largely imposed by immediate family, the dislocation seems magnified, somehow, by the foreign environs in which they find themselves.

Elsewhere, however, the depictions of life abroad are more benign, even playful. The second of Slattery's stories featured here, 'Marmalade', centres on a woman and a man with 'a clipped inflected accent' flirting in a German café, 'condensation rolling up in coils from their saturated coats'. Here Slattery's eye for detail and ear for dialogue carry echoes of Brennan's wondrous and often wondering evocations of New York and its inhabitants, enriched surely by her position as an outside observer of the city's idiosyncrasies. We are especially delighted to be able to share these two pieces by Slattery, published under her own name for the first time by kind permission of her family. The micro-fiction which closes the anthology, Denyse Woods' 'Wallpaper', is similarly vivid, depicting a woman who has come to live vicariously through the letters of an anonymous traveller to Bormio – again an outsider, in this case at not one but two removes from the society she emotionally inhabits.

Diplomacy is an intrinsically social occupation, revolving around the art of conversation, the building of networks and alliances. But, as the fixed communities with which diplomats interact can attest, it is also inherently unstable – a life lived in four-year cycles, a loop of introductory calls and farewells, of exile and return. Seldom dull, it can, nevertheless, be lonely – less for the diplomats themselves, perhaps, preoccupied with the day-to-day of Embassy life, than for the families they bring with them. Few writers better capture this than Maeve Brennan, a celebrated socialite, the model for Truman Capote's Holly Golightly, who died in the darkest loneliness. Her story, 'The Children Are Very Quiet When They Are Away', has a dog, not a diplomat, as its protagonist; but the unease of 'the lawn empty, shrinking into the mist … the air … turned to silence', the questioning 'what is away, and then, what is here?' will resonate with those who live their days knowing always that, before long, they will be moving on, setting down roots, only to pull them up again.

Although diplomats' lives revolve around politics, we are, instinctually and by training, careful to refrain from commenting openly or directly on political matters – domestic or international. And, indeed, most of the fiction gathered here is preoccupied with the personal, the inner life, rather than social commentary. Much of the fiction and all of the poems selected have in common that sense of a life behind a life, of hiding in plain sight, of sharing a secret but sharing it in code. Perhaps what truly attracts the diplomat to poetry is that opportunity to reveal something while revealing nothing, a sleight of hand which allows the writer, at work a very public and accountable figure, the chance to take a risk and let slip a little of the other side of their personality, while at the same time maintaining a metaphorical reserve, opening a door and closing it at the same time, betraying just a flicker of the room within.

Alongside Vivanti and, at times, Brennan, Eimar O'Duffy is a notable exception. His *Cuanduine* trilogy blends science fiction and mythology to present a searing – and deeply funny – satire of the emerging Irish state in the

1920s, pillorying revivalists like Yeats who, in Declan Kiberd's memorable phrase, sought to 'invent Ireland' by harking back to a Celtic past. *King Goshawk and the Birds*, the first novel of the trilogy, was written in the years immediately following the publication of *Ulysses*, and Joyce's influence is apparent in its rich, anarchic style, including in the newspaper clippings from the chapter anthologised here, parodies which seem fresh and perhaps still all-too resonant, a century later. But in his critiques, especially in those of received economic wisdoms, O'Duffy is also highly original. He was evidently an influence on later writers, including fellow satirist and civil servant, Brian O'Nolan (Flann O'Brien or Myles na gCopaleen).

Culture and creativity have long been emblematic of Ireland's international profile, not least in mediating multilateral relations. The role of culture in diplomacy was recognised with the establishment of the Department's Cultural Relations Committee in 1949. Committee member, Josephine McNeill – Ireland's first female diplomat when appointed to the Netherlands in 1949 – was a committed speaker and promoter of the Irish language, and her translation of Indian folk tales (*Finnsgéalta ó India*, 1932) only hints at her devotion to promoting Irish cultural heritage on the international stage. Other diplomats embraced the cultural life of their host countries. Sean G. Ronan's tireless research restored the almost-forgotten Greek-Irish Japanese writer Lafcadio Hearn to fame in his native country, and Brian Earls' lifelong fascination with folk traditions found entertaining and enlightening voice in his essay on the social and political function of *anekdoty* (jokes) in the Caucasus in the latter days of the Soviet Union. New York – so long a magnet for generations of Irish migrants and a thriving centre of Irish and Irish American culture – was home to a number of significant writers collected in this volume, including Maeve Brennan, Kate Cruise O'Brien and Eavan

Boland. In 1956, Boland's father, Frederick, became Ireland's first Ambassador to the United Nations in that city. The connections between the Boland family and the Department were honoured and renewed in 2018 with the commissioning of the poem, 'Our Future Will Become the Past of Other Women' by Ambassador Geraldine Byrne Nason of Ireland's Permanent Mission to the UN, reaffirming the enduring contribution of our poetry to diplomacy.

We deliberately decided not to organise these writings by theme or genre; each reader will find their own resonances and echoes and will, we hope, enjoy the sense of how the poems, fiction and non-fiction pieces speak to one another, across location and time. Many of the poems and short stories are set in winter, in tones of cold and snow and ice, perhaps expressing the essential loneliness of the diplomat/writer. Many, too, are preoccupied with ideas of identity and home, not surprising in a life where ultimately the diplomat is never really at home, despite having lived in many places, and often returns to Ireland with that sense of being a stranger, a sensation which caused us to find our title for this anthology in Richard Ryan's evocative poem, 'Winter in Minneapolis'.

We are indeed 'all strangers here', but we hope that you will enjoy that sensation of strangeness, and that at the end of this anthology you will feel a little more familiar with the inner world of diplomacy and with the officers and families of the Department. Their words have helped to shape policy and Ireland's place in the world over the last century, and their personal writing is brought together here for the first time, in a chorus of creativity and community. There is range in all of the work featured here, much as there is in the backgrounds of the diplomats who represent our state. But there are also those qualities common to all good diplomats and almost all good writers – a deep interest in and empathy for others; a curiosity about and dissatisfaction with the inconsistencies of the world they inhabit; and, above all, a concern with precision in language, rooted in the recognition that words matter.

NOTE

1 For more on the history of women in the Department, see Michael Kennedy, '"It is a Disadvantage to the Represented by a Woman": The Experiences of Women in the Irish Diplomatic Service', *Irish Studies in International Affairs* 13 (2002), pp. 215–35; Ann Marie O'Brien, *An Ideal Diplomat?: Women and Irish Foreign Affairs, 1946–90* (Dublin, Four Courts Press, 2020).

# Anne Anderson

## THINKING WITH MY PEN (*extract*)

I joined the Department in November 1972, just weeks before Ireland joined the then EEC on 1 January 1973. It was a large intake by the standards of the time: twelve Third Secretaries, of whom two were women – the late, wonderful, Clare O'Flaherty and myself. There was some comment at the time about this 'big influx' of women, which left me rather perplexed. I was told that, while of course there had previously been female Third Secretaries, this was the first time there had been *two* in a single intake.[1]

I married in 1974, and here is where the EEC entry in 1973 becomes very significant. Our EEC accession had forced the lifting of the ban on married women in the public service. Without this insistence from Brussels, the ban would undoubtedly have persisted for years further. Like generations of women before me, I would have had to choose between marriage and public service.

The early years went smoothly, even if there were some straws in the wind. When I kept my own name on marriage, the Head of Personnel at the time – otherwise a kindly and benign individual – told me that he didn't 'know what game I was playing' but he supposed it was up to me.

The first real difficulties arose in 1976 when I was posted to Geneva. I found myself with the distinction of being the first married woman to be posted abroad. At the time, as now, there was a different foreign service allowance for a married and single officer, and – less formally – a rent ceiling that differed depending on whether the accommodation was for a married or single officer.

Although the relevant regulations referred to 'married officer' or 'single officer', our Personnel section still felt it necessary to refer the matter to the Department of Finance: should a married woman officer be entitled to a married officer's allowance? The Department of Finance was sceptical: its view was that the Regulations were framed at a time when by definition a married officer could only be a married man. Therefore, at a minimum, the issue needed to be referred to the Attorney General for his advice.

My husband, at the time an Administrative Officer in the Department of Finance, was bearing the brunt of the extremely conservative mindset that prevailed in that Department. On the question of the rental ceiling, his superior officer told him of the terms in which the debate was being conducted: 'Why should a man be allowed hang up his hat in his wife's apartment, paid for the State.' Shades of the old *'fear isteach'* mentality of rural Ireland of decades ago!

A certain amount of steel entered my soul at that time. The whole discussion was patently ridiculous and I knew that, particularly in an EU perspective, it was legally unsustainable. I also felt that, if the file went to the Attorney General, it might languish indefinitely on his desk. I lodged strong objections and finally, on the eve of my departure, I was informed that married officers would be deemed to include female married officers, and my allowances would be the same as a married man.

Let me pause here and frame the issue.

The experience had not been a comfortable one for me. What 24 year old, still feeling his or her way in the Department, wants to be branded as a trouble-maker? And, in particular, what young woman wants to risk a reputation for being strident or shrewish?

But the lesson was important. The 'system' isn't always right, and we can't always wait and hope the cogs of justice will slowly turn. We need to choose our battles. But if the issue is important enough, we have to be ready to speak up and stand our ground.

Meanwhile, still across in the stone-age Department of Finance of 1976, my husband had applied for a career break to join me on my posting abroad – by definition, the first married man to do so. His application was refused right up along the line before, finally, it was granted following the personal intervention of the Minister for Finance. It required courage on my husband's part to persist against the hierarchy. We women are not the only warriors!

That first Geneva posting was interesting in a number of respects. A male 'traveling spouse' was still something of a novelty in diplomatic circles. My husband was very supportive and often cooked dinner for our diplomatic guests. He was regularly being congratulated on his selflessness and heroic readiness to subordinate his career to mine.

I had no doubt my husband deserved this acknowledgement. Yet something nagged. Lots of female spouses of male diplomats, who were equally supportive and some of whom had made similar career 'sacrifices', were not being acknowledged in the same way. And I often detected an undertone to these elaborate compliments. While praise was being heaped on my husband's selflessness, unspoken but implicit was a sense of an 'unmanly' choice, a more sophisticated expression of the naked prejudice we had experienced in the Department of Finance.

That was almost forty years ago [in 2014] and of course attitudes have evolved. But, even if to a lesser degree, I continue to believe and sense a societal attitude that is different in the case of male and female spouses, with a greater threat to self-esteem in the case of the male spouse. If this is true, there are knock-on effects. There will be a corresponding greater reluctance on the part of the female officer to put her husband in this position, and guilt if she feels she has done so.

I think this issue is too little understood, and it's important to identify it. Being a diplomat by definition implies service abroad; no one can expect to climb the ladder without foreign postings. Our own job satisfaction, and our progression within the Department, requires us to undertake and embrace that part of our career. Over time, in the majority of cases, this will mean finding an accommodation with our lives as wives and mothers.

Yes, we certainly need to think about working hours, child care, and those other very important issues. But we also need to consider deeply within ourselves, and with our partners, how we are going to live with our choices at a psychological level. The Department has an important role in helping to facilitate working spouses, irrespective of whether they are male or female. But, in dealing with the wider societal issue, we need to arm ourselves as individuals and within our partnerships.

The next jolt came in 1982, after I had been back in HQ for a couple of years. A post as Consul General, at First Secretary level, in the US came up and I applied for it, as did others. The posting was discussed at the Management Advisory Committee and subsequently – over coffee for members of our Division – our Assistant Secretary told us, quite openly and unselfconsciously, about what had transpired. He said a view had prevailed in the MAC that Irish America was not ready for women diplomats and that this needed to be taken into account in posting decisions. A male colleague was appointed to the Consul General post.

I found the episode very troubling: not that I or anyone else had an entitlement to this or any other post, but that such considerations should have swayed the choice. Together with another female colleague who had also been an applicant, we sought a meeting with the Secretary of the Department. I recall articulating very strongly my view that the Foreign Service must assert the image and values that define contemporary Ireland, and not try to refashion ourselves in a way that caters to prejudices, or perceived prejudices, of Irish America or any other grouping.

As the then Secretary is not here to relate his side of the story, I should say that he told us the MAC discussion had been misunderstood by our Assistant Secretary and that the posting decision had been made on other grounds.

I am sometimes reminded of that long ago conversation. I still believe, emphatically, that the integrity of our foreign policy requires that we are in all circumstances true to who we are as a people. There may be extreme cases – where, say, the laws of a particular country would make it impossible for a woman diplomat, or a gay diplomat, to function with any degree of effectiveness. But in all other cases – and this will include postings in more marginal countries – our own values will provide the true touchstone of our conduct.

Perhaps partly as a result of this bracing discussion in 1982, I was posted to Washington the following year. I stayed there until 1987, and my daughter was born in Washington in 1985.

Here, let me shift to something more personal.

I have exactly the same recollections of my daughter's infancy as are shared by every working mother: all the delights and all the conflicting pressures. One memory will never leave me: St. Patrick's Day, the Taoiseach's visit, a very long day with all hands on deck in the Embassy, one-year old Claire with a fever, plunging with her into a cold bath around midnight to bring her temperature down. I knew – or at least I felt – that I couldn't let the Embassy down, but I also felt utterly miserable: that I was falling short as a mother and as a human being.

But even if I will never forget that particular night, I think I knew even at the time that I was over-reacting. This was a routine childhood illness, nothing more serious; my daughter had been well cared for during the day. And I think there is a lesson here: we can't deny the reality of our feelings, but we have to go easy on ourselves, and not beat ourselves up unnecessarily.

I doubt there is a single address of this type without the 'guilt' word coming up. For a reason: because it's everywhere: this over-developed, misplaced, female propensity to feel guilt. Of course none of us is perfect, but we are sane, responsible, decent people trying to make the best choices we can. Let's make those responsible, balanced choices – and then live with them.

In 1987, I returned to HQ on promotion to Counsellor. At this stage, I had been thirteen years as First Secretary, including a couple of years as acting First Secretary. The Department had entered inter-Departmental competition for a brief period in 1986–1987, and I won my promotion through a competitive interview process. It was the only Counsellor post filled from that year's competition and I felt myself very lucky.

But I felt more than that. There was at the time – as there is now – a bottle neck from First Secretary to Counsellor and it felt like getting through the eye of a needle. Nevertheless, prior to the interdepartmental competition, First Secretary colleagues more junior than me had already been promoted to Counsellor through decisions of the Management Advisory Committee. I respected those who had achieved this promotion, but it was certainly not self-evident what accomplishments or aptitudes had seen them promoted ahead of myself and other colleagues. And, whether or not it was a relevant factor, these were male colleagues promoted by a male MAC.

I always considered the 1987 promotion as a watershed in my career, and the question remained open for me as to whether I would have had to wait years longer if I was dependent on a decision of my own MAC. Perhaps not –

and it was indeed a decision of the MAC that saw me promoted to Assistant Secretary in 1991. But the 1987 experience led me to believe that women are likely to fare better in more open, structured, competitive processes than in decisions taken behind closed doors.

I am well aware that interview processes carry their own risks and potential for unconscious bias. But I would prefer any day to take my chances in these more transparent processes. And that applies at every level – in the interest of honesty and completeness, I would add that I made my feelings in this regard clear both before and after the Secretary General appointment in 2009.

When I arrived back as Counsellor in 1987, I came to a busy Anglo-Irish Division, which was working through the implementation of the 1985 Anglo Irish Agreement. It was an exciting and invigorating time, and in many senses a Division in transition. There were still residual traces of earlier attitudes, when not just had Irish America been regarded as macho territory, but dealing with political figures in Northern Ireland had in some ways been seen so too.

It was definitely time to evolve, and I was glad to be there at the time of evolution and to be part of it. Today of course, Anglo-Irish Division is a very different place, with a strong female presence at senior level. But, more generally, the risk of stereotyping or clustering – certain jobs being seen as more male-oriented and others as more female-oriented – requires constant alertness.

In 1991, I was promoted to Assistant Secretary and Head of Administration and was in that role for a further four years. We pushed out a number of boundaries, including our first experiment with interview boards for internal promotions within the Department.

Overseeing the recruitment of Third Secretaries is one of the responsibilities of Administration Division. There was a puzzling aspect of what was happening in the early

1990s. More women than men were applying, but proportionately considerably fewer women were making it through the preliminary written general knowledge testing. We were losing too many women at the first hurdle.

We worked with the Civil Service Commission to try to figure out what was happening. The answer, we found, lay in a degree of unconscious bias in the multiple choice questions – there were, for example, sports related questions which would fit far more readily with traditional male interests.

And here let me say something in parenthesis: how often have we women sat around while our male colleagues, or male politicians and civil servants, bonded over forensic analysis of soccer or GAA results? Of course, we don't begrudge this interest, and may sometimes share it – particularly for the major GAA fixtures – but there is something amiss if it becomes workplace currency to an alienating degree.

Once the problem with the general knowledge questions was diagnosed and fixed, and they became more gender neutral, we started to see women coming through in proportionate numbers. So there's a lesson here too: if outcomes are skewed, the inputs and process need investigation to see where along the line the problem is occurring. The answer may not be immediately obvious, but if one keeps digging, it will be found.

NOTE
1   In 1947, the first three female Third Secretaries were appointed: Máire Mhac an tSaoi, Róisín O'Doherty, and Mary Tinney.

# Daniel Binchy

## ADOLF HITLER (*extract*)

I first saw Hitler on a murky November evening in 1921. A Bavarian fellow-student in the University of Munich had induced me to accompany him to a meeting of what he described as 'a new freak party' in the Bürgerbräukeller. The hall was not quite full, the audience seemed to be drawn from the poorest of the poor – the 'down and outs' of the city: indeed, except for a sprinkling of obvious ex-soldiers, I might well have believed myself assisting at a continuation of a Communist meeting which I had attended in a neighbouring hall a few nights previously. Hitler was the principal speaker, and as he sat on a platform waiting for the very prosy chairman to conclude, I remember wondering idly if it would be possible to find a more commonplace-looking man. His countenance was opaque, his complexion pasty, his hair plastered down with some glistening unguent, and – as if to accentuate the impression of insignificance – he wore a carefully docked 'toothbrush' moustache. I felt willing to bet that in private life he was a plumber: a whispered query to my friend brought the information that he was a housepainter.

He rose to speak, and after a few minutes I had forgotten all about his insignificant exterior. Here was a born natural orator. He began slowly, almost hesitatingly, stumbling over the construction of his sentences, correcting his dialect pronunciation. Then all at once he seemed to take fire. His voice rose victorious over falterings, his eyes blazed with conviction, his whole body became an instrument of rude eloquence. As his exaltation increased, his voice rose almost to a scream, his gesticulation became a wild pantomime, and I noticed traces of foam at the corners of his mouth. He spoke so quickly and in such a pronounced dialect that I had great difficulty in following him, but the same phrases kept recurring all through his address like motifs in a symphony: the Marxist traitors, the criminals who caused the Revolution, the German army which was stabbed in the back, and – most insistent of all – the Jews. There were some interruptions, and I gathered from Hitler's attempts to deal with them that he was utterly devoid of humour.[1] But there could be no doubt of his ascendancy over the vast majority of the audience. His purple passages were greeted with roars of applause, and when he finally sank back exhausted into his chair, there was a scene of hysterical enthusiasm which baffles description. As we left the meeting my friend asked me what I thought of this new party leader. With all the arrogance of twenty-one I replied: 'A harmless lunatic with the gift of oratory.' I can still hear his retort: 'No lunatic with a gift for oratory is harmless.'

I saw Hitler again nine years later at a meeting in the Sportpalast in Berlin to celebrate the success of his party in the general election of September 1930. I found little change in his appearance beyond a marked increase in his waist-line: 'the twentieth-century Siegfried,' as one of his followers called him, had developed a very unheroic *embonpoint*. In his speech I found no change at all. Allowing for the altered place and circumstances, it was substantially the same address which I had heard in the Bürgerbräukeller. There were the same denunciations, the same digressions – and the same enthusiasm. At the conclusion of his speech the vast throng cheered itself hoarse. The obscure housepainter was now the leader of the second largest party in Germany. In the interval which has since elapsed, he has gone from strength to strength, and today he is Chancellor of the Reich. One may well ask: what manner of man is this? [...]

How to explain his ascendancy over the masses? To millions of normal Germans he is a prophet and a hero. On what is this reputation based? Obviously not on his intelligence. Nor can it be on his political record, which makes poor reading. He has been invariably outwitted by more experienced statesmen and sometimes made to look intensely foolish. He has made bad mistakes in tactics: witness his decision to oppose Hindenberg for the presidency in March of last year. By this action he secured for the old Field Marshal a solid block of twenty million votes and therewith the claim to speak for the absolute majority of the German people. The story of the frantic endeavours to make him a German citizen in time for the fray raised much laughter at his expense.[2] And even now, before being entrusted with the Chancellorship, he has had his wings firmly clipped by the President. He has had to accept as colleagues most of the 'Government of Barons' which he was hysterically denouncing a few months ago. In addition he has the chief of the Conservative Nationalists, whose meetings were consistently broken up by the Nazis during the last election campaign, as well as the chief of the *Stahlhelm*, with which his Brown Army has had many a skirmish. He can hardly expect these men to swallow his programme. Accordingly his choice will be unenviable: either to scrap his more crazy objectives and govern Germany along bourgeois conservative lines, thereby risking the secession of his proletarian supporters, or to stage a fight with his 'reactionary' colleagues and return to the wilderness once more.

Some have attempted to explain Hitler's ascendancy by his eloquence, others by his genius for propaganda, others again by the fact that he stands on the same intellectual plain as the bulk of his followers. While these are contributory factors, the personality of the man himself cannot be left out of account. His personal honesty and disinterestedness are not disputed by any sincere opponent. But the real secret of his power lies in his fanatical, almost mystic, belief in himself and his mission. 'I am only forty-three years old,' he told his followers on the day after his defeat in the presidential election, 'and I am in perfect health. I am convinced that nothing can happen me, for I know that I have been appointed to my task by a higher power.' There are only two barriers to megalomania in public life: intelligence and a sense of humour. Either of these qualities would suffice to prevent it, but I believe Hitler to be lacking in both, and thus faith in himself and his mission has become for him a kind of religion. Such fanatical belief can easily be communicated to the masses, especially when it is accompanied, as in his case, by the gift of eloquence. It is not merely the right sort of faith which is capable of moving mountains.

I write while Germany is in the throes of the most bitter election in her history. Until the result is known, it would be idle to speculate as to the new Chancellor's future. But, whatever be the result of the gambler's throw, he himself will deserve the continued attention of the student of comparative politics. For the phenomenon of Hitler is not peculiar to Germany.

NOTES

1   I have since learned that not even his warmest admirers claim for him a sense of humour.

2   As Hitler declined to apply for naturalisation in the ordinary way, his friends sought to smuggle him into citizenship by getting him appointed to some nominal position in the public service of one of those federal states which had Nazi ministries. First, Dr. Frick, then Minister for Education in Thuringia and now Minister for the Interior in Hitler's Cabinet, proposed to make him Professor of Education in the University of Jena, but the Faculty protested. Frick then proceeded to nominate him head constable of the police in the little village of Hildburghausen, but amid general laughter the nomination was held to be unconstitutional on the ground of secrecy. Finally Dr. Klagge, the first Nazi minister in Brunswick, found the solution.

Hitler was appointed attaché to the Brunswick 'Legation' in Berlin, a post which involved neither work nor salary, but only an oath of allegiance to the Weimar constitution, which the new official apparently found no difficulty in taking.

Eavan Boland

EVICTION

Back from Dublin, my grandmother
finds an eviction notice on her door.
Now she is in court for rent arrears.
The lawyers are amused.
These are the Petty Sessions,
this is Drogheda, this is the Bank Holiday.
Their comments fill a column in the newspaper.
Was the notice well served?
Was it served at all?
Is she a weekly or a monthly tenant?
In which one of the plaintiffs' rent books
is she registered?
The case comes to an end, is dismissed.
Leaving behind the autumn evening.
Leaving behind the room she entered.
Leaving behind the reason I have always
resisted history.
A woman leaves a courtroom in tears.
A nation is rising to the light.
History notes the second, not the first.
Nor does it know the answer as to why
on a winter evening
in a modern Ireland
I linger over the page of the *Drogheda
Argus and Leinster Journal*, 1904,
knowing as I do that my attention has
no agency, none at all. Nor my rage.

# Eavan Boland

## Object Lessons (*extract*)

I had no choice. That may well be the first, the most
enduring characteristic of influence. What's more, I knew
nothing. One morning I was woken before dawn, dressed
in a pink cardigan and skirt, put in a car, taken to an
airport. I was five. My mother was with me. The light of
the control tower at Collinstown Airport – it would
become Dublin Airport – came through the autumn
darkness. I was sick on the plane, suddenly and neatly,
into the paper bag provided for the purpose.

I left behind fractions of place and memory, images
which would expose slowly. There was a lilac bush I had
pulled at so often its musk stayed under my fingernails for
days. I would remember the unkempt greenness of the
canal where it divided Leeson Street. The lock was made of
splintery wood, and boys dived from its narrow platform
in summer. Fields, fragrances, an impression of light and
informality – that was all. I held my mother's hand, got
into another car. I was in another country.

Hardly anything else that happened to me as a child
was as important as this: that I left one country and came
to another. That an ordinary displacement made an
extraordinary distance between the word *place* and the
word *mine*.

\*\*\*

We had come to London. It was 1950. I have a memory of
houses and moving vans, of adult voices late at night.
Then we were in a tall house, of dun-colored stone, with a
flagstaff fitted to a low balcony. In the hall, through doors
which were more like wooden gates, there was a kind of
chair I had never seen before. It was black leather, and the
top was rounded into a sort of hood, edged with brass

buttoning. It was called the Watchman's Chair. I was told a man sat in it all night.

Almost everything about this house was different from the one we had left behind. That had been family sized, with a flight of stone steps and a garden edging out into fields. There had been glasshouses and a raggy brown-and-white terrier called Jimmy. There had been lilac and roses along a stone wall. Nothing about it had the closed-in feel of this street. But that had been the house of a life in Ireland, of an Irishman and his wife and five children. And now my father had gone, all at once, it seemed, from being an Irish civil servant to being an ambassador in London. The life had changed. The house had changed.

I knew I was somewhere else. I knew there was something momentous – and for me alone – in the meaning of the big staircase, with its gilded iron fretwork and its polished balustrade; in the formal carpets, with the emblems of the four provinces of Ireland on them: the harp for Leinster, the red hand for Ulster, the dog and shield for the other two. I knew that the meaning was not good. But what was bad and what was good? Bad, it seemed, was dropping soft toys and metal cars down the stairwell. Bad was making noise and tricking with the fire hoses on every floor. Good was being invisible: spending hours in the sparse playroom on the top floor, with a blank television and the balcony which overlooked a dark, closed-in courtyard.

We turned the armchairs on their side there, day after day, and called them horses, and rode them away from this strange house with fog outside the window and a fiction of home in the carpets on the floor.

***

Exile is not simple. There are Irish emigrant songs which make it sound so; they speak of green shores and farewells. By and large, they fit into Valéry's description of

Tennyson's *In Memoriam*: 'the broken heart which runs into many editions.' Which is not to deny their melody, but it is a marketable one. In most cases those songs were composed in settled and hard-pressed communities of Irishmen and women – most of them in the New World – to reassure them that they still had noble roots as they branched out in a daylight which was often sordid and dispossessed.

I wanted simplicity. I craved it. At school I would learn Thomas Hood's poem: 'I remember, I remember / The house where I was born.' But as time went on, I didn't. Such memory as I had was constantly being confused and disrupted by gossip and homily, by the brisk and contingent talk of adults. 'Stop that. Settle down. Go to sleep now.'

The city I came to offered no simplicity either. The rooms to the east of the house looked out on gardens and railings. But the vista was almost always, that first winter anyway, of a yellow fog. If the windows were open, it drifted smokily at the sill. If the doors were open and you went into the street, you entered a muddled and frightening mime. Passersby were gagged in white handkerchiefs. The lights of buses loomed up suddenly. All I knew of the country was this city; all I knew of this city was its fog.

The first winter passed. In the conventional interpretation of exile I should, child as I was, have missed my home and my country. I should have entered the lift and regret of an emigrant ballad and remembered the Dublin hills, say, and the way they look before rain: heathery and too near. Instead I stared out the window at the convent school I attended in North London. It was March, my first one in England. A swell of grass, a sort of hummock, ran the length of the window and beyond. It had been planted with crocuses, purple, white, yellow. I may not have seen them before; I had certainly never seen so many. There and then I appropriated the English spring.

***

This was not ordinary nature loving. I was not really a nature lover anyway. I resisted walks in Hyde Park whenever I could, and I was restless when we went out at school, paired off in the dreaded 'crocodile,' to pick up polished chestnuts or gather acorns. This was different. Not a season but a place. Not an observant affection but a thwarted possessiveness: a rare and virulent homesickness.

Even good poets, Thoreau says, do not see 'the westward side of the mountain.' They propose instead 'a tame and civil side of nature.' My concept of the English spring was as makeshift, as simplified and marketable to my spirit, as the vision of Ireland in any emigrant song. English crocuses were always a brilliant mauve or gold. English cows – I had heard this somewhere – only grazed in meadows full of buttercups, flowers so called because they made the milk richer. The chaffinch was forever on the orchard bough. In the big woodlands south of London – I was sure of this, though I had never seen them – were acres of bluebells, harebells, primroses.

If it was a simplification, if it resembled in this the country of emigrant yearning, they had a common source. An emigrant and an exile are not necessarily the same thing. There is at least an illusion of choice about the first condition although, sooner or later, it will share the desolation of the second. But both need a paradigm: The disoriented intelligence seeks out symmetry. I wanted a shape which was flawless. If I had only known it, I wanted a country where I was the sole citizen, where the season was fixed in the first days of April, where there were no arrivals or departures.

The more I imagined that springtime, the more I became, in my imagination, the Victorian child suited to its impossible poise. It was not difficult. If Aristophanes called Euripides, as he is said to have done, a maker of ragamuffin manikins, maybe the remark can do as well for childhood make-believe. Certainly I had plenty of pictures to work from. There were old encyclopedias in the house with just the images I was looking for: English girls with well-managed hair, with lawn pinafores over sprigged dresses, with stockinged legs and buckled shoes. Alice without the looking glass.

Alice. The Looking Glass. An old England, unshadowed by the anger of the oppressed. It would have made better sense had the country I left behind not been engaged in a rapid and passionate restatement of its own identity. Ireland, after so many centuries, was now a republic. A text was being rewritten. Street names. Laws. School curricula. The writing went on and on. My childhood was merely a phrase in it.

II

My father enters here: a complicated man and, by all accounts, a Jesuitical negotiator. And a Jesuit boy he had been, going to Clongowes, the boarding school south of Dublin, where James Joyce, twenty years earlier, had wept and broken his glasses. My father may have learned there how to make a concept pliable. Later on, in our adult conversations, he would distinguish between Metternich and Talleyrand; between a diplomat who merely sold himself and one who sold his country.

He was a member of what may have been the last generation of European diplomats whose apprenticeship in pessimism was served between two wars. I see them standing on railway platforms, discoursing and wagering in first-class carriages, taking unreliable planes to theaters of crisis. They offered to chaos their skills of rhetoric and compromise and their unending gifts for finding the appropriate dress. Bowler hats, silk top hats, heavy ivory crepe evening scarves seemed to fill the house, marking my father's exits and entrances. He had been in Paris in the thirties. As assistant secretary at Foreign Affairs he had been one of the caretakers of Ireland's neutrality in the Second World War. During the forties he traveled from Dublin to London, arranging trade agreements, searching out the language, the exact form of words which would bridge the damage of centuries with the practicality of a moment.

In a sense, he is an anomalous figure against the backdrop of Irish political passion. While argument raged and the injuries of the Irish Civil War healed slowly, he went about his tasks and his travels. Paris. London. Rome. Photographs from the forties show him in a reticent coat of Irish tweed and a brown fedora. His Parisian training is shown only in the way he holds a pair of calf brown gloves, well folded, on the steps of St. Peter's.

In these journeys his accoutrements were talk and a pursuit of realpolitik. The Irish, after the war, were in need of coal and food and employment abroad – especially in England. It was not a time for expensive gestures or republican intransigence.

Observe him in the forties, just after that war, discussing coal with the Ministry of Supply in London. His country needs it, and he will get it. But the ironies are plentiful. Here is a man who studied classics at Trinity and political science at Harvard. He can quote Thucydides on the costliness of civil strife and Tacitus on the infirmity of rulers. He has a strong sense of historical absurdity and a true sense of patriotism. He will put all and any of that behind the attempt to bring heat and shelter from that country to his own. He will search hard for the right formula of words to achieve it. And yet will anything he says, anything he proposes, have the raw force of the nineteenth-century Fenian cry 'Burn everything English but their coal?'

\*\*\*

There were shadows. His grandfather had been the master of the workhouse in Clonmel. The historical ambiguity of a forebear who had harnessed his pony and culled his kitchen garden in the environs of fever and hunger would not have been lost on him. After all, he served political masters for whom the fever and hunger of the nineteenth century were some of the most persistent badges of honor.

His mother – another shadow – was illegitimate. Married to his father, a respectable and feared civil servant in the British service, she had suffered much. Once or twice, at a later stage, he hinted obliquely at her sufferings: She had kept to the house a great deal; her closest friend was the housekeeper.

And there had been – there always was in Ireland – an eviction. It had happened to the family his mother lived with; she had been a child at the time. They had been evicted from a smallholding near the river Barrow in Kildare. There were almost no details. Just the elegant un-Irish name of Verschoyle was carefully remembered: the hated middleman. But if there were no details, the image of an eviction was a brutal Irish generic. No cartoon, no sentimental drawing can have anything like the force or bitterness of folk memory: the dreaded bailiff, the furniture out of doors, the windows barred. The illegitimate child, dispossessed even of a foster shelter, was enigmatically factored into my father's intelligence. Years later he told me of a childhood memory: of standing on Dame Street in Dublin, holding his mother's hand. The viceregal carriage – this may have been in 1910 – clattered out of the gates of Dublin Castle. He went to doff his cap, not an unusual gesture on those streets at that time. His mother pulled away her hand. 'Don't do that,' she whispered.

Now it was 1948, and Ireland, having been a member of the Commonwealth since 1921, was suddenly, almost improvisationally, declared a republic. There was surprise, even shock. But there were pieces to be picked up, loose ends to be tied. The old profession of diplomacy had everything to do with loose ends and scattered pieces, and so my father was in London. It was the Commonwealth conference, and he was speaking to old colleagues as well as an old oppressor. But his speech had an unusual ending. He wished Canada and Australia well – they had decided to remain in the Commonwealth – and he understood that decision; indeed, he respected it. But the Irish would withdraw. 'There is not,' he said – and I am going on hearsay and his own account in this – 'a cottage in Ireland which has not shuddered at the words "Open in the name of the king."'

It was negotiating rhetoric; it was appropriate language. He was a trained man and would not have used it had it not fitted both requirements. But there was also, I am sure of it, an invisible darkness in the language: the parish lands of Kilberry to the east of Athy. In any case, Ireland was now a republic and needed an ambassador. And he was it.

I knew nothing. Nothing of nations or that Napoleon said, 'What is history but a fable agreed upon?' The truth was that by such words, such gestures – by hints and transits, negotiations and compromises I was utterly oblivious of – my fate was decided together with my country's. By a strange, compound irony, the same sequence of events which made me a citizen of a republic had determined my exile from it.

When night came, I balanced a heavy maroon volume on the sheet – the books had been carefully covered for me by my mother – and I was out in the air of an English spring. Never mind that I was called Ginger and Carrot-Top at school, that I had freckles and an accent. I was wearing muslin and those shoes, or maybe boots with impossible mother-of-pearl buttons joining the silky leather from toe to shin, which needed the curve of a silver buttonhook to undo. I was looking for a thrush's nest. I was in those places for which the English had fragrant, unfamiliar names: a copse; an orchard; a meadow. In the Irish usage they would have been mere fields and gardens. I was picking bluebells and primroses, going home with indigo- and lemon-colored handfuls. I was going home to muffins and clear, swirling tea surrounded by flowered porcelain. Then it was time for the light to be switched off, for the room to fill with shadows and lamplight.

'Language is fossil poetry,' says Emerson, and it may well be. But it is also home truth. Whatever the inventions and distortions of my imaginings, my tongue, the sounds it made in my mouth, betrayed me. I was no English Alice. I was an Irish child in England. The more time went on, the more my confusion grew. I knew, if only by vague apprehensions, what I did not own; I had no knowledge of what I did. The other children at school had a king and a country. They could be casual about the bluebells and chaffinches. They could say 'orchard' instead of 'garden' with the offhand grace imparted by nine-tenths of the law. I could not. When the king died and the reverend mother announced the fact to the whole school at lunchtime, the other children knew how to weep. I only knew how to admire their tears.

The inevitable happened. One day my tongue betrayed me out of dream and counterfeit into cold truth. I was in the cloakroom at school in the middle of the afternoon. A winter darkness was already gathering through one of the stubborn fogs of the time. A teacher was marshaling children here and there, dividing those who were taking buses from those who were being collected. 'I amn't taking the bus,' I said. I was six or seven then, still within earshot of another way of speaking. But the English do not use that particular construction. It is an older usage. If they contract the verb and the negative, they say, 'I'm not.'

Without knowing, I had used that thing for which the English reserve a visceral dislike: their language, loaded and aimed by the old enemy. The teacher whirled around. She corrected my grammar; her face set, her tone cold. 'You're not in Ireland now' was what she said.

Eavan Boland

OUR FUTURE WILL BECOME THE PAST OF OTHER WOMEN
(*extract*)

Show me your hand. I see our past,
Your palm roughened by heat, by frost.
By pulling a crop out of the earth
By lifting a cauldron off the hearth.
By stripping rushes dipped in fat
To make a wick make a rush light.
That was your world: your entry to
Our ancestry in our darkest century.
Ghost-sufferer, our ghost-sister
Remind us now again that history
changes in one moment with one mind.
That it belongs to us, to all of us.
As we mark these hundred years
We will not leave you behind.
[...]
If we could only summon
Or see them these women,
Foremothers of the nurture
And dignity that will come
To all of us from this day
We could say across the century
To each one—give me your hand:
It has written our future.
Our future will become
The past of other women.

Our island that was once
Settled and removed on the edge
Of Europe is now a bridge
To the world. And so we share
This day with women everywhere.
For those who find the rights they need

61

To be hard won, not guaranteed,
Not easily given, for each one
We have a gift, a talisman:
The memory of these Irish women
Who struggled and prevailed.
For whose sake we choose
These things from their date
To honour, to remember and to celebrate:

All those who called for it,
The vote for women.
All those who had the faith
That voices can be raised. Can be heard.
All those who saw their hopes
Become the law. All those who woke
In a new state flowering
From an old nation and found

Justice no longer blind.
Inequity set aside.
And freedom re-defined.[1]

NOTE

1  The following translations of the poem are available at
   https://www.irishtimes.com/vote100/eavan-boland-poem:
   Arabic by Reem Dawood; Chinese by Huiyi Bao; French by
   Clíona Ní Ríordáin; Irish by Aifric Mac Aodha; Russian by
   Grigory Kruzhkov; Spanish by Pura López-Colomé.

Eavan Boland

QUARANTINE

In the worst hour of the worst season
        of the worst year of a whole people
a man set out from the workhouse with his wife.
He was walking—they were both walking—north.

She was sick with famine fever and could not keep up.
        He lifted her and put her on his back.
He walked like that west and west and north.
Until at nightfall under freezing stars they arrived.

In the morning they were both found dead.
        Of cold. Of hunger. Of the toxins of a whole history.
But her feet were held against his breastbone.
The last heat of his flesh was his last gift to her.

Let no love poem ever come to this threshold.
        There is no place here for the inexact
praise of the easy graces and sensuality of the body.
There is only time for this merciless inventory:

Their death together in the winter of 1847.
        Also what they suffered. How they lived.
And what there is between a man and woman.
And in which darkness it can best be proved.

Eavan Boland

THE SINGERS
*for M.R.*

The women who were singers in the West
lived on an unforgiving coast.
I want to ask was there ever one
moment when all of it relented—
when rain and ocean and their own
sense of home were revealed to them
as one and the same?
                              After which
every day was still shaped by weather,
but every night their mouths filled with
Atlantic storms and clouded-over stars
and exhausted birds?
                              And only when the danger
was plain in the music could you know
the measure of their true rejoicing in

finding a voice where they found a vision.

# Eddie Brannigan

## REBEL RABBLE RUBBLE (*extract*)

PEARSE MCFIERCE: I think I'll read out the Proclamation now. And while I'm doing it, I want you to throw some money out to the crowd, to prove that we are not materialistic or out for financial gain ... Now, where did I put that Proclamation? So many pockets in these army uniforms ...

PRIVATE COONEY: You had it on Saturday night at the meeting when everyone was signing it ... remember, you gave it to Seamus Colony, Junket, and Cluck.

MCFIERCE: Did anyone else sign it then?

COONEY: Nobody asked me to sign anything at all.

MCFIERCE: Who had it last then?!

COONEY: I remember now. It was Níall MacEoin.

MCFIERCE: And who had it after him?

COONEY: Nobody. I don't recall anyone having it after him.

MCFIERCE: Well, where the hell is it then?! Don't tell me I forgot it!

INSURGENT SOLDIER (*calls out*): Troops coming from the bridge, sir! ... The Brits are coming!

COONEY: No!!! ... They're not British ... They've got Volunteer uniforms on ...!

MCFIERCE: Hurray! Reinforcements! ... I knew they would come ... Fairyhouse Races or not ...

COONEY: But ... They're stopping over at Clery's, sir!

(*Sound of glass windows being broken across street*).

MCFIERCE: What ... what are they doing? ... They're breaking into Clery's! ... Hey! ... Youuuu mennn! You men! ... It's not Clery's! ... We're over here! ... In the GPO!

COONEY: Sir, will you look who's leading them!!

MCFIERCE: Give me those glasses! … What? It's Níall McEoin …

COONEY: And hey… hey! … He's shouting something … no, he's reading something out!

NÍALL MCEOIN's voice from across the street: … *and Irishwomen* … *In the name of God, and of the Dead Generations*

COONEY: Oh my God … He's reading out *your* Proclamation …

MCEOIN: … *receives her old tradition of nationhood* …

COONEY: … from the front door of Clery's!

MCFIERCE: The Judas Iscariot! The Devil! … The humiliation! … Give me a rifle quick!

# Maeve Brennan

## A DAYDREAM

This is a daydream: I am lying in the sand just below the dunes on the beach in East Hampton, where I lived for several years. It is a warm, sunless day, with a cool wind blowing in from the ocean. My eyes are closed. I like the beach and the sand. There is a big Turkish towel between me and the sand, and I am quite alone. The cats and my dog, Bluebell, walked over here with me, but two of the cats dropped out at the walled rose garden a short distance back, and the four others are hiding in the long dune grass just above me. Bluebell is down by the water. She is a black Labrador retriever, and she swims and rolls in the water and watches for a seagull to play with, but the gulls fly off shrieking with outrage at the sight of her. I can't stay here much longer. In a few minutes, I'll get up and start for home – a five-minute walk through dune grass and between trees and across the wide, sloping lawn that leads to the big house where the walled rose garden is. I live at the foot of that lawn. I'll just lie here a few more minutes and then I'll go back.

But I opened my eyes too suddenly, for no reason at all, and the beach at East Hampton has vanished, along with Bluebell and the cats, all of them dead for years now. The Turkish towel is in reality the nubbly white counterpane of the bed I am lying on, and the cool ocean breeze is being provided by the blessed air conditioner. It is ninety-three degrees outside – a terrible day in New York City. So much for the daydream of sand and sea and roses. The daydream was, after all, only a mild attack of homesickness. The reason it was a mild attack instead of a fierce one is that there are a number of places I am homesick for. East Hampton is only one of them.

# Maeve Brennan

## THE CHILDREN ARE VERY QUIET WHEN THEY ARE AWAY

It is a winter-afternoon sky, very dark, and lowering itself now to thicken the heavy mist that is gathering over the dunes. The Atlantic Ocean, hidden by the fading dunes, is thundering today. The line of the dunes is growing dimmer, and the huge house that stands up there over the seas is becoming ghostly. It is an enormously clumsy house, with hundreds of diamond paned windows and a massive front door that has flights of stone steps going up to it. Inside, there must be at least eighty or ninety rooms, all of different shapes and some with balconies. In clear weather, some of the balconies can be seen from here.

'Here' is a small lawn that stretches its little length with modest satisfaction in front of a fat, romantic cottage that is very closely related to the amiable monstrosity on the dunes. The cottage might have been baked from a bit of dough left over after the giant's place on the dunes was made. They are alike, and the cottage has its own massive doorway and its diamond-paned windows and its big beams and its gingerbread roof.

The giant house is inhabited in the summertime by seven children, and the cottage is the home of a black Labrador retriever and six handsome mongrel cats. The retriever's name is Bluebell and she is almost six years old. On a bleak day like today, the cats stay indoors. They are asleep around the house, or they are at the windows, attentive to nothing. But at the edge of the driveway that separates the small lawn from the great one leading to the dunes, Bluebell lies on guard, with a large bone between her front paws and her head turned towards the big house away up there in the distance. Bluebell must wonder why the children do not appear. They were always appearing, from all directions, and descending on her, when she did not reach them first. They used to swoop down from their house and across the lawn in a flight of white shorts and white shirts, and Bluebell never crossed the driveway to trespass on their grass until she was certain they were coming to her. They used to call her name as they ran for her, and as their breath shortened and their voices came closer, her name sounded louder, and the sound of it filled her with a joy that could only increase, because there was no limit to the children's energy or to their affection for her. 'Bluebell. Good *Bluebell*. Good *Bluebell*.' There had never been so many voices calling her at once, or so many legs to charge at and then avoid, or so many admiring faces to watch and please. Please them all, always please, that was her duty, her only duty, and she had never before seen it so plain, or felt it to be so simple, or so interesting, or felt herself so valuable. She was a god and she performed like a dog. She forgot her middle age and her extra weight and her gray muzzle, and she frolicked like a puppy, and like a mustang, and like a kitten.

She found a treasure in the short grass and then, after smelling it importantly, she tormented it for a few seconds with her paws before she pranced away and left it as it was, invincible. She entertained like a dog. She lay stretched on her back with her huge chest heaving dramatically. Upside down she is grotesque, a vulnerable monster. She might be a sacrifice, on the lawn, in the sunlight. Her front paws hang in the air empty and aimless, and the big soft ears that make her look demure and mournful fade away, inside out, and leave her face exposed and wild. And her eyes are wild; they look at nothing. The children are astonished to see their familiar turn mysterious, and they make a circle around her. They are embarrassed, because she is shameless, and they try to clear the air with their laughter. 'Look at Bluebell. She is *funny*.' Who is Bluebell now, and what is she? She is not herself. The smallest girl decides that Bluebell is a bench, and she sits heavily down on the softest place, the stomach. Bluebell springs rudely up and resumes her proper shape. Now she is a dog again, and she stands on four legs again. The children welcome her return by telling her her name: Bluebell, Bluebell, Bluebell. Bluebell brandishes her heavy tail and challenges the eyes that watch her with her eyes, and then she races away and they all race after her. She has never been so pursued. She has never been so famous or so celebrated. Her name is on every lip. She has come into her own. She is the only dog in the world.

But here it is winter, with the cold winter weather that is so good for playing in, and she has been waiting for hours, ever since summer, and the children have not appeared. If she watches faithfully they will appear. They generally come out around this time. Whenever they come out is this time. Bluebell moves the old bone over to the middle of the driveway, and then she resumes her dignified attitude, with her paws precisely arranged, as though she were lying in wait on her own tomb. Her head is turned to the house on the dunes. It is lost in the mist. The house is gone. There is no sound except the pounding of seas in the distance, and that sound means nothing to Bluebell. What use to plunge into the sea and brave the waves when she has no witnesses? The lawn is empty, shrinking away into the mist, and the air has turned to silence. No voice is calling from up there on the dunes. There is no Bluebell. Her name is lost. She was the only dog in the world, but now she is only a dog. It is all the children's fault, all this absence. It is all their fault. They are too quiet. All this silence can be blamed on them, and all this waste. Bluebell takes her eyes from the dunes and puts her chin on the empty bone between her paws. She drowses. It is all the children's fault. Everything is too quiet. It is all their fault. The children are quiet because they are away. But what is away, and then, what is here? Bluebell is here. Bluebell sleeps. Now Bluebell is away where the children are who are so quiet here.

# Robert Brennan

## IRELAND STANDING FIRM:
## MY WARTIME MISSION IN WASHINGTON (*extract*)

In March 1941 I was instructed to inform the State Department that General Frank Aiken, the Minister for Defence, intended to visit the United States for the purpose of purchasing arms, munitions and ships. The official who received me was very cool indeed.

'We know nothing about this visit,' he said.

The attitude of this official whom I met officially for the first time was so glacial and unlike that of all the other U.S. officials that I suspected that the dice had been loaded against Frank from the very start. I was to receive confirmation of this fact later.

I explained as courteously as I could that the purpose of my call was to tell him of General Aiken's forthcoming visit, and he grudgingly noted this fact. When Frank arrived, I made the usual application for an interview with the President and the Secretary of State and was told that the matter would be arranged as expeditiously as possible but that there might be some delay in the case of the President as he was unusually busy. Meanwhile, I was to introduce General Aiken to Mr. Joseph Greene, the State Department official who was the liaison officer between representatives of foreign governments and the armed services. Joe, an old friend of mine, was as usual courteous and kindly. He introduced Frank to the appropriate officers in the Army, Navy and Air Force, and while awaiting the promised interview with the President, Joe arranged for Frank to visit certain airplane factories, air bases, etc., throughout the country. It was understood that as soon as I got word from the White House, Frank's tour would be cut short, and he would return to Washington.

Seventeen days elapsed before Frank rang me from California. He said he was returning to Washington to say goodbye before returning to Ireland. He had got fed up with the situation. He knew, of course, that I had been pressing the State Department every day about the interview with the President and that every day I had been put off with one excuse or another. He knew, too, that the treatment he was receiving at the hands of the White House was in strange contrast to that accorded to every other Minister of State who visited Washington and particularly to that accorded to Winston Churchill, who had been in Washington a few months before. Roosevelt had met and welcomed the British Prime Minister a hundred miles out in Chesapeake Bay. I saw Sumner Welles next day and told him of Frank's decision. He was genuinely distressed.

'Get him to wait,' he said. 'Give me a day or two more. This must not be allowed to happen. I may have a word for you tomorrow.'

And right enough when Frank came back the next day, I was able to tell him that the President would see him on the following day at 11.30 a.m. So there we were at the White House at the appointed time received in the outer room by Colonel Watson, the President's secretary, and conducted almost at once into Franklin D. Roosevelt's office. He was seated at this desk and his greetings for us seemed cordial enough. His technique with any visitor, particularly one who might have an awkward question to ask, was invariably the same. He would talk for twenty minutes, at the end of which time the visitor was supposed to leave. The signal that the interview was over was the entrance of Colonel Watson.

On this occasion F.D.R. surpassed himself. Having listened to Frank for about two minutes, he began to talk and he continued to talk of his great regard for Ireland. He told us all about the stories regarding Ireland which he had previously told Sean T. and myself and which indeed I had heard from him many times. I was made aware of the fact that the twenty minutes were up when Colonel Watson wandered in and began to pace up and down the floor.

Frank ignored the interruption. He had not yet got in his say and he was determined to do so. Colonel Watson went out and Frank began to talk. He said no one could doubt Ireland's attitude towards Fascism. We alone in Europe had actually defeated a threatened Fascist uprising in our own country. We would like to be in a position to meet an invader wherever he might come from, and that was why we needed arms, munitions and ships. We had recruited no fewer than 250,000 in our various forces. They were ready to defend our territory, but they were poorly equipped. The position was complicated by the attitude of the British, whose forces were massed on the unnatural border separating the six counties from the rest of the country. Roosevelt interrupted him.

'Listen, General,' he said. 'I believe in talking straight. You are reported as having said that it does not matter to Ireland whether England or Germany wins this war.'

'When and where am I supposed to have said that?' asked Frank.

I intervened and said: 'Mr. President, I have been present at very interview General Aiken gave, and I assure you he never said anything of the kind.'

As if there been no denial, F.D.R. went on to say that it was a stupid folly to say it did not matter if Germany won the war. If that happened, the whole world was in danger of coming under the heel of merciless tyranny in the form of a Nazi dictatorship. The American people in common with the peoples opposing this infamous attempt at world subjugation were very much concerned. F.D.R. himself had gone so far as to have the seas patrolled within a hundred miles of the American coast to spot the German submarines who were preying on their shipping. He intended to extend this patrol area to a thousand miles.

'There is something you might do,' he said. 'You might patrol the sea off the west and south coasts of Ireland to spot these same submarines. We could spare you a few planes for that purpose.'

Frank said that we had had no trouble from submarines. What we were afraid of was invasion. He took it that the people of Ireland would have the President's sympathy in case of aggression.

'Yes,' said F.D.R., 'German aggression.'

'Or British aggression,' said Frank.

The President became very angry. He said it was preposterous to suggest that the British had any intention of becoming an aggressor in the case of Ireland.

'If that is so,' said Frank, 'why cannot they say so? We have asked them to –'

The President interrupted him again.

'What you have to fear,' he said, 'is German aggression.'

'Or British aggression.'

At this the President gave striking evidence of his indignation. The Negro servants had entered, no doubt urged by Colonel Watson, and had begun to place a tablecloth and some silver on the President's desk, preparatory to serving his lunch. When Frank repeated 'British aggression', the President caught a corner of the cloth and jerked it across the table so that some of the silver was hurled across the floor.

'I never heard anything so preposterous in all my life,' he cried, jerking his head backwards and forward.

'Wouldn't it be a simple thing for them to give us a guarantee?' said Frank.

'Why, I could give you a guarantee right now,' said F.D.R.

'Perhaps Mr. President,' I said, 'you could do something along that line. Perhaps you could point out to Mr. Churchill that it would ease the situation very considerably if he would give us this guarantee.'

'Of course he'd give it,' replied the President. 'I could get it from him in the morning.'

This was a good note on which to end the interview, so we thanked him and withdrew.

John Campbell

FINNISH WINTER

Madonna on a wall,
Two photographs, a candle on a tray,
Books over your bed,
So few, each read,
So few your things.
A passport where you wear your sailor hat
Nine years ago, no younger,
The same face calm in the light,
The same eyes,
Only the yellow tulips dying.
I sit on the edge of the bed
And read a book that says Yvaskyla,
Waiting for you.
In the next room they play tangos from Majorca.
When you come we light the candle,
You are fragrant with milk
And with the snow.
When you smile the candle flames,
The room turns gold,
Light tumbles into leaves.
How should this time grow old?
We too, the stillness, your hand in mine.

John Campbell

HARMONY

As a Mycenaean formula embedded in the text of Homer
Or an agate set in winking silver
Or rime on puddles frozen in the yard
His new contains his old.
His hair is scanty, white,
Words bubble up, as quickly disappear,
The things that were the core of him
Have worked their own betrayal.
She swings a bucket on her arm,
The two of them in counterpoint,
She ripe with flowers, seedlings, plants,
He distant across the empty yard,
Hesitant, by the barn door
Where moody cattle chomp on rasp-dry hay.
Clang of bucket, tap of stick,
Their daily conversation shapes their love.
Beyond the yard the fields stretching away,
Beyond, the sea
And, faint, the far horizon.

John Campbell

SNOW

The silence of it
Or its warmth?
When the wolves came to tear her heart
They were calmed by it.
They looked into the distance,
Their breath like smoke,
Their fur encrusted with its whiteness.
He could barely remember his hatred,
The screaming of the birds,
The whale's yellowing jawbone
Drawn back from the torn mouth.
When they had finished their work
They sat reverently,
Old monks in a circle,
Their lips scarlet against the snow.

Siobhán Campbell

CALL OF THE CORNCRAKE

There is a tip of forever
in the wait for the cut
when you fly low on rufous wings
and call out your court.

Crane-necked, we hear you
rattle through grass
hoping to mate before meadows
are sheared.

A line that might stop.
No crex comes back
before the machine
grinds in the gap.

What sight is right?
We hope to spy
while you scour the meadow,
*high beak, high eye.*

Siobhán Campbell

## WHEN ALL THIS IS OVER

I plan to go north
by unapproved roads
where sniper signs rust on the trees.

I will cross the border
over and back
several times to see how it feels.

I will dance the pig's dyke
and taste mountain mayflower
on the breeze.

Near under-fished lakes
I will hear a blood-pause
in the reach of the night

when every word used for batter
and crisis will cruise with the ease
of what runs right through us,

when the shift and fill
of my own dear cells
is all they will tell as they breathe.

And out through the lanes,
I will lie in my form
in overgrown fields

not a chopper in sight.
And they say it is safe
and the weather agrees.

Siobhán Campbell

## WHY ISLANDERS DON'T KISS HELLO

And it's not just the bad-timing nose-grazing
jaw against pursed expectation, nor
is it because of Judas
(though he slips out the side door of this discussion)
but more that it seems too familiar
as we have not been to pre-school with your mother.
Perhaps we are not fully of *the Europe*
where the lean-to nature of a kiss can denote
who will be shafted in a vote.
Or is it just a fear of being wrong, two in
Paris, three in Zagreb and so on?
Right-left instead of left-right could affect the funding
for those new roads in Cavan.
It's not to do with hygiene;
we shake hands happily instead
but we've learned because we must,
being from the island of largesse,
to give that peck of venture in a shared future
where the view over one shoulder is as good
from this side as the other.

Kevin Conmy

CARIBBEAN

I'm rumpunched by the seashore
listening to each wave break
And the almost silence in between.

The nightbirds call: they say
"we're here but you can't see us,
you can't see us but we're near."

Leaning back I search the nightsky,
a dizzying puzzle of stars,
the universe in dot-to-dot.

The absence of pattern is not
a problem as you surrender
in the embrace of the Caribbean.

Kevin Conmy

FIRST DANCE

It was our way
to labour long
and hunt hard.
Moving fast
fierce and graceful –
movement was life to us.

Then once in quiet
nightrest moment
restless, I moved
without intent
without aim
except in answer to the need
the rhythm of
my possibilities.

I stretched
arched skyward
climbing high moonbound
swayheld, then followed
sweeping low ground
shadowing.

Aware only of
momentum pulsing
flamelimbed
in me spinning
dizzy the world
returned to stillness.

# Ragnar Deeney Almqvist

## THE STATUE ARTIST

He was a living sculpture. Unlike the charlatans who cluttered the city's high streets drenched in silver and gold, dressed as freaks, blowing bubbles, dancing, twitching, blinking, he did not move. He spent his days in back alleys, standing, staring at the dirt around him, rigid as marble. His eyes glazed over the shadows lengthening on the alley walls. His consciousness flickered, his heartbeat dulled. The greatest pleasures he knew were the searing aches that grew like foetuses within his muscles over the course of a day's stillness. He was an atheist, but the pain brought him closer to God than any believer had ever been.

He disdained money. Dressed as anyone else, hiding in dark corners, away from the city's tourists, he did not, at first, receive much, and so had little to disdain. But any coins flung at his feet he left there. Drunks and junkies would gather in his wake, and there was pleasure in this also, the misery with which they would clot their veins. Over months, as crowds began to form around him, regardless of how obscure the place he sought to exhibit, the offerings grew. By summer, his day's art complete, the concrete would often glisten, pools of gold and silver over which he stepped unheeding.

Adulation encircled him: pointing fingers, puzzled faces, murmurings, he took great pride in it all. He was an artist. Stillness was his art. The years he had wasted composing haikus, painting, scratching the viola, all those failures fell behind him now like the stage behind the curtain. In the stillness of the day all his miseries were hidden. Unmoving, he was transformed.

She had been there for many days watching him. Small and unobtrusive, she had dull fair hair, a porcelain face, chipped in places, as if several times dropped on carpeted floors. She avoided eye contact, spoke to his sneakers. 'I think what you're doing is amazing. I've never seen art so forceful.'

Blushing, he thanked her. 'How do you do it?' she asked. 'Stay so still, I mean, for so long.'

He shrugged, 'It's not so hard.'

The girl glanced up at him, eyes rimmed with shadow, pupils heavy. 'Yesterday you stood with your hands before your face for seven hours. You never twitched.'

Again he shrugged. 'If I twitched,' he said, 'then I would not be standing still.'

The girl smiled, looked once more at his feet. 'Would you like to go for coffee?' she asked.

He looked at her and nodded, slowly.

The city's coffee shops were all alike: petite Polish waitresses, carefully unsanded floorboards, framed posters of cult movies, cinnamon smells. These rooms were purgatory.

'Have you studied art?' she asked. Her hands, lying on the tabletop, pulsed like threatened starfish.

'Yes.'

'I study art,' she said.

'And do you like it?'

'Yes. Did you?'

'No.' His espresso was bitter. He felt the caffeine like tar in his throat and stomach, choking him. 'Studying art did me a lot of harm.'

The girl nodded. 'I have heard people say that.'

He looked at her sharply. Her dress was made of greyish-yellow wool, trimmed with red tassels. Her only make-up was dark eye shadow, liberally applied. Her cigarettes were rolled. She was in every way a typical student. 'You don't believe them when they say it?'

'No.'

'Why?' he asked.

'Those that say it are usually successes. Whatever harm it might have done has not hurt them much.'

He smiled at the implication. 'Successes,' he said, quietly.

Over by the counter, a plate was dropped. The coffee drinkers laughed, applauded boorishly. He scowled. 'Let's go somewhere else.'

She nodded, the tassels on her dress bobbing like apples on a string.

They went for a pint, smoked some cigarettes, and kissed under a dirty streetlamp. They got the bus to her place, a house on the city's outskirts, once her grandmother's.

'She died last year. Cancer. I nursed her through the last months.'

He nodded, asked her no more about it.

The house was small and cluttered, paperbacks scattered across the floor, easels bunched in every corner. She painted mostly still life, showed him sketchbooks filled with nudes and rotting aubergines. Though her draughtsmanship was excellent, he thought her work hollow. The vegetables looked like photographs, the people like waxworks, realistic but not real.

'I've drawn you, you know,' she admitted, blushing. She pulled a notebook from her bag, handed it to him. In dozens of pages he stood at the centre of charcoal crowds, scowling fantastically at himself. His chin hag-like, eyes vapid, the space around him loose and shadow-filled, he seemed a creature ripped from Gothic, caught within a nightmare. He set the notebook down.

'You don't like them?' she said, voice trembling.

He shook his head. 'Not that. It can be hard to see yourself.'

She frowned a moment, her small imperfect features knotting tightly together, lips whitening like a boxer's knuckles. 'I understand,' she said. 'I've often thought that too.' She glanced at the empty bottle before them. 'Would you like more wine?' Before he could answer, she was halfway to the kitchen. 'You know,' she called from behind the bead partition, 'I've never had a model like you. To stay so still, so long. It's incredible.'

He shrugged. Between the blood-red beads her silhouette worked the cork patiently. 'There's no easier thing in the world,' he shouted back, too loudly he knew at once. He drained what wine remained in his glass. 'Really I could stand much more. Sometimes, I think, well … I think I could never move again.' He laughed. 'I've dreamed that.'

'And why not?' she called. Her voice was distant now, her silhouette gone.

He sighed. 'I don't know. People grow indifferent, then soon resentful. Already I sense it, the way they mutter after me, the faked concern. They prefer the high street freaks and beggars, the sand sculptors, the doll dancers, the goldpainted whores. Try explaining art to them!' He shook his head. 'No, I'd be locked away, shot blind with electricity, if I pushed myself even close to where I can go.'

How long since he had spoken so much? He was drunk, he realised, his speech slurred embarrassingly. Suddenly she was beside him again, her hand pressed hard against his leg. 'You are a great artist,' she said, smiling.

He nodded, reassured. 'I think so.'

When she removed her dress, she pushed his face to her small white breasts and he breathed deep. She smelled of incense. Tiny scars ran along her stomach. He kissed each one, causing her to groan. Then she pushed him back, straddled him on the bed, pupils pulsing within their shadowed sockets.

It was bright when he awoke, sunlight so white it burned his retinas to look on it. His eyes did not shut. His hands did not move to his face. His mouth did not open wide in puzzlement. He heard sizzling, smelt bacon frying, and felt his tongue water in response, but when he went to move it, nothing.

Panic seized him, but the physical sensations that accompanied it, and that he knew so very well – the dry mouth, constricted breathing, sweating hands – did not appear. As his eyes burned, his mind locked, and for several seconds – it could have been minutes, hours, so timeless was the quality – no thought went through his head, just the purest terror.

Like a patient, he lay, propped high in the bed, pillows beneath him, arms resting neutrally over the paint stained duvet, beyond whose ends he could see his toes poking out. The room in which he had spent the night was heavy with light and shadow now, its bare walls flecked with paint. Books and bottles scattered everywhere, and in the furthest corner, an easel, its back to him, set beside a low table, more coloured than any rainbow.

A low hum joined the sizzling filtering through the beaded partition. Panic came again in waves, but though his mind thrashed, his body was a cadaver, and all the screams which pierced his inner ear could not cause his tongue to tremble.

At length, she appeared, dressed in a t-shirt only and carrying a plate piled high with rashers, eggs, buttered toast and in her other hand a pot of coffee, the smell of which now sickened him. She smiled. 'Do you like the music?' She set the breakfast down on the floor, laughed, sat beside him, cupped a hand to his face. 'You are such an artist,' she said. 'To stay so wonderfully still.' All he could do was look at her. She stared deep into his eyes, smiled. 'I painted you while you were asleep. You were so peaceful, I couldn't resist.' She rose quickly, went to the easel – her butt cheeks rising, falling – lifted the canvass from it and turned it to him. He couldn't but be impressed. Her lines were clear and well-drawn, as before, yet this composition was truer. She turned it back to herself again, scrutinised it, eyebrows drawing together. 'I'm not sure,' she said. 'There's something in it that I like, but it's not quite there, you know? Still,' she put her painting back on the easel, 'many more chances.' Grinning, she lifted the plate from the floor. 'Now,' she said, 'I imagine you're hungry,' She took a strip of bacon, and dangled it above his half open mouth. Oil dripped onto his face – he saw but could not feel it. 'Open wide,' she whispered. The scars on her stomach resembled train tracks. 'Open wide,' she insisted. Like a goldfish, he gaped at her. 'Not hungry then?' She shook her head. 'And me after going to all the trouble. Well, I guess I'll just leave the plate here, your lordship. Take some when you feel up to it.'

In the background, the music twanged on.


Some time before dusk she would push his eyelids shut. Then came the sound of the needle's preparation – he had been in hospital before and knew the clicks and hisses well. He could not feel the injection, of course, but, having seen the pocks on his arms the days she swabbed him, realized where he was being shot. What he was being shot with, where she got it, he had no idea – perhaps her grandmother's, he thought. It didn't matter – he had accepted that he would never leave this bed.

During the day she would paint him, and at night too, after the drugs had wiped his senses clear. She showed him the sketches, the paintings. By them, through a methadone mist, he tracked his own deterioration. She cooked for him frequently, but never fed him. Often the uneaten food – steak, pasta, once even a takeaway – appeared in her portraits, propped on his thinning chest, or beside him, on the locker, between novels and political treatises, leather covers ringed with coffee stains.

The drugs – he presumed at least it was the drugs – prevented him from hungering. But they could not dull the hate which gripped him, nor the weary fright of the passing days, as through her paintings – often nudes – he watched his ribs grow ever more pronounced, his skull begin to force its way out from behind his features.

'Such an incredible model,' she would repeat, running her hands almost lovingly across the paper covering his skeleton. When propped at certain angles, eyelids open, he could see his heart sighing within his chest; through the grey of his skin purple veins showed like silhouettes.

She would read to him sometimes, extracts from novels, poems. Her hands waved expressively as she read, as if to an audience of schoolchildren. Her voice drilled like a migraine.

Gradually, to his relief, he began to deafen. All sounds became thuds, then just an ocean, as from the inside of a shell, then not even that. His vision too started to blur, so that all her paintings came to resemble blobs, and her face, pressed to his, a blur, and he could see his suffering no more. At last, his senses were stripped entirely and there was only his mind, warped and ethereal. And relief came to him, as his soul filtered from its cage, and hung over his shattered body, and he was perfectly, completely still at last, and ever would be.

It was several days before she realised he was dead. His eyes had died before his body, which clung to life still, just as her grandmother's had, long past its time.

Weeks ago she had run out of medication. For nights, visions of him rising from the bed, taking her neck in his skeletal grip played endlessly in her dream. On the day of his last injection, after much thought, she hamstrung him. The mattress soaked with blood, more than such a tiny frame could possibly contain. He whimpered – a first sound in thirty-seven days – then nothing once more, and she went back to her easel and painted.

Her last portraits were of his skeleton, the organs decomposed, ripped from his bones by the cats she had let in through the room's back window and the tiny larvae she sensed but could not see. In the end, there were well over a hundred paintings. Spread one side of the house to the other, she thought them a work of some magnitude, even brilliance. She exhibited them at a city gallery, where they aroused a mixed response, with critics admiring the excellence of her draftsmanship, but dubious as to the work's originality, and unhappy with its scope. 'What is offered here is nothing new,' one wrote, 'and lacks authenticity. This is the work of a gifted imitator, not an artist.' She read the reviews with disdain, tore them into tiny pieces, and buried the remnants in her garden, alongside his bones, where they were dug up by dogs, and scattered across the grey and artless suburbs.

# Eamon Delaney

## The Casting of Mr O'Shaughnessy (*extract*)

At 4.45 p.m. I came down Clonskeagh Road from Loyola and, as arranged, met Wycherley and Tess sitting on the railings of Isaac Butt's house. Like birds of prey they were both quietly looking across the road at the dark trees surrounding Mossbawn House and, to my irritation, appeared to be less-than-well dressed for the great patriot's dinner table: Tess decked out in a floppy brown suede jacket and ranch-hand Levis, and Wycherley looking pale and thin inside his grey shirt and soot-black mohair suit from the Lemass era. They didn't see me so I dived into a suburban garden, crossed a low fence (Butt's windows were open so someone must live there after all) and crept up behind them.

Pushing a broken twig into the back of Tess's neck, I shouted, 'Stop your statue or I'll cut your throat!'

'Shane!' yelped Tess, springing from the wall.

Wycherley cringed with disgust and made a cutting remark about the nation letting its orphans on the loose. His red-eyed face was the pallor of unsalted butter and he appeared to be holding his stomach; hangover or the psychosomatic tension of the big job.

'You look like you're going to a funeral, there, Bob.'

'Hush, Shane,' said Tess. 'He's in a fragile state.'

'And I'll put you in one if you're not careful,' he grumbled.

'Come, come, let's have a ceasefire. It's all the rage.'

'It won't be what we'll be doing,' he said with determination.

'No?'

'No. The unveiling ceremony has to be on his ninetieth birthday and I want what we've been forced to do finished a week before that.'

'That's very tight.'

'The whole project depends on it,' he said impatiently. 'It has to be done. After what happened yesterday there's no question about it. Our reputation depends on it. Yours as well as mine. And the government's. I gave them a commitment.'

'All according to plan.'

'That's right,' he said softly, avoiding looking at me.

We watched Wycherley. He looked weary, tired of the whole affair. Again he expressed, or pretended to express, his disappointment and annoyance at the government's narrow terms for the O'Shaughnessy project. The philistines, he said, any abstraction was beyond them. Don't worry, they would get the super-realism they were looking for. The whole project had caused him nothing but grief, from beginning to end. He wanted to see the back of it. Now it was reported that Forbes was thinking of suing him which was ridiculous. Out of order. Even if he did perhaps over-hastily blame Forbes for the early threats and was now prepared to acknowledge that there was probably more than a spurned sculptor behind the AVNS, it still did not justify going to court over what were merely word-of-mouth allegations. Slander was one of the city's liberties – couldn't he handle the cut and thrust? Look at all the people the media and politicians and experts on the street slandered by linking them with the AVNS. Would be UDA be taking action, or M15, or the South African Security Service (suspected because of Corry's anti-apartheid activities)?

He would give as much time to the Forbes court case as he had given to the AVNS 'threats' that caused it, which was very little. The campaign of the faceless and, for all we knew, personless Captain Moonlight had got far too much notice. Redmondites, my eye. They had done – Wycherley looked around here as a woman had entered an adjoining garden – they had done, he said in a lowered voice, nothing except write a few letters and now they were pompously calling a ceasefire! Pending further developments! Well, ceasefire or not, Wycherley would go on with the job. Same as always. He would see a memorial of O'Shaughnessy erected in St Stephen's Green on his ninetieth birthday, regardless of the stymieing efforts of Forbes, Redmondites or the Commemoration Committee. OK?

'OK,' we answered.

'No problem,' said I, touching his arm.

'Thank you,' he said and a soft grateful smile played about his lips and twinkling bloodshot eyes. 'Thank you so much.'

Dishevelled and drained as he was, a proud craggy glamour emanated from his wax-and-cotton features during this touching if slightly embarrassing moment of suffused affection. We, his adopted, had seen him through thick and thin, and we would see him through to the end.

'Come on.' He touched my elbow and we rose from Butt's wall.

'Let us go and see this man we're to encase in bronze.'

A clear grass verge sided the slipway from the kerb to his gates. On two granite pillars, small signs read respectively, 'Mossbawn' and 'House'. We passed in and crunched up the short curve of gravelled driveway. Trees surrounded us on all sides, linking densely above our heads to give the effect of a tunnel through which sparkling fingers of sunlight managed to penetrate. Bright yellow dandelions shot up from between years of broken twigs entangled in the thorned undergrowth. Suddenly, driveway parted and trees thinned, the house was clearly visible. A chocolate-brown Volkswagen sat squatted in the sunlight, toy-like and incongruously innocent, given its owner. He'd driven it himself until recently, but now the daughter took the wheel.

A swathe of grey gravel semi-circled the front of the house and our heavily scrunching soles signalled our approach. It was very quiet. The greying whitewashed house bore little sign of internal life. The upstairs windows were veiled as was, further up, a loft skylight. The spacious downstairs windows, however, had their velvet curtain folds pulled back and belted at the waist and as we mounted the first of the seven stone steps to the blue front door, I caught an intriguing glimpse of bookshelves, oil paintings and mantelpiece within.

We stood before the front door. Wycherley, out of polite habit, wiped his winkled George Webbs on the doormat, and rearranged the remaining bits of his hair with tremulous fingers.

Tess, fidgeting with the last walnut button left on her jacket, smiled and said to me, 'Shane, there's no bell.'

In other words, they were waiting for me to knock. Me – the silver-fingered Corny of the Squad, whose gentle knock, knock, knock brings them out. I lifted the heavy head of his Anna Livia knocker and far from gentle was its resounding clack-clack! The whole door (house? bed? Corny?) shook with the iron thuds. We waited. Footsteps approached. Fairly fast ones for an old man. Was he already trying to impress us? A tiny telescopic spyhole eyed us and, for a laugh, I put my fingertip over it, blotting out the old boy's world. Wycherley, far from laughing, knocked my arm down.

Jesus – just in time, for the door pulled swiftly back to reveal, not the old man we expected, but a wondrous young creature in a black sleeveless dress, whose wonderful wet wound of a welcome mouth asked us who we were. The apparition of this radiant creature – with big soft Bambi eyes and tangled wreath of Rossetti hair, of my own height (age? generation? political import?) – took me by pleasant surprise. What, pray, was such a splendid creature doing treading or, should I say, daintily toe-kissing, the floors of Corny's abode this soft Saturday afternoon? His granddaughter? If so, I'm a Provo tomorrow. His mistress? If so, I'm a reincarnated Black and Tan come to kill the cradle-snatcher.

'Oh, I am sorry!' she flustered when Wycherley explained who we were.

'Mr Wycherley and company – of course. Do come in!'

A bare arm ushered us into the hall.

We had nothing to offer the coat-and-hat stand, already overburdened with galoshes, worn slippers, walking sticks and about fifty hanging coats (his victims at a rough count) and so, coatless and awkward, we stood around waiting for the poor dear to finish relocking the door. In fact, poor Vanessa (she introduced herself while she was on her knees – like so many of Corny's victims) had to work the rust-tough bottom bolt up and down, to get it across and into its stubborn ring. With the vigour of the yanking effort that ample woolwork of tendril hair shook loose around her head like an unravelled tea cosy. And, just as unseemly, but even more becoming, her straining dress gradually worked its way up a freckle-speckled full-white thigh, closely followed, as you can imagine, by my beady eye.

'Do you want a hand?' asked Tess, casting an accusatory glance at her gentlemen companions.

'No thanks,' came a strained voice. 'I've just got it – there!'

'Goodness me,' declared Vanessa, rising to her feet with a flush of colour and smoothing her dress. 'You can never be too careful about security these days. Especially the last few days. Mr O'Shaughnessy has been very laid back about it, but I think it is terrible. How anyone would want to terrorise an old man about things that happened seventy years ago – isn't it just terrible?'

'Shocking,' I said, measuring the concern in those green doe-eyes. Stone the bleeding crows – his mistress at ninety?

'Do you have a police watch on your premises, Mr Wycherley?'

'Not since last night and the so-called ceasefire,' replied an abrupt Mr Wycherley, brazenly looking about the place. 'Quite honestly, I share Mr O'Shaughnessy's laid-back attitude. I've taken little notice of the whole business. Cranks through and through. Shall we go in here?'

'Oh … eh.' Vanessa's little face fell. 'Why, yes. Yes, do,' she cried, nervously slipping behind us. 'Do go on into the living-room. Mrs Williams will bring you in some tea. Sit down, please.'

On seeing Mr Wycherley proprietorially head for the fireside leather armchair, Vanessa bashfully bounced forward (she does skip!) to clear from its squashed cushions a heap of books and journals, and on seeing Mr Wycherley agreeably ease into the leather she retreated from the room smiling apologetically. She was off to fetch the man himself, perhaps waking him from an early slumber.

'Nice girl,' ventured Tess after the door shut.

'Yes, very,' snapped Wycherley, glumly peering into the empty grate.

'Sorry I spoke.'

'You will be, the place is probably bugged. Shane! Sit down out of that, and stop snooping around the man's house.'

'I'm just looking at his bookshelves,' I protested, already up and about and, I have to admit, absolutely enthralled by the room's shelves and trappings.

'Tess, dear, you wouldn't fetch me a glass of water from the kitchen?'

The 'living area' was very much as Joe had described it. It was a hybrid of two rooms – a front living-room in which we three had quietly sat before Tess left and I began scouring, and an attached drawing-room – the two rooms successfully de-partitioned in the way Corny wished the country was, with two big bright windows at either end.

Though the walls were crowded with paintings and pictures of dead friends and relatives, it was very obviously a 'living area': his last retreat. Unwashed tea cups and crumbed plates were discreetly stuck in between the neat piles of papers, journals and files that grew Manhattan-like from polished tables. Let's hope our quarry – the tell-tale papers – is downstairs and not up here or we'll never find them, I thought, and let's hope Joe comes up with a better description of what they're sheathed in. At the foot of one of the many bookcases that reached to the ceiling was a line of tiny shoes, a heap of recent newspapers and a vat of what looked like home-made wine but could have been diluted blood (take it easy, Shane). In a corner there was, indeed, a row of those big pin-stripe suits he swims around in. They were hanging on a rail and they looked amazing. A fully open wardrobe! I'd have shown them to Bob if he wasn't busy fighting a hangover and reading some notes.

'What are you looking for?' Wycherley called, wiping Solpadeine from his mouth and taking out a fag.

'A skeleton,' I said and there was a titter.

'Shane,' scolded Tess, almost presciently, before laughing herself.

'Good evening,' announced Mr O'Shaughnessy, and the laughter stopped like that (I click my fingers).

'Oh, good … good evening,' we all murmured, stunned by the silence of his entry.

He shut the door gently, coughed and came over to shake hands. Hushed, we rose to greet him, and he tottered towards us, smiling wanly with those wet lizard's eyes of his bulging out of a grey-skinned skull. It was a shock to realise how old he was, and looked, seen in the flesh. One forgot because of the high public profile, the speeches, the court cases, the activist politics, that this was one of the oldest of the old fighters, a man who defended Boland's Mills with de Valera.

We warmly shook. I could feel the bones moving within, reasserting the great O'Shaughnessy, a hand that had killed many a bad and fine man. I was finally happy in his company. He'd soon be in theirs.

Loose-fingered Wycherley appeared to receive the withered paw less warmly, perhaps afraid he might pull off some of the flesh he hoped to sculpt, a tactile reminder of his own mortality.

'You must forgive my delay,' croaked Mr O'Shaughnessy in that familiar coffee-percolator voice. 'I was in the shower.'

'The shower?' said Tess, speaking for all of us. Sure a shower would kill him. Or would it? He was fast on his feet and he swung around.

'For a wash, young lady. And who are you?'

'Oh,' she said, a bit flustered, and stepping forward while a waxen claw patted her to sit. 'Tessa Masterson's my name. I'm so pleased to be working on –'

'Yes, I know your mother,' he interrupted and clutching her hand for safety he plopped down beside her, his little shoes rising as he landed. Black Winstanleys, I noted with secret satisfaction. My shoes!

'She was a wonderful actress in her day,' he expanded, leaning back and roving his pink-rimmed eyeballs across the three of us. On 'actress' I noted the furious French phlegm gargling its way up his turkey-throttled throat.

'But she's still an actress now,' Tess gently pointed out. It was a sore point with the family.

'Yes,' he said softly and paused, crossing his thin legs. He was moving around inside one of those greatly oversized pin-stripe suits, this one of thick navy wool, worn over a wrinkled white shirt and a floppy yellow tie. Oisin would have loved it. I loved it. Him. Now. I could see what Sharon Travers saw. He was a dapper little dote, as cute as a rat in an overcoat. Preserved, he'd make a lovely sculpture.

'McArdle, is it?'

'It is,' I said, but you don't know my mother.

'McArdle … Shane,' he said to himself, a fact which made me nervous. 'Shane is a fine name. There's not enough Shanes around.'

'One is enough,' muttered Wycherley.

'I am grateful to you,' he announced, after another awkward pause, 'for your patience.'

'Nonsense,' said Wycherley. 'You were only a few minutes.'

'I mean,' he explained, 'for sticking to the commission to do my statue. Despite all these threats and trouble the minister tells me that you have no intention of pulling out. I am most grateful. You must have suffered a great deal of distress from this' – he gesticulated vaguely, and prematurely, towards the fireplace – 'this absurd mischief … fomented trouble. Never did I think a memorial to me would come to this' – hand flapping loosely at the grate – 'though, now that it has, it doesn't surprise me.'

'I can assure you, Mr O'Shaughnessy,' declared Wycherley with confidence, 'we were never too alarmed. How could we take any of this AVNS business too seriously? Cranks from beginning to end, and quite honestly –'

'Be careful,' interrupted O'Shaughnessy, the fleshy lid of one round eye rising ponderously. 'Be careful.'

The now-customary pause followed. We waited in the intimidating silence. Not a sound. Only the noise of O'Shaughnessy's gums engaging in a bout of lubricious saliva-swallowing.

'The British,' he said, licking one lip and linking his hands.

'Oh,' said Wycherley.

'I see their hand in this.' He nodded and on cue, a right hand once again floppily gesticulated to the fireplace. 'The whole thing smacks of amateurs, masquerading as historically concerned politicals. Redmondites, they call themselves! In 1986! He coughed energetically, shaking inside the oversized suit, and brought up tears. 'How could such people be still around, threatening to blow up statues, or those gifted enough to make them.'

Wycherley nodded.

'It is all too much to believe. Too fantastic for this day and age.'

'Very true,' I judiciously interjected.

'The AVNS.' He spat out the initials with great sarcasm. 'Running around with their contemptible little letters, calling me a retired terrorist – how dare they!?' he said raising his voice, and veins.

Denis Devlin

A Government official dressed in grey minor
Slipped into a low pub
At the end of the world;
Outside, the rain was falling in millions.

An ancient like a frittered, chalk hill
Monocled the evening paper through a chip of window-
    pane:
The disgraced words took on dignity.

'Will he tout me for a drink?' feared the Government
    official
Though the ancient stirred no more than thought in a
    new-dead man.

Denis Devlin

ANK'HOR VAT

The antlered forests
Move down to the sea.
Here the dung-filled jungle pauses

Buddha has covered the walls of the great temple
With the vegetative speed of his imagery

Let us wait, hand in hand

No Western god or saint
Ever smiled with the lissom fury of this god
Who holds in doubt
The wooden stare of Apollo
Our Christian crown of thorns:

There is no mystery in the luminous lines
Of that high, animal face
The smile, sad, humouring and equal
Blesses without obliging
Loves without condescension;
The god, clear as spring-water
Sees through everything, while everything
Flows through him

A fling of flowers here
Whose names I do not know
Downy, scarlet gullets
Green legs yielding and closing

While, at my mental distance from passion,
The prolific divinity of the temple
Is a quiet lettering on vellum.

Let us lie down before him
His look will flow like oil over us.

Denis Devlin

The General Secretary's feet whispered over the red carpet
And stopped, a demure pair, beside the demure
Cadet, poor but correct,
Devoted menial of well-mannered Power.
"A word with you." "Yes, your Excellency."
Excellency smiled. "Your silk shirt is nice, Scriptor.
But listen. Better not let these private letters
Reach the President. He gets worried, you know,
About the personal misfortunes of the people;
And really, the Minister is due to arrive.
It is surely most unseemly
To keep the State in the waiting-room
For God knows what beggars,
For totally unnecessary people."

Their mutual shirtfronts gleamed in a white smile
The electorate at breakfast approved of the war for peace
And the private detective idly deflowered a rose.

Denis Devlin

Here are empty quaysides
It might be midnight nearby
Or a searchlight stripe on midnight.

Enter, stealthy, who-you-know
Propelled along in torpor
He might be a river flowing
Back to the source, its author

He is pulled up short
By stacks of sacked grain. He
pushes, his legs move
Up and down and free.

Denis Devlin

## FROM GOVERNMENT BUILDINGS

Evening lapses. No pity or pain, the badgered
Great get home, and the little, tomorrow's anchorage,
All smiling, sour the milk of charity,
Like the pyrrhonist poets, Love's saboteurs.

The clerks fan out and the lamps; and I look inwards:
What turns amuse you now? with whom, not me! do
You cower in Time, whose palsied pulse is nimbler
A hair's breadth when want and have are equal?

My room sighs empty with malignant waiting;
The November wind slows down outside, wheeling
Twig and awning on the brick balcony,
A wind with hackles up. In Rome at evening

Swallows traced eggshapes on the vellum sky,
The wind was warm with blue rain in Dublin;
When the culture-heroes explore the nether world
It was voiceless beasts on the move made Death terrible.

Friendship I will not, barring you; to have witness does:
Doll birds, dogs with their social nose, by day
Are touchstone. But at night my totem silence
With face of wood refuses to testify.

The famous exile's dead, from many on many
Deportations, from Spain to Prague to Nice,
Kaleidoscopic police, his Danse Macabre;
One of the best the worst had never feared.

You, you I cherish with my learned heart
As in the bombed cathedral town, doubly

A tourist trophy now, the dean shouted: "At last!
At least and at last we have stored the windows away,

The fabulation of my Lord's glory, by
Seven and by seven and by seven multiplied!"
So is my care though none your mystic I,
Nor you like the painted saints but breath and more.

And do not pace the room haunting the furniture
But be my insular love; and I would have you
Fingering the ring with its silver bat, the foreign
And credible Chinese symbol of happiness.

Denis Devlin

TANTALUS

The diplomat has bared his head,
The wine spreads across the cloth.
Give me stones for leavened bread?
My spine's pipette will fume in wrath.

I knew a gifted girl, she spoke
Languages more than Noah's beasts,
She took the veil and loathed the yoke,
Flirting despair with Mormon priests.

What will you give me if I tell?
I cannot speak, my hands are tied.
Shame like an Alderman in Hell
Has broke me down till I have cried.

# Noel Dorr

## IRELAND AT THE UNITED NATIONS (*extract*)

Spell a word of nine letters: l-a-n-d-s-w-e-r-k. If my memory is correct it was a Saturday night in 1960 or 1961. I was a very junior official in the Department of External Affairs and I had been called into Iveagh House to decode an urgent message from Ireland's UN mission in New York. At the time we used an old-fashioned code book for coded messages of a relatively low level of security, and of course the code book, which was a kind of dictionary of words alongside their code equivalents, had no entry for 'landswerk'. So, in decoding, I had to spell out this strange word one letter at a time.

The message, when decoded, proved to be a request from the Irish contingent with the UN force in the Congo: they were asking for a number of the Swedish armoured cars that were then in service with the Irish Defence Forces to be shipped out to them from Dublin. Communication systems at the time were not good. As a result the message had to be sent by a very indirect route – from the Mission to the UN and so on to External Affairs in Dublin for transmission to the Department of Defence.

Thinking about this long-ago incident reminds me that Ireland's involvement in UN peacekeeping operations spans the whole of my own diplomatic career, and more; back indeed to 1958 – only three years after Ireland took its seat for the first time in the UN General Assembly on 14 December 1955. Over the period since then, tens of thousands of members of the Irish Defence Forces have served in trouble spots in all corners of the world; and Ireland's record of participation in peacekeeping over half a century is a matter of justified pride for Irish people.

Unlike the more robust concept of enforcement action, UN peacekeeping is not mentioned explicitly in the UN

Charter: it is a creative development based on the general principles of Chapter 6, which allow the Security Council to make recommendations in regard to the 'Pacific Settlement of Disputes'.

UN peacekeeping can be said to have started in 1948 when UNTSO – a corps of unarmed military observers drawn from other Member States – was placed along ceasefire lines to help maintain a truce between Israel and its Arab neighbours. A similar observer group was interposed between Indian and Pakistani forces in 1949. Peacekeeping, in the more usual sense of a small, lightly-armed military force – a symbolic line of 'blue helmets' interposed with their consent between warring parties – dates back to the Suez crisis of 1956.

At that time, after Israel had gone to war against Egypt, two European powers, the UK and France, in secret collusion with Israel, intervened and attacked Egypt. Their overt purpose was to separate the original combatants, Israel and Egypt. In reality they wanted to re-establish control over the Suez Canal, which had been nationalised by Egypt's President Nasser a short time before. Their attack on Egypt was inept and their action was widely condemned. After a week of fighting, Egypt and Israel agreed to a ceasefire and the UK and France came under very strong international pressure, not least from US President Eisenhower and Secretary of State John Foster Dulles, to end their attack and withdraw. The UN Secretary General, Dag Hammarskjöld, with the support of Lester Pearson of Canada and others, devised a proposal for a UN peacekeeping force and the General Assembly agreed to send a UN Emergency Force of some 6,000 – known for short as UNEF – to the Sinai to take up position between the Egyptian and Israeli forces. Its arrival in the area allowed the UK and France to withdraw their forces, without too much loss of face, from what by then had become a disastrous situation for them.

This first full UN peacekeeping force became a model for other such forces over the years. As it happened it was established in 1956 just as an Irish Delegation attended the full session of the General Assembly for the first time.

Two years later, in 1958, Ireland dipped its own toe in the water: at the request of the UN it sent unarmed officers of the Defence Forces to serve for several months as members of the UN Observer Group in Lebanon (UNOGIL). Eventually some fifty Irish officers were involved. This group of unarmed observers was not quite comparable to UNEF, which was an organised military force, but it marked the first involvement of members of the Irish Defence Forces in a UN peacekeeping operation of any kind, or indeed in any kind of international service abroad.

In 1960 Ireland went much further: for the first time in its history it contributed an armed military contingent to a full-scale peacekeeping force – the UN operation in the Congo, which came to be known as ONUC, an acronym based on its title in French. This operation lasted four years and, before it concluded, it came close to bringing about the break-up of the UN. It also cost the lives of a number of members of the Irish Defence Forces. A great deal has already been written about the operation as a whole and about Ireland's participation in it. In writing about it here, I will draw largely on personal memories from the period just after I joined the Department of External Affairs. [...]

The request arrived in Dublin through the Irish Mission to the UN in New York in the early days of July 1960, just six months after I had joined the Department of External Affairs. I remember helping colleagues in the Political and UN section, under the direction of Conor Cruise O'Brien, to put together material for a memorandum to the Government. This was the formal submission in which the Minister for External Affairs, Frank Aiken, with the agreement of the Minister for Defence, recommended to the Government that it should agree to the UN request. On 19 July the Government decided to do so.

This was a historic decision: it means that, for the first time ever, units of the Irish Defence Forces, bearing arms, would serve abroad. As we look back today at Ireland's participation over the years in many different UN peacekeeping forces around the world, it is easy to forget just how strange and novel it was for the Ireland of 1960 to decide to send a contingent of soldiers, all of them volunteers, to join the new UN Force in the Congo.

Ireland has never had compulsory military service. The Irish Defence Forces were small and poorly equipped, and I think I am right in saying that they still used some First World War weapons at the time. They enjoyed good standing at home but they had never served overseas – indeed, Irish law did not permit such service outside the jurisdiction of our own State. And the Congo was a faraway country of which we knew little and with which we had no obvious connection. Why then did the Government decide to send first one battalion, and then two – at one time perhaps one-ninth of our armed forces in all – to serve in that distant country in Africa?

Under Article 25 of the Charter UN Member States agree to accept and carry out the decisions of the Security Council. But a decision authorising a peacekeeping force like that which the Council had adopted on this occasion does not impose an obligation on any particular Member State to contribute a contingent. The main reason for the positive recommendation was undoubtedly a belief that Ireland, when asked to support the UN in a practical way, should live up to what it had been saying for four years now in the General Assembly.[1]

Irish Governments have always believed that small States, in particular, have need of an effective international organisation to limit conflict and promote the rule of law in international life. I explained in an earlier chapter that this had been a theme of the Irish Delegations to the League of Nations in the 1920s and 1930s and one that had been repeated over the years since Ireland had been admitted to the UN.

Frank Aiken had now been Minister for three years. He had made some thoughtful speeches in the General Assembly in favour of decolonisation in Africa and elsewhere; and he had argued that, since there was now an organisation such as the UN to support their case, it was no longer necessary for national liberation movements to resort to the use of armed force, as he himself had felt obliged to do in Ireland in an earlier era when no such organisation existed. He had also argued in the Assembly for the gradual development of what he called 'areas of law'; and, more controversially, he had offered a plan for phased withdrawal along lines of longitude by US and Soviet forces that were confronting each other in Central Europe. Furthermore, he had proposed and advocated what was still a novel, and indeed controversial, idea at the time – the negotiation of a treaty to prevent the further spread of nuclear weapons. This proposal, which I will describe in a later chapter, eventually came to fruition with the signature of the Nuclear Non-Proliferation Treaty in 1968.

This was all admirable in its way. But now, unexpectedly, in mid-1960, came a test of whether Ireland was ready to live up to the rhetoric of its Minister and his delegation. Was it prepared to give practical evidence of its support for these ideas and principles by responding to the request of the UN Secretary General to send a contingent of Irish soldiers into Africa? Aiken and the Department believed that it had a moral obligation to do so.

There were other reasons too. The Irish Permanent Representative (that is, Ambassador) to the UN in New York, Freddie Boland, was at the time running a hotly contested campaign against two opponents for election as

President of the UN General Assembly: he won the election two months later.[2] Undoubtedly, there was a belief that a positive response to the request from the Secretary General would help his campaign by showing that Ireland was a 'good UN member'. The Defence Forces too, whose officers had tasted UN service in the Lebanon two years before, probably saw the possibility of service abroad in a good cause as a help to morale and to recruitment.

It is possible that there was also one other, less tangible, reason why the Government responded favourably to the UN request. This was the fact that a positive response would mean providing help in its difficulties to the Congo in particular. Frank Aiken, like some other older members of the Government, had been active as a young man in the Irish independence struggle in the early part of the century. He had joined the Volunteers as early as 1913.[3] Undoubtedly he would have remembered Roger Casement, whose name in Irish minds of that generation was indelibly associated with his heroic exploits in reporting atrocities in King Leopold's Congo Free State and against the Putomayo Indians in Peru, and with a later doomed effort to import arms to Ireland from Germany in the *Aud* in 1916. Indeed, although he was only a teenager at the time, Aiken, like other members of the old guard, might even have known Casement personally. Perhaps he saw the decision to respond to the request to send Irish troops to help the UN in the Congo as a fitting closing of the circle that Casement's work there had opened half a century before. [...]

I think back with sympathy to those heroic members of the first Irish military contingent to serve overseas on a UN mission, in a country about which they could have known very little at the time. They were transported out to the Congo from Dublin in huge US military aircraft in late July and early August 1960. Their equipment was, to say the least, rather outdated – bolt-action Lee-Enfield rifles, I think, of First World War vintage – and their communications equipment was poor. Their uniforms were those they would have worn in Ireland: the 'bull's wool' of which they were made was more suited to the rigours of the Irish winter than to the steamy heat of an equatorial climate. Then, and long afterwards, their ranking system was deliberately kept low so that, for example, a captain in the Irish army might well be the equivalent of a major or perhaps even a lieutenant colonel in other contingents. Nevertheless they went out with enthusiasm and *élan* to serve in a country that was soon to prove itself to be indeed the 'heart of darkness'. [...]

That November, the great adventure of Ireland's venture into the heart of Africa on behalf of the UN turned to tragedy. An Irish patrol in Kivu province in the eastern Congo ran into an ambush at Niemba, and nine Irish soldiers were killed by Baluba tribesmen armed with primitive weapons. These were the first soldiers of the Irish State to die abroad on active international service. Their bodies were brought home for burial. Like thousands of others, I went down to O'Connell Street to see the funeral cortège pass. Standing on the pavement I listened to the sombre music of the Dead March – a sharp and poignant counterpoint to the cheerful, spirited music to which they and their companions had marched out and into Africa some months before.

Ireland was sobered by this tragedy: this was no longer a great adventure; these deaths were real. But if the innocent idealism of the initial decision to join the UN force was tempered by the stark reality of Niemba, it was not diminished. I do not recall that there was any serious proposal at the time that the Government should withdraw the Irish contingent – as has happened more recently with larger countries that suffered similar losses in support of UN operations in Africa. Rather, there was a kind of sad pride in the fact that Irish peacekeepers had given their lives for an international ideal, and a belief that continuing the commitment would give meaning to their sacrifice.

Over the following months, the UN was drawn deeply into the quagmire that rapidly developed in the Congo. Indeed, in the following years, the organisation almost broke apart under the stresses set up by the task of nation-building in a country that was really at that stage no more than a colonial assemblage of disparate tribal regions; a country where post-colonial interference by European powers was a major factor; and a country that was eyed by both sides in the Cold War as a region of possible strategic value.

NOTES

1   Skelly (1997) p. 269.
2   The General Assembly elects an individual each year to preside over its sessions. The post, which is a prestigious one, is generally rotated among regional groups and is often filled by agreement among members of the group. In 1960, however, in addition to Boland, there were two other candidates from Europe – Jiri Nosek of Czechoslovakia and Thor Thors of Iceland – and Boland who had to run a vigorous campaign. He was successful and was elected to the post when the Assembly opened in mid-September.
3   See previous chapter.

# Brian Earls

## THE SEA OF ANECDOTES (*extract*)

There can come a moment in the experience of travel when
a shift in understanding occurs – that instant when, as it
were, the curtains begin to part – as a previously elusive
society seems to reveal something essential about itself. I
experienced one such moment on a summer evening in the
early 1990s. Together with a Moscow friend, I had gone on
a walking holiday and found myself spending the night in
a mountain hut in the southern Russian republic of
Kabardino Balkaria. Apart from myself, the remainder of
the company, a group of about six climbers, were
Russians. I had at that time been living in Moscow for
about a year, and was slowly and with an effort that was
scarcely matched by the meagre results, making my way
into the beguiling but unyielding Russian language. I and
my companion were mere hill walkers, but the others in
the hut were serious climbers, who the following day
planned to climb the nearby Mount Elbrus. As this
involved setting out before sunrise, and thus before the
summer heat had begun to melt the snow, the climbers
were not inclined to sleep. Instead they passed the time
exchanging what they called *anekdoty*. It was evident that
these must be jokes, as in the darkened hut the speakers
were regularly greeted with laughter. While occasionally
this was loud and heartfelt, more often it was knowing and
subdued and seemed to imply some complicity between
narrator and audience. The laughter was, it seemed clear,
an essential component of the occasion, encouraging
performers to embark on new jests and prompting the
previously silent into speech.

While this merriment was afoot, I lay on my bunk
straining to understand, and to be admitted to some small
share of the pleasure which the rest of the company
evidently derived from the recitals. At first the rapid flow

of speech and varying voices and styles proved impenetrable. When at last something began to cohere, to my surprise I seemed to be listening to a narrative in which a number of characters from Tolstoy's War and Peace featured. While the presence of Natasha Rostova, Prince Andrei, and Pierre Bezukhov seemed improbable in this particular setting, the stylised and simplified tsarist Moscow which provided the setting for the *anekdot* left little doubt regarding the identity of the protagonists. Somewhat puzzlingly, alongside these familiar figures, another individual, Poruchik Rzhevsky, who I could not recall from Tolstoy's novel, was also a prominent actor in the laughter-provoking antics.

As the jokes flowed back and forth, with one speaker complementing another and occasional pauses in the succession of jests signalling some shift in joke type or focus, other characters joined Natasha and Poruchik on stage. In addition to Lenin, his unfaithful wife Krupskaya and her lover Felix Edmundovich (Dzerzhinsky), there was Vovochka the hooligan schoolboy, Chapaev the Red Army commander, Rabinovich the melancholy and unillusioned Jew, and Stirlitz, an adroit Soviet spy in Hitler's Germany. These were joined by characters from the fiction of Turgenev and the poetry of Nicolai Nekrasov, Timur and his Band from the works of Arkady Gaidar, a popular children's writer of the 1930s, Ilya Muromicz, Baba Yaga, and Ivanushka Durachok from the world of folktales, and a host of characters from Russian cinema of the 1960s and 1970s, including such exotics as Winnie the Pooh, Holmes and Watson and even Mowgli, the hero of Kipling's Jungle Book. Together with these named characters the jokes contained an interminable succession of students, policemen, army recruits, hunters and talking animals, together with an amiable ethnic carnival of Ukrainians, Moldovans, Georgians, Estonians, Armenians, Jews and Chukchas (a Siberian people). Perhaps the most frequently encountered protagonists were an anonymous, but often surprisingly individualised, man and woman, who in jest after jest acted out a dialectic of good and bad manners, refined and coarse language, sobriety and drunkenness, and the confusions and hypocrisies of sexual desire. When towards dawn the narrators fell silent, it was clear that I had heard not an assortment of jokes, but rather glimpsed an entire world of stories, with its own cast of characters, cycles and conventions, themes and sub-genres.

The origin of Russian jokes seems uncertain. While some trace them back to the rich folklore of laughter of the tsarist era, others argue that they are linked to the specificities of the Soviet experience, to the ending of the freedoms that existed as late as the period of the New Economic Policy, and to the gap between the inflated language of the new state and the banalities of daily existence. When viewed through Western eyes, as in Ben Lewis's *Hammer and Tickle: the History of Communism Told Through Communist Jokes*, the emphasis has tended to fall on their political content. While such a reading has its obvious truth, and it is well attested that *anekdotchiki* (joke-tellers) were among those swept into the Gulag, it risks distortion by privileging a single category. Once the Stalinist fury had exhausted itself, the state seems to have taken little interest in those who told jokes – or at least resigned itself to the inevitability of such mockery – and accounts of the Brezhnev years speak of jokes as an amiable and ever present feature of the urban scene.

Certain conventions were nonetheless observed. Those who came of age in the 1970s recall learning in childhood, as one of those pieces of social information that help you negotiate the world, that jokes were to be told in small groups made up of people you knew and trusted and that political jokes were never to be recited in the presence of strangers. Such caution was not always observed. In the USSR vodka was an accompaniment of all kinds of sociability, with the result that prudence could be eroded, as with every drink narrators grew more daring until caution was largely thrown to the winds. It was not, however, totally discarded; in such circumstances a narrator might engage in a precautionary manoeuvre, ostentatiously interrupting the flow of *anekdoty* to address a (presumed) listening device concealed in the corner of the room. The unseen listener might be the recipient of a brisk 'Slava KPSS' (Glory to the Communist Party of the Soviet Union) or be assured: 'We have everything we want. We are very happy.'

As the listening device was imaginary, for it would have been impossible to have monitored every apartment in Moscow, an undertaking which could only have told the authorities what they already knew, the aversion-of-evil formula was itself a jest. It was, as it were, an acknowledgment that the jokes were at once part of the scheme of things and incompatible with official rhetoric. The *anekdoty* of the final decades of the USSR were not so much anti-Soviet as standing in an oblique relationship to Soviet accounts of reality. By creating an alternative verbal universe, whose currency was laughter, they constituted a muted commentary on the hortatory and optimistic language of the state. The *anekdoty* did not contradict, or in most cases even explicitly engage with, public doctrine, but rather, by tactics of indirection, called the latter into question by the realism of their own vision.

The *anekdoty* had their self-reflective aspects. One told of a competition in which the prize for the best joke would be ten years in prison, the second prize a tour of places associated with Lenin (Siberia), and the third a meeting with Lenin (execution). Although at such moments they might have appeared subversive, viewed through Soviet eyes they had their reassuring aspect. Not only did they not openly question the architecture of power, but the minutiae of Soviet life, which constituted the background to their narratives, were assumed to be normative. This ambiguity was reflected in a conceit of the time, which held that the *anekdoty* were produced by a special department of the KGB. (A friend whom I asked if he had ever invented a joke immediately replied: 'I'm not a KGBshnik.') The muted admiration extended to the KGB did not embrace those lower down in the power chain. A man with a few drinks taken tried to tell a joke to a member of the militia. The latter bridled. 'Do you not know I'm a militia man,' he said. 'Don't worry,' replied the other, 'I'll tell it to you twice.' Although those in authority may have smiled at the unending jokes of their citizens, their sober view is likely to have been that, unlike earlier cultural forms which could be appropriated, these were unamenable and could not be accommodated within a stylised and formulaic official discourse. It must have been for this reason that the jokes were an entirely oral form.

There were of course occasional individuals, such as Sergei Tichtin, who began collecting as early as 1956, who wrote down jokes which came their way. It was, however, only possible for Tichtin to publish the material he had collected following his emigration to Israel in 1977. For those who remained behind, the outcome of their curiosity and desire to document were manuscripts or typescripts known only to the individual collector or to a small circle of friends. These collections could be seen as resembling the manuscript songbooks compiled during the same period. The latter recorded courtyard songs, a narrative genre of deep romantic impulses, which were immensely popular in the 1950s and 60s among young people living in the apartment blocks of the big cities. The songs, which chronicled love affairs and conflicts between hooligans and the militia, but also exotica such as the adventures of cowboys or of sailors in Marseille bars, were disliked by the young people's organisation Komsomol, which resented the private nature of their imaginings and their indifference to the political. In the Soviet period, when the state possessed a monopoly on printing and distribution, *anekdoty*, like courtyard songs, were a tolerated but subterranean form, which were not admitted to print. The exclusion of *anekdoty* extended even to places, such as the comic journal *Krokodil*, where they might not have seemed out of place. Although the latter carried translations of Western jokes, it found no room in its columns for the domestic item.

In the early 1990s, following the ending of the Soviet Union, in what may well be the last example Europe will witness of an extensive oral genre making such a transition, jokes exploded into printed form. During those years *anekdoty* were everywhere. Collections, extending from flimsy, cheaply printed items of about thirty pages to substantial hardbacks of several hundred pages, were to be encountered on the stalls in Moscow metro stations and the city's underpasses. Such was the demand, and, as it seemed, the unending supply of new material that, if one chanced to pass by a week later, what one would have seen before would have been replaced by new collections. (During that period, having decided to buy anything new that I happened to see while travelling by metro, I assembled a collection of over eight hundred items.) Like earlier oral genres, such as fairytales and legends, that had been flattened into print, the result of this process was a loss of context, as the personality of the narrator and the response of the audience alike disappeared and performance became text. It was also observed that *mat* – vulgar or obscene language – which was a feature of some categories of *anekdot*, had been largely edited out. In spite of such losses, the collections proved immensely popular, and it was a common sight in the metro to see people reading *anekdoty* they had just bought.

Joe Hayes

CHERNOBYL

In April 1986 I was in the final months of a four-year posting as First Secretary at the Irish Embassy in Moscow. I can still recall the unseasonably mild spring weather with clear blue skies signalling the end of the long Russian winter.

We were looking forward to the International Labour Day holiday on 1 May, a key date in the Soviet calendar when the leadership gathered on top of Lenin's Mausoleum in Red Square for an orchestrated show of workers' solidarity.

A year previously the Politburo had elected the reform minded Mikhail Gorbachev as General Secretary of the Communist Party but the Cold War was still the determining context in East-West relations. Despite Gorbachev's embrace of 'perestroika' and 'glasnost' the Soviet Union remained a totalitarian behemoth with a huge nuclear arsenal. Together with Ronald Reagan's America it was locked in a shared strategic belief in collective nuclear annihilation. The terrifyingly apt acronym was MAD – mutually assured destruction.

Shortly after 1am on Saturday, 26 April, an explosion in reactor number 4 at the nuclear power plant in Chernobyl, less than one hundred kilometres north of Kiev, capital of The Ukraine, precipitated a catastrophic radiation leak.

It was the following Monday, 28 April, before word of the explosion filtered out and several days later before the full extent of the disaster became clear.

In the early hours of Monday a Swedish nuclear power plant logged a spike in radiation. It quickly became clear that the leak was not from the Swedish plant but that the particles were specific to Soviet nuclear plants.

The Swedish Government contacted Moscow and Monday night's news bulletins carried the first, reluctant, understated acknowledgement of the catastrophe in Chernobyl.

Reading from a statement by the Council of Ministers the newsreader spoke soothingly of 'an accident' at the Chernobyl power station but reassured listeners that the consequences were being taken care of. She concluded: 'A Government commission has been established.'

Moscow's diplomatic community was accustomed to these opaque official announcements. Few paid heed to them. The sun was shining, winter was over and a long holiday weekend awaited.

It was Wednesday before the first intimations of the disaster reached the Embassy.

We had just opened when a call came through on a bad line from Dublin. In 1986 phone calls from home were rare. It was the news-desk of *The Irish Press* in Burgh Quay.

'ABC News in America is carrying a report of a nuclear explosion in the Soviet Union. Do you know anything about it? What steps are you taking to safeguard the Irish community?'

My heart stopped.

Could the unthinkable have happened?

A nuclear war broken out over-night?

'This is a terrible line,' I told the caller from Burgh Quay. 'I can't hear a word. I'll call you back.'

Our Ambassador, the late Tadhg O'Sullivan, was on leave and not due back until after the May holiday. Tadhg was one of the best – agreeable, good-humoured and wise. The first thing he'd do was establish the facts.

I called the American, German, and British Embassies.

The Americans had satellite images of an explosion at Chernobyl showing a far bigger blast than the 'accident' referred to in the bland Soviet news bulletins. They also had reports that the Ukrainian town closest to Chernobyl, Pripyat, was being evacuated. Someone in the German Embassy had been to the Moscow train station serving trains from Kiev – Kievski Station – and seen hundreds of frightened passengers. The Nordic countries were registering alarmingly high radiation levels and were certain that it was being carried on the prevailing winds from the Soviet Union.

It was clear that something serious had happened and that the Soviets were determined to play it down but at least I could reassure Iveagh House, *The Irish Press* and our small resident Irish community that it wasn't nuclear war.

The May Day celebrations went ahead across the Soviet Union. In Kiev smiling young women in Ukrainian national costume led the parade but secretly party officials who knew the extent of the radiation leak from nearby Chernobyl had evacuated their children and family members.

Ambassador O'Sullivan returned from Ireland the following week bringing with him a Geiger counter supplied by the Department of Defence.

I remember the two of us standing on the flat roof of the Embassy trying with little success to interpret the strange sinister clicking sounds. 'I don't suppose we'll be having many high level visitors this year' remarked Tadhg drily.

Over the weeks that followed we developed a protective veil of dark humour. We joked about Chernobyl lettuce and radioactive radishes. Looking back now, thirty years later, it wasn't funny. My wife and I had three young children under six and a colleague at the Embassy had an infant son. Was it safe to let the children eat the spring fruit and vegetables from Moscow's street markets, most of which had come from The Ukraine? Were there long-term health implications?

As it transpired seventy per cent of the radioactive fallout landed in Belarus, Ukraine and Western Russia.

Moscow escaped relatively lightly. Over the years Adi Roche's Chernobyl Children International marked Ireland's generous and compassionate response to the legacy of contamination and ill health.

I left Moscow that September. Tadhg O'Sullivan went on to serve as Ireland's Ambassador to France. He died in 1999. Mikhail Gorbachev, the last leader of the Soviet Union is 88 this year. He set out to reform the Soviet Union but the failed cover up of the Chernobyl disaster marked the first steps in the inevitable collapse of the Union of Soviet Socialist Republics. That at least was one positive outcome.

Valentin Iremonger

## CLEAR VIEW IN SUMMER

Heavy with leaves the garden bushes again
Sun, and the trees admire them, lazily.
Cabbages and carnations, drills and beds of them, droop
    tiredly
And far away the hills, like dry dogs, crouching, squeal
    for water.
Love, who is it whispers everything is in order
On this summer afternoon, when nothing moves, not even
the flies, strangely,
As we relax by the lawn, here under the pear-tree,
    watching idly
The leaves declining, the shadows surely lengthen.

But it won't be always summer—not for us; there are bad
    times coming
When you and I will look with envy on old photographs,
Remembering how we stood, there in the sun, looking
    like gods,
While the days of our lives, like fruit, swelled and
    decayed,
And how, by the lake,
Its surface, one August evening, unchipped, walking, we
    laughed
As love slipped his arms through ours and we gladly
    followed
The path he showed us through life's valley running.

There'll be much to recall, then, when, like wet summer
    leaves,
The days under our tread don't rustle, no other summer
    waiting
Around the turn of a new year with rich clothes to grace
    us

Whose subtle beauty will have long since languished;
And Nature's flashing greenness will stitch up our hearts
    with anguish
Each day when August with sunlight riddles the branches,
the leaves taking
Voluptuously the south west wind's caresses
Year after drying year.


And yet the declension of each following season, each
    day's
Defection, splits open our hope only and not our courage,
    safe and sound
In the deep shelter of our awareness; the bushes and tall
    trees
Flourish and go down unconsciously in defeat
While full-grown man, whose pride the angels weep,
Watches love itself gutter out some dull evening, nobody
    around,
Winter moving in, no fuel left, the lights not working, the
    lease
Unrenewable, summer a seldom-remembered scat-phrase.

Valentin Iremonger

## THE COMING DAY

'Every man has his price.' The cyclist rode by
His comment to his comrade on the rackets
Of politics and business nuzzling in my ears.
I walked steadily on, hands in dustcoat pockets,
Knowing that, no matter how much I tried,
I could not stop the thought that slipped and veered

By the foreshore of my mind like a water-wag
Disturbing the calm of my sleep for nights to come
Or tilting the horizon-line of my day and age.
Suppose that for some guarantee of peace and ease, or some
Other form of happiness, my now taut ideals sag
Letting my life absorb the shocks of joy and rage,

What then? What, indeed, then. I do not know.
To-day my left hand is on my desk and the sun shines on
The long curious fingers that people admire. It is early
To be regretting the things that will be gone,
The fine-drawn skin, the midday sun, the hot ideals that show
Indulgence, lack of integrity or false sympathy rarely.

Yet now, in my twenty-sixth year, the questions are being
    written down
And the day upon which I must reply draws near.
I have no answers ready; so I am not much surprised
That every sentence strips some nerve of fear,
Or that, walking in streets or sitting in rooms, the sound
Of voices frightens me, their menace being so thinly
    disguised.

Valentin Iremonger

## Due to a Technical Fault

Three days gone now
And no letters.

They've stopped delivery because
It doesn't matter any more

To them or to
Us.

Communication is through.

I don't know what's happening
Do you?

Over there in Mount Pleasant
They're counting sacks of mail

Not, of course
For you
Or me.

What a life of idle grace
They're having.

Tomorrow
Will be the fourth day.

Will anything happen

Tonight?

*Stockholm*

Note: Mount Pleasant is the
London postal sorting office.

Valentin Iremonger

THE EVE OF DESTRUCTION
*for Suds and Gibbles*

One daffodil
So brilliantly yellow,
Its head hanging over
On a piece of waste ground
In this cruel arctic April.

Two cosmonauts
In space now.
Let's pretend, darlings,
We don't know
What they're doing.

Marginalia these words, maybe,
Such as the old wise
Monks left us.

For the record, then,
If it survives,
I'm sorry our grandchildren
Won't be able even to

See

Such a yellow
Daffodil.

*Stockholm 1966.*

Valentin Iremonger

## THE OLD HOUSE

Simply to come to it again, having been absent
For many years—marriage, children, the tiring
Duties of provision: things in a dubious world
Themselves worthy enough.

Often he wondered whether the new wing he added
Shortly before he left had a sure foundation,
A good dampcourse; and whether the timber, carefully
    fitted,
Had been sufficiently seasoned.

Looking at it now from the roadway, it seems to stand
Solidly against the main building, not too brash, ageing
In a dignified reticence as the evening cool sun
Slants over the hill just westward

And along the drive, slowly, as becomes a prodigal
Knowing the family, curious, detached, watching,
Heir now to the whole house and its rich broad acres,
He moves towards possession.

## Valentin Iremonger

### SANDYMOUNT NOW
*for Frank Biggar*

No one should go
Back to the old places.
Too many one knew
Are dead,
Old slow remembered customs
Gone with them.

And the streets, besides,
Seem narrower
In any event.
The Green tidied up
By the Municipal Council,
The rough fields covered
By semi-detacheds
With tiny gardens,
The teeming tumultuous sea
Pushed further back
By a new wall;
All disturbing elements
Pretty nearly
Accounted for

—Including, alas,
Regret,
Which, at any time,
Is irrelevant.

Biddy Jenkinson

I MÚRASCAILL SARONIKÓS TÓLOS

Ní rabhas ag súil le sonc faoin gcroí
agus an bád ag fágáil
caladh Hydra,
ach shroicheas an Sceilg.

An fharraige, an charraig, an spéir
na trí nithe is buaine.

Ba Ghréagach mé
Le gean tíre.

Biddy Jenkinson

## Iníon Léinn i bPáras

Iníon léinn
ar bheagán *francs français*
a chaill an bus deiridh
go Provence
is a chaith an oíche
gan baint di
in óstán
*de la troisième*
*catégorie*

is a luigh
gan suipéar
go maidin
os cionn
*les couvertures*
cathaoir faoi *buton* an dorais
ag éisteacht le doirse ag oscailt
ag dúnadh
spriongaí leapan
ag gíoscán

Daol dubh baineann
ar an tsiléal
Os cionn na cúl leapan
Fógra clóscríofa
'*Défense d'émettre des cries de joie*'
Uimhreacha teileafóin faoi
Is luígh an iníon léinn
gan bogadh

ar an *dessus de lit* breac uaithne
ar nós *effigie* ar thuama

an *cafard* ar an *plafond*
á síneadh féin le macnas.

Scriob scriob spriongaí
Doirse ag agallamh
Boladh sean allais
Ón oreiller ar an dtalamh

Is é nár fhéad sí bogadh
Chuala siseadh beag sa súsa
Sioscadh insan líonadh
Flaspóg óna íochtar
Is tháinig daol dubh fireann
Ag bóiléagar thar an tsíleáil

Mar thraein ag tógáil rithime
Na roth chuige féinig
Bhíog an t-ósta beagán
Chuaigh an lampa dearg ag léimrigh
Luasc an fógra rabhaidh
Ina chormhéar údarásach
Nuair chuaigh an *cafard* fireann
In airde ar a pháirtí

Cling cnaipí teilgthe
Síos sipeanna ag géilleadh
Clitear cleatar leamhan oíche
Slupar slap discréideach
Gur choirrigh gach aon mhoiliciúil

De shlaod-aer marbh an óstáin
Gur mhothallaigh, gur ramhraigh
Is gur thuirling ar an ógbhean

Fúth fáth fuadh dá haltóir í
Ag arrach atmaisféarach

A dhein dá asanálú féin
Ionsparáid na hógmhná

Is lean an tigh ag sioscarnach
Le slupar slapar méine
Lean an gliog glea gliogar
An liútarléatar leathair
Is an dá dhaol dhubha ag léimrigh

Gur spreag giorra anála an arrachtaigh
A chothram inti féinig
Is gur sáraíodh *tous le règlements*
Le héamh ón iníon aonair.

Biddy Jenkinson

SRÁIDEANNA SARAJEVO

Fuinneog caifé.
Sicíní á róstadh.
Gach uair a chasann an bior
geiteann sciatháin.

Falla an tsiopa
criathraithe ag piléir.
Poill á ndruileáil
do chomhartha nua.

Thit buama san Afganastáin.
Sceith siopaí
scairfeanna ildaite
a cheannaigh feiminigh.

# Niall Keogh

## CON CREMIN (extract)

The members of the Irish legation [to Vichy] had very little communication with their families in Ireland.[1] In Kenmare few letters arrived and very little information came from the Department.[2] The communications in the form of personal telegrams consisted of Christmas greetings and announcements about births in the family.[3] One source of considerable news and information was the Counsellor of the Canadian Embassy to France, Pierre Dupuy. Ireland and Canada were the only Commonwealth countries that did not break diplomatic links with Vichy France.

> Dupuy ... had been many years in France and was a very good friend of the Irish Mission. He came back quite often for a few days to Vichy from London and was always a good source of comment on what people in London were thinking of Vichy and events generally.[4]

Dupuy made three missions to Vichy France in November and December 1940. He met Pétain, and reported the Marshal was still hoping for a British victory. Dupuy made three more visits to Vichy, in February and August of 1941 and July 1942.[5] While his visits brought news to the Irish legation, Dupuy's 'reports, which continued to be upbeat and hopeful, were increasingly out of touch with the reality of the situation'.[6]

Even with the visits of Canadian friends, the conditions in Vichy continued to be grim. The first three months saw the legation staying at the Hotel des Lilas which they abandoned in October, due to the lack of heating, for the Hotel Gallia which was to provide accommodation for the legation for the next four years.[7] The winter of 1941 was 'what Frenchmen said was the coldest winter in ninety years' and the diplomats accepted visitors while wearing their overcoats.[8] There was continuous overcrowding in Vichy as it was only a small spa town.

Life for the Irish delegation in Vichy was not exciting and the diplomats as a group clung together as they were all quite young.[9] The French historian Azema stated 'the order of the day was austerity, if not virtue' and distractions were few apart from the cinema, a multitude of galas, playing bridge or tall stories, and Sundays provided an opportunity to make excursions into the countryside to gather food and take the air.[10]

The Irish legation also distracted themselves by playing golf. Seán Murphy 'sublimated his hostility [to the Vichy regime] by regular rounds of golf',[11] Cremin admitted that they 'just played golf all the time'.[12] The Irish legation was hostile to the German presence and this was manifested by the fact that the Irish legation in Vichy was the only delegation not to invite Germans to their receptions.[13]

The Cremin family were reunited when Cremin returned to Dublin for debriefing in March of 1941 and he brought his family back to Vichy, via Lisbon. Far from believing in Britain's 'inevitable defeat', Cremin stated: 'By the end of 1940 I had come to the conclusion that we had to reckon with a long war and, therefore, that I should bring back my wife and children'.[14] The Hotel Gallia was not suited for family life and within two or three weeks they found a villa in Cusset, two miles from Vichy.[15] Cremin commuted to work by bike or on a small motorcycle,[16] for which he was issued diplomatic licence plates.[17]

The unoccupied zone was not self-sufficient in food and in September 1940 Murphy telegraphed to report that 'severe food restrictions have come into force at noon today received by public with resignation. Severity is attributed to requisitioning on a large scale by German authorities and to fact that free zone is poorest in food.'[18] By January the situation had become more serious.[19] For the Cremin family the food situation improved when they found out that:

> the owners of the villa came from farming stock and we were thus able to get a fair quantity of food from the farm. It was of course rather expensive but in the circumstances very well worthwhile.[20]

An indication of the economic situation of unoccupied France was that one of Cremin's official duties was to sit on a committee with other members of the diplomatic corps to decide which other members of the diplomatic corps would be allowed petrol coupons. Cremin related that:

> The group met each working day for an hour over several months, in an alcove off the main lounge of the Hotel du Parc and we listened with great sympathy to an extraordinary variety of reasons as to why a 'client' should have a coupon.[21]

After several months the committee was disbanded when the Romanian legation sent a supply of petrol to provision the diplomatic corps in Vichy.[22] The legation was presented with 7000 litres of petrol for use by the legation's vehicles.[23]

As the war progressed the number of legations in Vichy dwindled because when countries went to war on Nazi Germany, the Nazis demanded the removal of their representatives. By December 1942, only eighteen missions remained.[24] In January 1943, the diplomatic missions of Brazil, Peru, Colombia and Ecuador left Vichy under escort by German troops.[25] In February 1943, the Venezuelan, Uruguayan, Paraguayan, Bolivian, Honduran and Chinese missions left as well.[26] By June 1943, all legations were restricted to within 50 km of Vichy by rail or road unless they had special permission.[27]

NOTES
1    Donal Ó Drisceoil, *Censorship in Ireland, 1939–1945: neutrality, politics and society* (Cork, Cork University Press, 1996). Ó

Drisceoil stated 'A 100% censorship was applied to correspondence to and from the continent of Europe for the entire duration of the Emergency', p. 62. In correspondence with the Military Archives, 16 October 2003, Comdt. Brennan informed me that there is 'no material in the G2 (Intelligence) or Office of the Controller of Censorship 1939–46 collections relating to Con Cremin. There is mention of his name, which indicates that his correspondence was being examined. However, this was standard practice and a file was opened if any material or information came to notice. Quite clearly, this did not occur'.

2   Cissy Crussell interview, 10 March 2001.

3   NAI, DFA 243/873.

4   Earlier draft of Con Cremin's 'Memoirs' compiled by Mgr. Frank Cremin.

5   R.T. Thomas, *Britain and Vichy, the dilemma of Anglo-French Relations 1940–42* (London, Macmillan, 1979), p. 215.

6   http://www.dfait-maeci.gc.ca/hist/Dupuy-e.asp. Churchill was 'deeply grateful ... for Dupuy's magnificent work ... The Canadian channel is invaluable and indeed at the moment our only line'.

7   Cremin, 'Memoirs', p. 18.

8   William Leahy, *I Was There* (London, Victor Gollancz, 1950), p. 15.

9   Correspondence with Dr Aedeen Cremin, 16 March 2001.

10   Azéma, *From Munich to the Liberation*, p. 93.

11   Keogh, *Ireland and Europe*, p. 139.

12   Mahon Hayes interview, 31 October 2003.

13   Maurice Martin DuGard, *La chronique de Vichy: 1940–1944* (Paris, Flammarion, 1975). This indicates an anti-Fascist mentality. (I am very grateful to Prof. M. MacNamara for this reference.)

14   Cremin, 'Memoirs', p. 22.

15   Early draft of Con Cremin's 'Memoirs' compiled by Mgr. Frank Cremin.

16   Cremin, 'Memoirs', p. 23.

17   Creeda FitzGibbon interview 29 March 2001.

18   NAI, DFA P 12/1, Murphy to Walshe, 29 September 1940.

19   Leahy, *I Was There*, p. 23.

20   Early draft of Con Cremin's 'Memoirs' compiled by Mgr. Frank Cremin.

21   Cremin, 'Memoirs', p. 23.

22  *Ibid*, p. 24. Romania was the main producer of oil in Europe at this time.

23  NAI, DFA Paris 48/11, Murphy to Walshe, 17 May 1941.

24  NAI, DFA P 12/1, Murphy to Walshe, 11 December 1942.

25  *Ibid*, 25 January 1943.

26  *Ibid*, 4 February 1943.

27  *Ibid*, 2 June 1943.

# Gerard Keown

## FIRST OF THE SMALL NATIONS (*extract*)

### *Flags and Anthems: Promotional Difficulties Abroad*

Efforts at promotion would only prove partially successful as long as the British foreign service was responsible for Irish representation overseas. Visits by Irish sportsmen to the continent were occasions of vigilance by Irish representatives, lest the British flag and anthem feature on the programme. Here the Free State was at a disadvantage against the superior manpower of the Foreign Office, with British consuls making a point of showing up to local stadiums armed with flag and score. The presence of a Free State representative was not always a guarantee that the correct procedure would be followed, as became clear in April 1926 during an international athletics meeting in Brussels. Things got off to a bad start when the Irish team, accompanied by Minister J.J. Walsh, arrived without prior notification to the trade commissioner in the city, Count O'Kelly. A veteran of the flag wars, he had the foresight to send in advance a tricolour and the score of the national anthem to the organisers. He was somewhat taken aback to see the Union flag and British anthem greet the arrival of the Irish team at the stadium. After much embarrassment on the part of the organisers, the correct flag was found but the music was not. As the Belgian army band did not know the tune, and O'Kelly was unable to hum it, the victorious Irish athletes took their lap of honour to the bars of the Norwegian national anthem, presumably in the hope that there were no Norwegians present to object.

This unedifying episode illustrates the problems the Free State encountered in promoting itself abroad. The name itself was a constitutional mouthful, one indirectly derived from a decision by Sinn Féin in 1917 to use the word 'saorstát' (literally 'free state') to translate 'republic' in Irish in place of the more usual word 'poblacht'. Saorstát appeared on official Dáil documents including the letter paper of the delegation sent to London to negotiate the Treaty with Britain in 1921. In the course of the negotiations, the British seized upon this when naming the new country the Irish Free State. It presented the new state with a challenge in communicating to the outside world. Count O'Kelly put it succinctly when he observed that, whereas 'Ireland' was one of the oldest countries in Europe, the 'Irish Free State' was part of the post-war 'political mushroom growth.'

Steps were taken when circumstances permitted to reinforce the country's image abroad through 'soft' diplomacy. Military visits to foreign academies and the success of Irish equestrian teams all contributed to raising the profile of the Free State in their own way. The League had recognised the Free State as a custodian of Celtic culture, but little was done to act on this: finance officials blocked funds for a Celtic congress in 1925 while doubts were voiced about the pan-Celtic movement lest it complicate relations with France. International soccer fixtures presented both opportunities and challenges, given the problems with flags and anthems and the existence of two rival football associations on the island. Efforts were made to promote links with the diaspora through the Tailteann Games, a kind of ethnic Olympiad held in Dublin in 1924. Overseas competitors, including the future Tarzan actor Johnny Weissmuller, were invited to participate in an array of Celtic sports and pageants, which bore little relation to their daily lives back home or with contemporary conditions in Ireland.

Relatively little was done to construct a clear set of images for promoting the country abroad. Uncertainty regarding which version of the national anthem was to be preferred, *Let Erin Remember* or *The Soldier's Song*, was one obstacle. A lack of publicity materials was another. Michael MacWhite drew attention to the large amount of publicity by the new states of Eastern Europe, and Seán Lester, in his capacity as director of publicity was anxious that the Free State should emulate them. J.J. Walsh put forward plans for a publicity book to coincide with the Tailteann Games and British Empire exhibition in 1924, but a combination of financial difficulties and a dearth of statistics saw the matter shelved until 1929. One of MacWhite's proposals to publicise the Free State included a booklet of Irish versions of town names and using Gaelic script in official correspondence. The cost of equipping ministries with new typewriters put paid to these suggestions, as did the gap between aspiration and linguistic proficiency of many a civil servant.

## 'A Mission of Thanks':
### W.T. Cosgrave's Visit to the United States in 1928

There was little over a month between the cabinet's decision to proceed with the visit on 13 December and Cosgrave's arrival in America on 20 January. The speed with which a programme was assembled featuring captains of industry, politics and the arts, reflected both the influence of the Irish-American organisations and the extent to which [Timothy] Smiddy's efforts had established the Free State. Dubbed by Cosgrave a 'mission of thanks to the American people' for their support for Irish independence, the journey was evocative of de Valera's progress across the States nine years earlier. Smiddy predicted it would be a 'grand triumphant march.' The visit took him to New York, Chicago, Washington and Philadelphia, with a detour to Ottawa. Cosgrave did not visit that other capital of Irish-America, Boston, on the advice of both the State Department and sympathetic Irish-Americans, who warned a hostile reception was likely. The visit was a whirlwind of meetings and public engagements. Even before his liner had docked on 20 January, Cosgrave had wired a message of thanks to President Coolidge. An editorial in the *New York Times* the following day asked 'what guest could be more welcome to the majority of the American people?'

On arrival in New York, he set off for Chicago by train where he was the guest of the Irish Fellowship Club. He was met on arrival by mayor 'Big Bill' Thompson, whose trademark racoon coat and trilby hat made the local headlines and contrasted with the 'sea of silk toppers' as Chicago society turned out to meet the Irish leader. Among them was a brother of Michael Collins serving in the Chicago police force. The police had prepared for demonstrations but none materialised; the icy January weather was hardly ideal for protesting. Cosgrave used a speech broadcast live from Chicago on national radio to paint a picture of the Free State as a respectable, forward looking European country that had set the divisions of the past behind it. The message was almost entirely economic, emphasising growth in trade and agriculture, reduction in the national debt and government spending on infrastructure. There was a clear appeal for investment and a call for Irish-Americans to visit. 'Ireland has a big heart for all her children,' he assured his audience, 'she will greet you as a mother.'

Irish-American money paid for the private train carriage that transported the visiting party, giant portraits of Cosgrave that adorned the Chicago streets and the syndicated radio broadcast of his Chicago speech, which reached an estimated audience of thirty million Americans. The broadcast was made possible by Owen Young, whose efforts to resolve the reparations problem the following year would result in the Young Plan. The Chicago Irish-Americans even supplied a doctor and dentist to accompany Cosgrave in case of medical emergency. The émigré largesse contrasted with the public messaging of a government and people intent on paying their own way.

Cosgrave called on President Coolidge in Washington on the 23rd and lunched with him the following day. The cabinet and leaders from both sides of the aisle on Capitol Hill turned out for the occasion. A former governor of Massachusetts, Coolidge was no stranger to Irish politics or the weight of the Irish vote. Secretary of State Kellogg also threw a dinner in Cosgrave's honour. He refused to be drawn on the country's prohibition laws, commenting that 'the air here is like champagne.' He was greeted on Capitol Hill as 'America's most welcome guest' and visited both houses of Congress. The Senate was temporarily recessed to enable him to speak and he renewed his thanks, describing his visit as a return for that paid by Benjamin Franklin to the Irish parliament in 1771. The last Irish leader to address the Senate had been Charles Stewart Parnell in 1880. An early morning canter was the occasion for a meeting with Senator William Borah, chairman of the Senate Foreign Relations Committee who had thwarted US ratification of the Treaty of Versailles. The overlapping worlds of Ireland and Britain were evident in a reception thrown by the Cork-born military attaché at the British embassy, Colonel L.H.R. Pope-Hennessy who, a decade earlier, had been a leading light in the Irish Dominion League. In Philadelphia, Cosgrave was presented by the Friendly Sons of St Patrick with a replica of a gold chain given to George Washington made especially for the occasion. In Atlantic City, he toured the famous Boardwalk.

The programme in New York was focused on Wall Street, with visits to a number of banks including the National City Bank that had overseen the Free State's national loan the previous year, a trip to the New York Stock Exchange and a meeting with the *Wall Street Journal*. Several of the banks Cosgrave visited would be among the first to suffer in the financial crash the following year. The government was keen to highlight the sound finances and credit worthiness of the Free State following reports from Washington that the government's weakened position and the growing strength of Fianna Fáil following the second general election in 1927 had adversely affected the country's credit rating. Fiscal rectitude, market confidence and financial probity were the watchwords along with an appeal for tourism and investment dollars. Criticism of high American tariffs as an obstacle to Irish exports to the United States prompted Mayor James J. Walker to mention low Free State taxes.

With an eye to the Irish community in the city, Cosgrave was invited to inspect the 'Fighting 69th' Irish American regiment, where the band drowned out a small republican protest. A round of receptions, lunches and dinners with city dignitaries and Irish-American politicians was capped by a gala Emerald Ball at the Waldorf Hotel. De Valera travelled to the United States at the same time, to raise funds and to mark Cosgrave's cards. Despite staying in the same hotel, he did not attend the ball while Cosgrave appeared only for a few minutes, ostensibly because he was tired but in reality to avoid any unpleasantness should he encounter anti-Free State protesters. Both men avoided meeting and referred only in passing to the presence of the other on American soil.

Cosgrave's visit was choreographed from start to finish to present the best image of the Free State for consumption by the American media. Speeches emphasised the journey the country had travelled since the treaty, the return of internal stability and external respectability. The legation even got in touch with the 'moving picture organisations' to ensure the best shots of Cosgrave would be used in cinema newsreels. If the State Department dubbed it a pilgrimage, it was one performed as much before the altars of the American republic as the shrines of Irish-America:

Washington's grave at Mount Vernon, the tomb of the unknown warrior at Arlington and the battle site at Valley Forge. A call on the elderly Fenian, John Devoy a few months before his death, and dinner hosted by the former judge Daniel Cohalan, who had spear-headed the pro-Free State campaign, paid respect to both sides of the split in Irish-America.

The reception was more restrained but no less warm in Canada, where Cosgrave was the guest of Prime Minister McKenzie King, even if icy weather conditions derailed Cosgrave's train outside Montreal, killing the driver. The travelling party was visibly shaken on arrival in Ottawa while an anxious McKenzie King confided to his diary his fears for the Empire had Cosgrave been killed, leaving the way clear for de Valera to take the helm in Dublin. After paying a visit to the Canadian parliament, he was guest of honour at a state dinner. In Ottawa, too, the financial message was paramount in public, while discussions in private focused on Commonwealth developments and Irish-Canadian cooperation at Geneva.

If Cosgrave began his American odyssey aboard the *Homeric*, it was somehow fitting that he returned home triumphant aboard the *Olympic*. An airplane escort, gun salute and fireworks greeted his return to Dublin, providing a welcome lift for a party still bruised from the electoral tribulations of the previous year. The visit surpassed expectations, casting Cosgrave in the role of a statesman received on equal terms in the capital of the most powerful country in the world. Ever-ready to detect a British plot, J.J. O'Kelly used the pages of the *Catholic Bulletin* to accuse Cosgrave of travelling to the US at London's behest to pacify Irish-America. The *Irish Times*, which generally took a cool view of Irish diplomatic activity, believed relations between America and Britain were better 'because Mr Cosgrave is a prime minister in Dublin.'

# Michael Lillis

## RIDDLED WITH LIGHT (*extract*)

Oral tradition and scholarly reconstruction from references in the poems concur that Aogán Ó Rathaille was born in Scrahanaveel, ten miles east of Killarney, around 1670, and there is corroborated evidence that he died in poverty in the region in 1728 or 1729. He clearly saw himself as a professional poet of the ebbing phase of the post-bardic tradition and he passionately asserted his family's immemorial connection as men of learning to the great families of West Munster; this may indeed reflect the role of his mother's family the Egans (hence Aogán) as lawyers to the family of Clancarty (an Cárrthach Mór). [...]

His easy familiarity with the vocabulary and content of later medieval and bardic Irish literature and history; his acquaintance with Irish, Greek and Roman mythology; his own work in copying earlier manuscripts and his evident mastery of English and Latin, all bespeak a privileged education, perhaps by the clergy and other men of learning at one or several of the surviving great houses of the locality, such as the homes of the many septs of the McCarthys or of Ó Donnchú of Glenflesk. [...]

Following the disasters of the Boyne and Aughrim, the Gaelic chieftains of West Munster, including an Cárrthach Mor, had been dispossessed or exiled. Ó Rathaille, a retainer, was forced from his home in Sliabh Luachra to live in poverty by Tonn Tóime's Atlantic storms in approximately 1694. The paradox of his importance as a poet lies in the fact that it was this experience of hardship and neglect which continued for the rest of his life that inspired almost all of his greatest lyric poems. Ó Rathaille had already found the voice of mature poetic authority. The title of the poem he wrote at this time is "An Tan d'Aistrigh go Duibhneachaibh Láimh le Tonn Tóime I gCiarraí" (Poem VII – On His Removing to Duibhneacha, beside Tonn Toime in Kerry) and it is the most accessible of the most powerful lyrics. The remarkable opening lines convey in their rhythms and flowing vowel sequences, as Ó Tuama noted, the billowing and fury of the ocean. The poet's indignation at his enforced expulsion to a humiliating backwater is dramatised in the sharp contrast both in meaning and sound between the clustered g-sounds of comfort in line seven and the bleakness of line eight with the stark-meaning and stark-sounding dealbh (dirt poor) and the striking alliterations between the d- and bh- sounds, each reinforcing the sensation of misery:

Is fada liom oíche fhír-fhliuch gan suan, gan srann,
Gan ceathra gan maoin, caoire, na buaibh na mbeann;
Anfhaith ar toinn taoibh liom do bhuair mo cheann,
Is níor chleachtas im naoin fíogaigh na ruacain abhann.

Da maireadh an rí díonmhar o bhruach na Leamhan
'S an gasra bhi ag roinn leis ler thruagh mo chall,
I gceannas na gcríoch gcaoin gcluthar gcuanach gcam,
Go dealbh I dtír Dhuibhneach nior bhuan mo chlann
(ls.1–8)

The drenching night drags on: no sleep or snore,
no stock, no wealth of sheep, no horned cows.
This storm on the waves nearby has harrowed my head
– I who ate no winkles or dogfish in my youth.

If that guardian King from the banks of the Leamhan lived on,
with all who shared his fate (and would pity my plight)
to rule that soft snug region, bayed and harboured,
my people would not stay poor in Duibhne country.

The poem concludes with one of his most stirring Envois, shifting in rhythm to a raw peremptory snarl:

A thonnsa thíos is aoirde géim go hard,
meabhair mo chinnse cloite od bhéiceach tá;
cabhair da dtíodh aris go hÉirinn bhán,
do ghlam nach binn do dhingfinn fein id bhráid.
(ls.17–20)

You wave down there, lifting your loudest roar,
the wits in my head are worsted by your wails.
If help ever came to lovely Ireland again
I'd wedge your ugly howling down your throat! [...]

None of Ó Rathaille's Aislingi, unlike his more overtly military or political verse, fulfils the conventional role of its day of encouraging Jacobite hopes of inevitable military victory. While his versions of the formula begin with a visitation by Ireland in the image of a young beauty, and while they all rehearse the Jacobite dream of restoration, the poet's conclusion is invariably despairing. In the contrast between the Jacobites' surging tribal hope and the poet's barren despair, Ó Rathaille's personal pessimism is searingly grounded. [...]

"Gile na Gile" (Poem IV – Brightness of Brightness) appears from the manuscript record to have been composed before the Jacobite invasions of Scotland of 1715. It was widely transcribed within a few years. Its unique and intricate metrical structure is so perfectly sustained and its word-play so elaborate that it has sometimes been described as an exercise in the "baroque" and read primarily as an extraordinary tour de force of versecraft. It fully merits such a description, but that is to miss the core substance of the poem which is its most fascinating level and which is artistically reinforced by the complex artistry. It belongs to the Aisling genre but is utterly sui generis by almost any standard of literature. [...]

Ó Rathaille begins with two stanzas which describe his vision with concentrated deliberation:

Gile na gile do chonnarc ar slí in uaigneas
(11)

Brightness of brightness I saw on the way in loneliness.

Each of the two phrases "Gile na Gile" and "ar slí in uaigneas" immediately present, especially in juxtaposition, connotations of the unfathomable. The impressionable and confused young reader of Juan de la Cruz (whose "En una Noche Oscura" and rendering of the Canticle of Canticles could be read as the Aisling version of religious experience), as I then was when listening to these phrases in West Kerry in 1962, heard echoes of profound mysticism. I still hear them. Years later I found that Yeats's magnificent trope "riddled with light" came closest to conveying Ó Rathaille's intent in English. It is distilled by the startling image reinforced by dazzling word play in the final lines of the second stanza:

Iorra ba ghlaine na gloine ar a broinn bhuacaigh
Do ginneadh ar ghineamhain di-se san tír uachtraigh.
(ls.7–8)

A jewel more glittering than glass on her high bosom
created, when she was conceived, in a higher world.

The rhythm of the third stanza starts to speed up and sets out the Jacobite vision, but with several twists: why is the maiden Ireland go fíor-uaigneach (most forlorn) as she shares this great news and what are the tidings the poet dare not mention? The word fios (tidings, knowledge), repeated here five times, also connotes magical knowledge:

Fios fiosach dhom d'innis, is isse go fíor-uaigneach,
fios filleadh don duine don ionad ba rí-dhualgas,
fios milleadh na druinge chuir eisean ar rinnruagairt,
's fios eile na cuirfead im laoithibh le fíor-uamhan.
(ll 9–12)

Mysterious tidings she revealed to me, and she most forlorn,
tidings of one returning by royal right,
tidings of the crew ruined who drove him out,
and tidings I keep from my poem from sheer fear.

The word speed increases as the speaker confesses that he became the erotic prisoner of the vision and that she disappeared when, St Anthony-like, he called on Mary's Son to protect him (against sexual evil):

Leimhe na leimhe dom druidim 'na cruinntuairim,
im chime ag an gcime do snaidhmeadh go fíorchrua mé;
ar ghoirm Mhic Muire dom fhortacht, do bhíog uaimse,
is d'imigh an bhruinneal 'na luisne go bruín Luachra.
(ls. 13–16)

Foolish past folly, I came to her very presence
bound tightly, her prisoner (she likewise a prisoner).
I invoked Mary's Son for succour; she started from me
and vanished like light to the fairy dwelling of Luachair.

Ó Rathaille achieves the pinnacle of pyrotechnics in Irish verse in the following stanza when, without varying the metrical structure, he takes the rhythm to a vertiginous gallop as the speaker rushed after the visionary maiden and, with a series of stunning word-games (tinne-bhrugh ... tigim – ni thuigim ... ionad na n-ionad do cumadh), the poet captures the grotesqueness of the druidic palace where he found her:

Rithim le rith mire im rithibh go croí-luaimneach,
trí imeallaibh corraigh, trí mhongaibh, trí shlímruaitigh;
don tinne-bhrugh tigim – ni thuigim cen tslí fuaras-
go hionad na n-ionad do cumadh le draiocht dhruaga.
(ls.17–20).

Heart pounding, I ran, with a frantic haste in my race,
by the margins of marshes, through swamps, over bare moors.
To a powerful fire-palace I came, by paths most strange,
to that place of all places, erected by druid magic.

There the poet encounters his maiden being groped by a lumbering brute in a brothel-like den surrounded by goblins and sluts. They take him prisoner but he confronts the girl:

D'iniseas di-se, san bhfriotal dob fhíor uaimse
nar chuibhe di snaidhmaedh le slibire slímbhuartha
's an duine ba ghile ar shliocht chine Scoit trí huaire
ag feitheamh ar ise bheith aige mar chaoin-nuachar.
Ar gcloistin mo ghutha di goileann go fíor-uaibhreach
is sileadh ag an bhfliche go life as a gríosghruannaibh;
cuireann liom giolla dom choimirc on mbruín uaithi –
's í gile na gile do chonnarc as slí in uaigneas.

(ll 24–30)

I said to her then in words that were full of truth,
how improper it was to join with that drawn gaunt creature
when a man the most fine, thrice over, of Scottish blood
was waiting to take her for his tender bride.
On hearing my voice she wept in high misery
and flowing tears fell down from her flushed cheeks.
She sent me a guard to guide me out of the palace
that brightness of brightness I saw on the way in loneliness. [...]

"Gile na Gile" is an extraordinary vision of mysterious delight and knowledge which, once the Jacobite content is declared, descends into a squalid, erotic nightmare of despair. Its pace, imagery and verbal brilliance have not been equalled in Irish and, while obviously inspired by political passion, the poem remains difficult to interpret.

For Dineen, Ó Rathaille's sublime production was his "Deathbed" poem (Poem XXI), now more commonly known by its first words "Cabhair ni Ghoirfead" (I'll Not Ask for Help). Yeats introduced its famous last line to the world in "The Curse of Cromwell" as: "His fathers served their fathers before Christ was crucified". While Ó Buachalla has argued that "the death-bed was a common trope in eighteenth century poetry" (The Poems p 40) and that it is not necessary to read it as written literally during the poet's last days, many readers like myself find the tone and content powerfully redolent of final days. Ó Rathaille launches his theme with typical defiance:

Cabhair ni ghairfead go gcuirtear me i gcruinn-chomhrainn –
dar an leabhar da ngairinn nior ghaire-de an ní dhomh-sa.
(ls.1–2)

No help I'll call till I'm put in the narrow coffin.
By the Book it would bring it no nearer if I did!

Do thonnchrith m'inchinn, d'imigh mo phríomh-dhochas,
poll im ionathar, biorra nimhe trim dhrólainn.
(ll 4–5)

Wave-shaken is my brain, my chief hope gone.

There's a hole in my gut, there are foul spikes through my
bowels.

In a brilliant image from chess he castigates King William
for cheating James out of his rightful throne:

Com Loch Deirg 'na ruide 'gus Toinn Tóime
o lom an cuireata cluiche ar an ri coróineach.
(ls. 9–10).

Reddened are Loch Dearg's narrows and the Wave of Tóim
since the Knave has skinned the crowned King in the game.

He hears the onset of death in the grunts of the
mythological Pig or, according to some, the noise of the
Torc waterfall – or, possibly in Ó Rathaille's intention,
both:

Fonn ni thigeann im ghaire ' s me ag cuí ar bhóithre
ach foghar na Muice nach gontar le saigheadóireacht.
(ll 15–16).

No music is nigh as I wail about the roads
except the noise of the Pig no arrows wound.

He reverts to his protest against the Kenmare family,
accusing Sir Valentine Browne of usurping the ancient
rights of the McCarthys:

An seabhach ag a bhfuilid sin uile 's a gcíosóireacht
fabhar ni thugann don duine , ce gaol dó-san.
(ll 19–20).

A hawk now holds those places, and takes their rent,
who favours none, though near to him in blood.

The last stanza is stark and imperishable:

Stadfadsa feasta – is gar dom éag gan mhoill
o treascradh dragain Leamhan , Léin is Laoi;
rachad 'na bhfasc le searc na laoch don chill,
na flatha fá raibh mo shean roimh éag do Chriost.
(ls. 25–28)

I will stop now – my death is hurrying near
now the dragons of the Leamhan, Loch Lein and the Laoi are
destroyed.

In the grave with this cherished chief I'll join those kings
my people served before the death of Christ.

For more than forty years I have travelled the world as a
diplomat or businessman. Ó Rathaille's greater poems
recited aloud inside my head, and quite often "outside",
have more than any other literary resource, however
cherished – even more than Joyce or Shakespeare – helped
sustain my days and nights. Poetry recited in one language
is notoriously opaque even as an oral experience to those
who do not understand it; to my surprise I have found that
the unique phonetic intricacies of "Gile na Gile" recited
slowly aloud have fascinated Brazilians, Colombian,
French or even American listeners. How much richer that
experience is when enhanced by the poem's complex and
profound intelligibilities! How sad it is, how deplorable,
that our educational system does not make the endless
variety and the thrilling power of this feat of native genius
more accessible to today's seventeen-year-olds.

## P.D. Linín [Róisín O'Doherty, later McDonagh]

MAIDHC SA DANMHAIRG (*sliocht*)

Dordán bagrach trom inneall scairdeitleáin a dhúisigh Maidhc.

Shín sé a lámh amach agus thóg sé uaireadóir ón mbord beag in aice leis an leaba. É fós leath ina chodladh, bhreathnaigh sé ar an am. Cúig nóiméad roimh a hocht. Nárbh aoibhinn dó? Na leathanta saoire ag tosú inniu.

Léim sé as an leaba agus rith sé trasna do dtí an fhuinneog. Roimhe amach chonaic sé an Mhuir Bhailt leathan agus an ghrian ag scalladh anuas uirthi. I bhfad uaidh bhí cósta na Sualainne go soiléir le feiceáil. Cheana féin bhí roinnt mhaith bád amuigh, na seolta beaga bána in airde. Bhí kyak amháin ann, fear ann i gculaith snámha, dath donn órga ar a chraiceann.

B'iontach go deo an aimsir í. B'iontaí fós do Mhaidhc an lá seo. Sea, inniu ar a dó a chlog bhí sé le dul ag aerfort Kastrup le casadh as Chian agus ar Cholm a bhí ag teacht le hAer Lingus ó Bhaile Átha Cliath. Bliain ó shin d'fhág sé slán acu, é tromchroíoch ag dul i gcéin uathu nuair a ceapadh a Dhaid mar thaidhleoir sa Danmhairg.

Bhí míle rud le hinsint aige dóibh anois agus é ag súil leis na scéalta a chloisteáil uathasan. Fan go gcloisfidís ag labhairt Danmhairgise é, fan go gcasfaidís ar Sven agus Jan. Mura mbeadh a dheirfiúr Síle a bheith imithe go teach Nuala i mBaile Átha Cliath seans go mbeadh sise leo. Ar chaoi ar bith bheadh na leadanna ábalta na heachtraí ar fad a insint do Nuala ar ball.

Nigh Maidhc é féin agus é ag smaoineamh siar ar na heachtraí a bhain don cheathrar acu i mBaile Átha Cliath. D'admhaigh sé dó féin go raibh sé ag tnúth go mór le teacht a seanchairde, cé go raibh sé sásta go maith leis an saol i gCopenhagen.

Chaith sé air a chuid éadaigh agus rith sé síos an staighre. Chuir sé na céimeanna deireanacha de de léim agus isteach leis i seomra an bhricfeasta áit a raibh Mam agus Daid fós ag ithe.

'Hé! a Dhaid, hé a Mham.' Shuigh sé síos. 'Beidh siad anseo inniu. Fan anois,' bhreathnaigh sé ar a uaireadóir, 'i gceann ceithre uaire, caoga nóiméad agus fiche seacht soicind!' B'ait leis an ciúnas sa seomra.

'Drochscéal ar maidin, a Mhaidhc.' Shín Daid sreangscéal chuige. 'Tháinig sé sin go luath ar maidin. Tá an tAire ag teacht le haghaidh an Mhórchruinnithe úd in Odense. Beimid ag dul go dtí aerfort Kastrup le casadh air ar a dó dhéag.'

'Féach, a Mhaidhc,' arsa Mam, 'tá ar an mbeirt againn imeacht inniu ar feadh seachtaine go dtí Odense. Beidh bean an Aire in éineacht leis agus ní foláir domsa dul leo. Tuigeann tú go mbeidh Príomh-Aire na Danmhairge agus an lucht Rialtais ar fad nach mór bailithe ann. Beidh maithe agus móruaisle na Germáine Thoir agus go leor ó thíortha eile na hEorpa ann. Ceist bás nó beatha, nach mór, dúinne in Éirinn na socraithe tráchtála a bheidh dá bplé. Beidh ar Dhaid obair mhór a dhéanamh le linn na Comhairle seo le cás na hÉireann a chosaint.'

'Ach ... Cian agus Colm ...'

'Tiocfaidh tú linn go dtí Kastrup agus féadfaidh tú fanacht go dtí an dó agus fáiltiú rompu tú féin,' arsa Mam.

'Sea, ach seachtain anseo linn féin!' ina olagón ó Mhaidhc.

'Ní bheidh sibh libh féin ar fad,' mheabhraigh Daid dó. 'Tá Elsa anseo leis na béilí a ullmhú agus an teach a chóiriú. Fágfaidh mé airgead agat le taxi a fháil le sibh a thabhairt abhaile ó Kastrup agus roinnt bhreise le caitheamh i rith na seachtaine. Beidh sibh in ann seachtain shuimiúil a chaitheamh agus go leor spraoi a bhaint amach ag an am céanna. Féach na hiarsmalanna breátha atá i gCopenhagen.'

'Fan go bhfeicfidh Colm agus Cian Tivoli,' arsa Mam. 'Níl áit is mó spraoi sa domhan mór.'

Tháinig lasadh in aghaidh Mhaidhc.

'An bhfuil cead agam iad a thabhairt go hElsinore le Caisleán Hamlet a thaispeáint dóibh?' as sé.

'Cinnte,' arsa Mam. 'Is dócha go bhfuil *Hamlet* ar an gcúrsa acu agus nach mór go mbeidh sé le rá acu nuair a théann siad abhaile gur sheas siad ar na ballaí ceannann céanna ar a sheas an Taibhse.'

Thosaigh Maidhc ag gáirí.

'Ach, éist a mhic.' Bhí Daid an-dáiríre. 'Tá Mam agus mé féin ag brath in iomlán ort nach ndéanfaidh sibh rud ar bith a thabharfadh droch-chlú ar an Ambasáid nó ormsa nó ar thír na hÉireann.'

'Beimid an-chúramach,' gheall ar Maidhc dó.

'Rud eile,' arsa Mam, 'beidh sé deacair teagmháil a dhéanamh linn in Odense. Beidh an clár againn an-trína chéile. Glaofaidh mise ar an fón anseo nuair a fhaighim caoi. Ná bíodh imní ar bith ort, tá an cailín sealadach sin san oifig go maith agus má bhíonn géarghá leis, beidh sise in ann Daid a fháil ar an fón.'

Dhein Maidhc tréaniarracht an díomá a mhothaigh sé a cheilt. Thuig sé na dualgais a bhí ar a mhuintir ach mar sin féin …

'Ceart mar sin,' ar seisean. 'Rachaidh mé anois féachaint an bhfuil an seomra ullamh ag Elsa do na buachaillí. Caithfidh mé an liathróid peile agus liathróidí leadóige a chuardach.'

Níor mhothaigh sé an t-am ag sleamhnú thart agus bhí a chulaith snámha aimsithe aige go díreach nuair a chuala sé Daid ag glaoch air.

'Táimid réidh le himeacht anois, a Mhaidhc,' ar seisean.

Ar an turas go dtí Kastrup – bhí an tAerfort tamall fada ó lár na cathrach – bhí Maidhc ag machnamh dó féin ar na rudaí a dhéanfaidís. Rinne sé pleananna do chuile lá den tseachtain, fiú amháin na béilí a d'iarrfadh sé ar Elsa a ullmhú dóibh triúr. Ní fheadar, ar sé leis féin, ar chuimhnigh Colm ar na prátaí-bhrioscaí a thabhairt? Bhí sé chomh fada sin ó bhlás sé iad.

Bhí an-fhuadar faoi Dhaid nuair a shroic siad an aerfort. Bhí air bainisteoir an aerfoirt a fheiceáil agus socraithe cinnte a dhéanamh go mbeadh seomra feithimh ar leith in áirithe don Aire. Bhí air freisin cúpla glaoch gutháin a chur isteach.

'Slán leat, a Mhaidhc,' ar seisean. 'Tabhair aire duit féin.'

'Bí go maith,' arsa Mam, ag breith barróige air.

Chuaigh Maidhc trasna go dtí an siopa agus cheannaigh sé cúpla leabhar cúl-pháipéir. Shuigh sé síos ar an mbinse breá compordach ag feitheamh.

D'ith sé na milseáin a cheannaigh sé dó féin agus bhí sé socair sásta go ceann uair a chloig. D'éirigh sé mí-fhoigneach ansin agus chuaigh sé in airde le breathnú ar na heitleáin ag tuirlingt. Bhí sé seo chomh suimiúil gur ar éigean a chuala sé an glór ag teacht thar na miocrafóin á rá go raibh an t-eitleán ó Bhaile Átha Cliath ag teacht ar an bpointe.

Rith sé síos an staighre arís agus ar éigean a bhí sé ann nuair a chonaic sé Colm agus Cian ag teacht anuas an staighre mhóir. Bhí fuinneog idir é agus iad ach bhí sé in ann beannú dóibh, agus d'aithin siad ar an bpointe é.

Nuair a thángadar amach sa halla ba dheacair dóibh comhrá a dhéanamh ar feadh cúpla nóiméad. Bhí an áit plúchta.

'Bhfuil na prátaí-bhrioscaí libh?' an chéad cheist a chuir sé orthu. 'Seo! Leanagaí mise,' ar sé, gan fanacht le freagra, ag tabhairt sonc an duine dóibh. Idir an triúir acu thugadar an bagáiste amach go dtí an cosán.

'Seo duit iad.' Bhain Colm paicéad mór as an mála láimhe.

'Míle buíochas! Féach, tacsaí anseo faoi dheireadh,' arsa Maidhc.

Nuair a bhí siad socraithe sa charr agus ar an mbealach, 'Conas atá Nuala?' ar sé, agus é ag líonadh a bhéal le prátaí-bhrioscaí.

'Thar cionn,' arsa Colm. 'Gheallamar di go gcuirfimis litir fada chuici gach seachtain ón triúir againn ag insint di faoi na heachtraí a bhain dúinn anseo.'

Mhínigh Maidhc dóibh go mbeadh a thuismitheoirí as baile ar feadh seachtaine agus thosaigh sé ag tabhairt eolas an bhaile dóibh.

'Seo anois, breathnaigí uaibh. Sin í an Mhuir Bhailt. Nach álainn go deo inniu í? Dá bhfeicfeadh sibh mí ó shin í, bhí sí reoite ar fad. Shiúil mé dhá chéad slat amach ar an bhfarraige maidin Domhnaigh amháin.'

'Shiúil tú ar an bhfarraige!' arsa Cian.

'Ní amháin gur shiúil mé amach ach bhí snámh agam inti trí sheachtain go díreach ina dhiaidh sin. Ní mhaireann an tEarrach ach coicís ar éigean.'

'Caithfidh go raibh sé fuar go maith le snámh.'

'Bhí sé damanta fuar, ach bhí teas sa ghrian nuair a tháinig mé amach.' Ansin, 'An bhfeiceann sibh? Sin Pálás an Rí.' Shín sé méar i dtreo an fhoirgnimh ársa dhú-dheirg a raibh na Gardaí ina seasamh taobh amuigh de.

'Meas tú an bhfeicfimid an Rí?' arsa Colm.

'Cá bhfois! ach tá go leor eile le feiceáil,' arsa Maidhc.

'Mar shampla?'

'Ar éigean is féidir liom fanacht,' arsa Maidhc, 'le Tivoli a thaispeáint daoibh. Ní fhaca sibh riamh áit chomh hiontach nó chomh breá le Tivoli. An cuimhin libh an Fête úd a bhí thíos ar an gcé i mBaile Átha Cliath?'

'Sea, nach cuimhin liom,' arsa Colm, 'agus chaith tusa an réal deireanach ar an Roulette agus b'éigin dúinn siúl abhaile go Domhnach Broc.'

'Ná tosaigh arís ar an gclamhsán,' arsa Cian.

'Sea,' arsa Maidhc, 'ach fan go bhfeicfidh sibh Tivoli. Tá sé chomh mór le Faiche Stiabhna agus gach orlach de clúdaithe le hábhar caitheamh aimsire agus le hiontas den uile shórt, agus mar Fhaiche Stiabhna, tá sé i lár na cathrach.'

'Bhfuil sé an-daor le dul isteach?'

'Níl, ach deirtear go dtógtar milliún punt isteach gach samhradh, idir chuairteoirí ó thíortha eile, mhuintir Chopenhagen féin, agus mhuintir na Danmhairge in iomlán. Ní dóigh liom go bhfuil áit ar bith cosúil leis murab é Disneyland 'sna Stáit é.'

'Idir an triúir againn bainfimid scléip as,' gheall Colm.

'Bí cinnte,' d'aontaigh Maidhc leis. 'Sin í Halla na Cathrach.'

'Ní lár amháin atá i gcathair Chopenhagen ach trí nó ceithre lár,' arsa Cian ag breathnú timpeall.

'Feicfidh sibh lá eile iad. Ach ní fada anois muid ón teach. Táimid cheana féin i Charlottenlund.'

Bhain siad teach Mhaidhc amach gan mhoill agus isteach leo tar éis do Mhaidhc costas an turais a íoc.

'Bhfuil ocras oraibh nó ar mhaith libh snámh ar dtús?'

'Snámh ar dtús,' arsa Cian agus Colm d'aon ghuth.

Rith Maidhc istead agus lig scread – 'Elsa, táimid anseo.'

Tháinig Elsa amach. Cailín óg ón tuaith a bhí inti agus bhí sí beagán cúthaileach. Chuir Maidhc na buachaillí in aithne di.

'Velkommen,' as sise ag fáiltiú rompu.

'An féidir linn béile a fháil i gceann uair a chloig?' d'fhiafraigh Maidhc.

Bhain an bheirt eile an-spraoi as a bheith ag éisteacht leis ag labhairt Danmhairgise. D'aontaigh Elsa go fonnmhar an béile a chur siar.

Bhí an teach suite caoga slat ón áit ba bhreátha snámh i gCopenhagen, Klampenborg.

'Ní áit nádúrtha snámha é,' a mhínigh Maidhc dóibh. 'Tógadh an gaineamh ó áiteanna éagsúla sa Damhairg agus rinneadh trá álainn do mhuintir Chopenhagen. I rith an tsamhraidh bíonn an trá dubh le daoine. Is deacair troigh cearnach a fháil le suí síos nuair a bhíonn an samhradh breá té. Bíonn na sluaite ann óna hocht ar maidin go dtína naoi nó a deich tráthnóna.'

Rith na buachaillí síos go dtí an trá, na cultacha snámha leo. Léim siad isteach san fharraige agus cé go raibh an t-uisce fuar ar dtús, ba mhór an taitneamh a bhaineadar as, ag bá a chéile le sáile. Nuair a thángadar amach shuigh siad síos ar an ngaineamh.

'Bhí sé sin thar cionn.' Lig Cian osna sásaimh as.

'Tá ocras orm anois,' arsa Colm.

'Conán Maol agus tú féin. Bíonn ocras i gcónaí oraibh!' Rinne Maidhc gáire. 'Fág seo, beidh an béile ullamh anois dúinn.' Ar a mbealach ar ais bhí sé ag insint dóibh faoin saol a bhí aige féin le bliain anuas.

'Tá mise sásta go maith anseo,' ar sé, 'Ar ndó tá an saol dian go leor sa scoil. Bíonn orm bheith istigh gach maidin ag a hocht agus ní bhím sa bhaile arís go dtí leathuair tar éis a sé. Deirimse libh gur deacair é sin a dhéanamh sa gheimhridh mar go mbíonn sé dubh go dtína naoi a chlog.'

'Céard faoi na cairde seo ar scríobh tú chugainn fúthu?' a d'fhiafraigh Colm.

'Sea,' arsa Maidhc, 'Sven agus Jan. Tá mé an-mhór leo. Tá siad in aon rang liom sa scoil agus cónaíonn siad in aice liom. Tabharfaidh mé cuireadh dóibh teacht anocht, b'fhéidir, agus beidh cluiche peile againn.'

Bhain siad an teach amach agus d'fháiltigh Elsa rompu. 'Croch na culachta snámha sa ghairdín,' ar sise, 'agus suígí chun boird.'

# Irene Christina Lynch [Irene Duffy Lynch]

## BEYOND FAITH AND ADVENTURE (*extract*)

My life is as I would have dreamed it to be. There have been terrible ups and downs but if I had it over again, I wouldn't change a thing. To have been able to pioneer something completely new, to have had the opportunity to be involved in development projects which worked hand in hand with the people of Igalaland and to have been able to benefit from the knowledge of so many world class experts for more than thirty years, has been truly fulfilling.

Born into a family of five girls in Lisselton, Co. Kerry, Nora McNamara joined the Missionary Sisters of the Holy Rosary in the early 1960s largely because she had a wish since childhood to help the poor in Africa. 'I got to know the Holy Rosary Sisters through the mission magazines and I first approached them in 1962. My early years in the convent were quite difficult largely because I felt my free spirit was curbed. I don't mind observing rules but I don't like to be tied down. When I went to University College Cork to study social science, I experienced a liberating force and I began to envisage how my studies would help me with my future work in development in Africa.'

We crossed the Niger River at Agenebode, to visit Sr. Nora, coordinator since 1971 of the Diocesan Development Services (DDS) in Idah, capital of Igalaland – which now forms part of Kogi State. It was Fr. Christopher who took us to the crowded and colourful river bank to bargain and huckster with the many boatmen lined up for business. Though it was a February morning in the middle of the dry season, stormy rain clouds threatened a safe crossing. Urgent discussions in high decibels and in many languages were taking place – *what if the wind whips up? No, there are no life jackets! By the grace of God, we will cross.* The seasoned boat men were cautious, watchful – and then suddenly, the sky cleared and all were directed to the boats. We were a party of five: my sister Bernadette and her husband James, my husband and I and Fr. Christopher, who took up a standing Christ-like stance beside the boatman – a position which took on a certain symbolism some twenty minutes later when we were half way across the wide expanse of water, rolling black clouds, whipped up by angry winds stirred up the majestic waters and brought from the heavens the mother of all cloud bursts. I speculated on what future lay beneath us in the event of the boat capsizing – images of crocodiles and God knows what else were not comforting. 'I'm an optimist' was Bernadette's retort! Nothing but a forced calm could be read on the faces of James and my husband who were seemingly absorbed in the newness of our surroundings. We know that Fr. Christopher resorted to prayer and the 'calming of the waters' and yes! miraculously, we reached the bank at Idah. If ever there was the image of drowned rats – shivering with the cold!

Sr. Nora was our ministering angel when we reached the DDS headquarters. In no time at all, she had us all togged out in traditional costumes which were borrowed from her many staff members and was able to produce on request, hot whiskeys from a bottle of Irish normally reserved for benefactors and other important persons!

She came to Idah as a newly qualified social scientist in 1970. Her first impressions of the country in which she was to spend the most of the next thirty years of her life were not good. 'It was September, just nine months after the end of the Biafran war. The countryside was wet, dirty and altogether miserable. Buildings everywhere were full of bullet holes and Jim Reeves records were playing all over the place. When I arrived in Idah, my heart sank further. There were signs of dire poverty everywhere and all I could sense was apathy and depression. Many things have improved since those days but there is still considerable poverty. Today, we have telecommunications advances but they are not matching existing needs. There are many more good roads but there's still no ferry between Agenebode and Idah.'

# Irene Duffy Lynch

## TITEANN RUDAÍ AS A CHÉILE LE CHINUA ACHEBE – RÉAMHRÁ
### (sliocht)

Baineann an t-úrscéal *Titeann Rudaí as a Chéile* a thideal as an dán 'The Second Coming' de chuid William Butler Yeats:

> Turning and turning in the widening gyre
> The falcon cannot hear the falconer;
> Things fall apart; the centre cannot hold;
> Mere anarchy is loosed upon the world.

Féachann Chinua Achebe siar ar a shochaí Íogbóch, go háirithe i rith an tréimhse ar bhris an fear geal isteach inti, mar mhisinéir, mar thrádálaí, mar riarthóir. San úrscéal seo, atá molta ó thús ina shárshaothar, déanann sé cur síos ar threabhacas a bhí in ann smaoineamh air féin mar aon phobal amháin, tráth dá raibh, a labhair d'aon ghuth amháin, a bhí páirteach sa stór coiteann eolais acu, agus a ghníomhaigh mar phobal amháin. Tháinig an fear geal agus bhris sé an aontacht sin. Agus sin ag tarlú, tugadh isteach sa treabhchas foclóir, smaointe agus gnása nua, agus de réir a chéile, ghéill an tseansochaí slí don riaradh coimhthíoch, agus thit gach rud as a chéile.

Príomhcharachtair san úrscéal is ea Okonkwo. I dtús an scéil, tá sé in ard a réime. Tá a cháil is a stádas bunaithe ar éachtaí tathagacha pearsanta atá curtha i gcrích aige. In aois a hocht mbliana déag, faigheann sé an ceann is fearr ar Amalinze, ar a nglaotaí 'an Cat' mar nár bhuail a dhroim an talamh riamh agus é ag iomrascáil. Uaidh sin amach, is léir go bhfuil saol mór i ndán do Okonkwo. Chomh maith le bheith ina iomrascálaí clúiteach, feirmeoir saibhir le triúir ban céile is ea é, agus dhá ghradam bronnta air. Is é a athair Unoka an t-aon duine a chuireann smál ar a cháil: fiachóir, cladhaire agus caimiléir a chuireann náire ar Okonkwo.

I gcompal Okonkwo agus lastall de, is léir a shaibhreas agus a rath. Ina ainneoin sin, is beag duine a thuigeann go bhfuil a bheatha faoi smacht ag an eagla – eagla roimh theip agus laige a athar, agus eagla go bhfágfaidh sé a cháil agus a shaibhreas le hoidhreacht ag a mhac míthiúntach Nwoye (lch 50 thíos):

'Ní churifidh mé suas le mac nach féidir a chloigeann a choinneáil in airde ag tionól na muintire. Ba thúisce liom é a thachtadh le mo lámha féin. Agus má sheasann tú ag stánadh orm mar sin,' a mhionnaigh sé, 'brisfidh Amadiora do chloigeann duit!'

Cothaíonn an eagla seo an lámh ládir lena rialaíonn sé a theaghlach. Ina aigne seisean, ní fiú rud ar bith a léiriú ach láidreacht. Mar nach dteastaíonn uaidh mothúchán ar bith a thaispeáint ach an fhearg, cuireann sé é féin lasmuigh de ghnása agus béasa réasúnta a mhuintire, nach rachadh chun troda riamh gan cúis shoiléir dhlisteanach a bheith acu. Os a choinne sin, is mion minic a ghníomhaíonn Okonkwo go tallanach, mar is é an fhearg an fórsa tiomána a spreagann é. Is tríd an fhearg agus an eagla a thuigimid Okonkwo. Is í an fhearg a chuireann air a bhean is óige a bhualadh i rith sheachtain na síochána; is í an fhearg a chuireann air gunna a scaoileadh lena dhara bean, Ekwefi. Tarraingíonn sé a mhaiseite chun Ikemefuna a leagadh mar tá eagla air go gceapfar go bhfuil sé lag. Ansin maraíonn sé mac Ezeudu, gníomh a tharraingíonn seacht mbliana ar deoraíocht óna threabhchas mar phionós air.

I gcuid a dó den úrscéal, feicimid Okonkwo ar deoraíocht i dtír dhúchais a mháthar, agus ainneoin gur cuireadh fáilte roimhe agus gur cabhraíodh go mór leis, is olc leis na blianta fada a chailliúint le heasumhlaíocht shíochánta. Gníomhaíonn a chara Obierika mar dhroichead idir Umuofia, tír dhúchais a athar, agus Mbanta, tír dhúchais a mháthair agus ionad a dheoraíochta. Le cabhair Obierika, éiríonn leis cuid dá shaibhreas a thógáil as an nua. Tugann Obierika gach eolas dó ar na forbairtí ina shráidbhaile féin, eolas a chuireann go mór lena éadóchas. Ag an phointe seo i mbeatha Okonkwo, déanann Achebe an cur síos seo air (lgh 134–5):

Bhí a bheatha faoi réir ag aon uaillmhian mhór amháin – a bheith ar thaoisigh mhóra an treabhchais. Ba é sin fios fátha a bheatha. Bhí a dhúil beagnach bainte amach aige, ach ansin thit gach rud as a chéile. Caitheadh amach é ar nós éisc ag cneadach ar chladach tirim gainimh. Ba léir nár dhual éachtaí móra dá dhia pearsanta nó dá *chi*. Ní féadhfadh duine dul thar chinniúint a *chi*. Níorbh fhíor nathán na seanóirí – dá ndéarfadh duine 'Sea' go ndéarfadh a *chi* 'Sea'. Seo duine a ndúirt a *chi* 'Ní hea' d'aineoinn a dhearbhaithe féin.

Céard iad na forbairtí seo a dtugann Obierika tuairisc orthu? Níl sráidbhaile Abame ann a thuilleadh. Scriosadh é mar go raibh a mhuintir easumhal dá n-oracal féin. Tá na misinéirí tagtha go Umuofia agus eaglais bunaithe acu le cabhair roinnt iompaitheach díograiseach. Tá Nwoye, mac Okonkwo, ina measc siúd. Mar bharr ar an donas, tá siad tagtha go Mbanta freisin. Feicimid an eaglais i rith na mblianta tosaigh ag iarraidh ionad coise a fháil le dua i sochaí atá faoi ghéarsmacht traidisiúin chianársa, faoi gheasa ag chleachtais ar leith.

Tá mífhoigne Okonkwo ag méadú agus níl sé sásta leis a chaoi fhadfhulangach a gcuireann na daoine suas le teacht na gCríostaithe. Níl siad ullamh rud ar bith a dhéanamh (lch 160):

'Ná smaoinimís ar nós cladhairí,' a duirt Okonkwo, 'Má thagann fear isteach i mo bhothán go ndéanann sé a chac ar an urlár, céard a dhéanaim? An ndúnaim mo shúile? Ní dhúnaim. Tógaim bata agus brisim a chloigeann. Sin é dhéanann fear. Tá na daoine seo ag doirteadh salachair anuas orainn gach lá, agus deir Okeke gur chóir dúinn ligean orainn nach bhfeicimid.' Rinne Okonkwo fuaim a bhí lán le samhnas. Treabhchas baineanda ab ea é seo, a mheabhraigh sé. Ní fhéadhfadh a leithéid tarlú in Umuofia, tír dhúchais a athar.

Agus Okonkwo ar tí Mbanta a fhágáil, tá imni an treabhchais faoin reiligiún nua soiléir nuair a éiríonn duine de na seanóirí chun labhairt (lch 167):

Tá reiligiún déistineach i ndiaidh socrú in bhur measc. Anois is féidir le fear a athair is a dheartháireacha a thréigean. Is féidir leis mallacht a chur ar dhéithe a aithreacha is a sinsear ar nós gadhar seilge a théann ar buile go tobann agus a thugann faoina mháistir. Tá imní orm fúibhse; tá imní orm faoin treabhchas.

I gcuid a trí den úrscéal, filleann Okonkwo ar Umuofia agus é lán le dóchas. Comhlíonfaidh sé traidisiúin a threabhchais, déanfaidh sé baill de chumann *ozo* dá pháistí, agus taispeánfaidh sé a láidreacht is a shaibhreas arís. Cuifidh sé deireadh leis an sciúirse nua atá tugtha leo ag na Críostaithe. Ach tá athrú tagtha ar Umuofia i rith blianta a dheoraíochta, agus duine eile tar éis áit Okonkwo a ghlacadh. Fiú fir a raibh gradaim acu, mar Ogbuefi Ugonna, tá siad imithe leis na misinéirí. In éindí leis an eaglais, tá an fear geal i ndiaidh rialtas le cúirteanna agus breithiúna agus teachtairí cúirte a thabhairt leis. Agus na deacrachtaí seo go léir ina bhealach, tá mearbhall ar Okonkwo (lgh 174–5):

'B'fhéidir go raibh mé rófhada as baile,' a dúirt Okonkwo leis féin, nach mór. 'Ach ní féidir liom na rudaí seo a deir tú liom a thuscint. Céard atá tar éis tarlú dár muintir? Cén fáth a bhfuil cumhacht na troda caillte acu?'

Tugann Obierika freagra (lgh 175–6):

Cé mar a cheapann tú gur féidir linn troid agus ár mbráithre féin iompaithe inár gcoinne? Tá an fear geal an-chliste. Tháinig sé lena chreideamh go ciúin síochánta. Chuir a amaideacht gáire orainn, agus ligeamar dó fanacht. Anois tá ár mbraithre tugtha leis aige, agus ní féidir lenár dtreabhchas gníomhú d'aon uaim a thuilleadh. Tá scian curtha aige sna rudaí a choinnigh le chéile sinn agus táimid tite as a chéile.

I rith n ama, leanann deacrachtaí is dúshláin na heaglaise nua, an teannas idir í agus an treabhchas ag méadú i gcónaí. Faoi dheireadh, agus in ainneoin an srian a mhol seanóirí áirithe, is bocht an chinniúint atá i ndán do Umuofia. Bailíonn na néalta, agus níl dabht ar aon duine faoin stoirm atá i ngar. Déanann Okonkwo iarracht Umuofia a dhúiseacht agus a spreagadh chun cur i gcoinne an fheillbhirt agus an choillte. Teipeann air: ní leanann duine ar bith é. Go luath ina dhiaidh sin, tar éis dó gníomhú as a stuaim féin le fearg agus fuath, cuireann sé lámh ina bhás féin, rud atá ina oilbhéim don treabhchas. Dearcann Obierika ar an chorp ag liobarnail ón chrann agus, mar a bheadh feartlaoi á rá aife, deir (lch 202):

> Bhí an fear seo ar dhuine de na fir ba mhó le rá in Umuofia. Thug tú air lámh a chur ina bhás féin; agus anois adhlacfar ar nós madra é ...

Adhlactar Okonkwo ar nós madra. Tragóid phearsanta is ea é sin, ach is tragóid don treabhchas é chomh mhaith, atá mearaithe briste anois le gach a bhí tagtha ina measc.

Joseph Lynch

SKELLIGS

Morning sun at Portmagee so journey on
To the unseen islands. We set off in calm bay waters
Germans, French, an older American couple
Tourists on a sort of pilgrimage
Seated windward, leeward, back to back:
Strangers in search colliding with the open sea.

The full Atlantic surge was quite a shock,
The boat rode windward bucking left and right
Plunged into troughs and barely snouted over
The hills of sea to plummet down again:
The ocean tossed us back as we ploughed on
Flotsam in its rolling maw; but on our way.

Atop a crest two crags appeared like grim
Portals to an eternity beyond our sight.
The sea was levelling out as we approached
This desolate jag of rock, its surface bleached
By myriads of gannets nesting there
Or skimming waves out from their awesome home.

Off green Skellig Michael the boat hove to, too rough to
    land.
The boatman pointed to a sheerdown path
From the church atop the rock right on the edge:
How the monks built that, he told us, no one knows.
How they came and how they stayed and died,
Built their clochans as close to God as they could be.

They planted and they prayed, cowled presences.
Six hundred years these men endured
Ascetic solitude to be with God.
Then, they withdrew again and pulled away.

And still the gannets wheeled and screeched and cried
Oh God, they cried, eight hundred feet above the waves.

The boat turned landward, the sea now with us
We rode the waves in their eternal tide.
A dolphin escort tore along our side
As if they recognised this hallowed route.
We stepped ashore exuberant, yet chastened by
That mystic force once wakened, now no more.

Around the ledge of those six beehive huts
The oceans surge, storms rage and wrack, the stars
     accelerate.

# Piaras Mac Éinrí

## BRITAIN AND IRELAND – LIVES ENTWINED (*extract*)

Like many Irish people of a certain age, I grew up in a strongly republican household. To my parents' generation, independence was hard-won and recent. They, and their parents before them, had been involved in different ways in the project of nation building – they remained deeply committed to and intensely proud of it.

Independence may have been hard-won but it was not simple and involved a certain amount of manipulation of our memories myths and narratives of the past. A black-and-white view of Britishness and Irishness was part of the new official Ireland's self-image; the struggle for freedom became the central myth of nationhood. As a boy of almost 12 years of age my proudest moment in 1966, the 50th anniversary of the Easter Rising against British Rule, was to read out, in Irish (although it had, of course, been written in English), the proclamation of the Republic, the founding text of the State, over a tinny public address system to the massed crowds of our local parish. [...]

It gradually came home to me that the divide was not so neat. Perhaps this is best illustrated, in my own case, by my grandfather's story. Sergeant Eddie Henry, from Kilmovee, Co. Mayo, served in the Royal Irish Constabulary or RIC, a police force that was later vilified by some republicans and nationalists as pro-British, although it also contained a fair number of rural Irish recruits for whom a life in policing was a respectable and honest career. I am one of the relatively few people, compared to the legions who used to assert it, who can say with confidence that my grandfather spent Easter Week 1916 in the General Post Office with Connolly, Pearse and their forces. That said, the factors that led to his presence were rather complex. He was wearing a British uniform, as he was at the time on loan to the Dublin Fusiliers to teach them marksmanship. His precise motives are still something of a family mystery, although we know that he roomed with Harry Boland, militant nationalist and later government minister, and may have been driven by solidarity or curiosity to become involved (another version simply says that Boland feared for his friend as the rebellion broke out and invited him into the GPO for his own protection). In the GPO, as a trained medical orderly, he assisted the grievously wounded Scottish-born socialist leader James Connolly, who was later executed while tied to a chair. The Freeman's Journal records that my grandfather and a few others who had been detained by the insurgents as 'prisoners of war' were released towards the end of the week. His career in the RIC continued after the Rising, but he also worked for Michael Collins, passing information about impending Black and Tan raids to the IRA. His house, as an RIC sergeant's house, was never raided, making it an excellent safe house and location for IRA arms. My grandmother never spoke of these times in her long life. [...]

In 1976 I joined the Irish Foreign Service – the Department of Foreign Affairs. Looking back now, my memory of my first posting to Brussels in 1978 is that I expected to find my British counterparts to be somehow more plausible, smoother, and smarter than I was. I am not proud of this, but I believe that many of us in those days subliminally thought something similar. It was a shock, then, to find that we were as good as anyone else and better than some, that our natural counterparts were as likely to be Danish or Dutch as British and that the British had their own difficulties in adjusting to the business of being a middle-sized, post-Empire state off the north-west coast of Europe. [...]

As Ireland itself began to change and old moulds were broken, I only gradually realised that my own views of

Britishness were not the whole story, even as seen from a narrowly Irish perspective. There were many Britains and many kinds of Britishness and my own identity and culture was far more influenced by them than I had ever realised or admitted. It was time to think again.

For one thing, there was the matter of class and diaspora. The nationalism of the middle classes who controlled Irish society after independence had little enough to offer the poor and the marginalised. Some of the smug moralists who were such strong supporters of Irish independence were also glad to see the back of these same poor and unemployed who emigrated, if only because, had they stayed, it would have posed a potentially revolutionary situation. In reality those with few prospects left for the neighbouring island in a constant flood for most of the 20th century. The reception they got may not have always been the warmest, but as one elderly returned migrant put it to me in Connemara, 'marach f...ing Sasana, ní bhéadh f...ing tada a'ainn' ('if it wasn't for f...ing England we'd have f...ing nothing'). Such migrants did not have the luxury of unalloyed nationalist politics, or at least they were aware of the hypocrisies and doublethink that could arise. The complexity of national and linguistic identity was brought home to me when we became regular visitors to the Irish-speaking heartland of South Connemara in the late 1980s. We met children who spoke perfect Connemara Irish and broad Cockney English, and adults who sang sean-nós and read English tabloids. This hybridity is, of course, mirrored in turn by generations of Irish in Britain, yet unlike Irish-Americans, they do not even seem to have a name. [...]

Samuel Beckett is famously said to have replied, on being asked if he was English, 'au contraire'. Too often in the past, the British were the 'not' of our identity; being Irish was sometimes collapsed to a mere 'not Britishness'. They were the Outside to our Inside, a reductionist and truncated view of identity that was probably commoner on this side of the Irish Sea than the other one. Confident nations do not need to assert their identity at the expense of others and especially at the expense of the other within themselves. There is more than a little British in the Irish and something of the Irish in the British as well.

## Eóin MacWhite

### THOMAS MOORE AND POLAND (*extract*)

Apart from his role in the development of Irish national feeling and as an important figure in the history of European Romanticism, Moore occupies a definite place in the history of the development of an independent Irish 'image' in Europe, both East and West. The first distorted glimmers came with the Ossianic wave, which only barely lapped the shores of Poland, though represented, for example, by Niemcewicz in his earlier ballads.[1] In Russian literature the Ossianic impact was a veritable tidal wave.[2] But after the picture of Ireland seen through the emerald-tinted filter of Moore comes a new image, that symbolised by the diffusion of two words into most of the Slavonic languages – *miting*, as a mass political manifestation, and *agitator* in its political sense, originally an English sneer which O'Connell made more honourable than a decoration.

These two words came into Polish relatively late, probably in the 1860s through Russian.[3] The phenomenon which they represent, reflected in the personal and political relations of Thomas Moore and Daniel O'Connell, is perhaps neatly symbolised in a couple of the earliest examples of their use in Russian. Prince Vyazemskii, who has already come into our story, recorded in his diary[4] a visit on 28 September 1838 in London to Lady Morgan, also known as Sydney Owenson, the author of *The Wild Irish Girl* and a personal friend of Moore. The Irish problem and O'Connell were discussed, and in his account Vyazemskii, a very fastidious man about language, very self-consciously writes the English word 'meeting', but for agitation he wrote *azhitatorstvo* – with a soft, instead of the later accepted hard, *g* – underlining the word. Yakov Tolstoy was in 1819 the chairman of a radical literary club, The Green Lamp, whose membership included Pushkin and Zhukhovsy. He was involved in the Decembrist movement but found himself abroad on the fatal day, and he remained abroad until his death in 1867. But by 1836 Tolstoy had become an informer in the pay of Nicholas I's notorious Third Department, in fact the Emperor's political police, reporting direct to its chief, Count Benkendorf, who showed most of his accounts to the Czar. In a report sent from Paris, dated 30 January 1838,[5] Tolstoy ascribed criticisms made by certain Catholic members of the French Chamber of Deputies of the treatment of Catholics in Poland to the inspiration of O'Connell, and here the Russian form *miting* is used. The monster meeting replaced 'The Meeting of the Waters' and the agitator took over the role of the bard.

NOTES

1   Manfred Kridl, *A Survey of Polish Literature and Culture* (The Hague, 1956), p. 187.

2   For this see V.I. Maslov, 'Ossian v Rossii, bibliografia', *Trudy Pushkinskogo Doma* (Leningrad, 1928), pp. 9–57; D.N. Vvedenskii, *Etyudy o vliyanii ossianovskoi poezii v russkoi literature* (Nezhin, 1918); E.J. Simmons, *English Literature and Culture in Russia, 1553–1840*; *Harvard Studies in Comparative Literature*, xii (1964), pp. 123–133; R. Iezuitova, 'Poeziya russkogo ossianisma', *Russkaya Literatura* 3 (1965), pp. 53–74.

3   A terminus *post quem* is given by the absence of these two words from Samuel Bogumil Linde's dictionary, *Slownik Jezyka Polskiego* (Lvov, 1854).

4   V.S. Nechayev (ed.), *P.A. Vyazemskii, Zapisnyye knizhki (1813– 1848)* (Moscow, 1963), p. 249. Vyazemskii played an important part in popularising Moore in Russia and translated 'Whene'er I see those smiling eyes', *Severnyye tsvety* (1829), p. 191.

5   E.V. Tarlé, 'Doneseniya Yakova Tolstogo iz Parizha v III otdelenie', in *Akademik Yevgenii Viktorovich Tarle, Sochineniya VI* (Moscow, 1959), pp. 585–6; Tarlé's article was originally published in *Literaturnoye Nasledstvo*, 31/32 (1937), pp. 563–62.

Aoife Mannix

A NIGHT OUT IN TAIPEI

What I taste most is the kindness
as I squeeze ancient Chinese wisdom
into a cup of hot water
and swirl my oxygen dreams
against cubic squares of light.

Apparently you can buy bottles of unconditional love
from a twenty four hour supermarket here.
A young man gives me a gift of his words
even though he knows I cannot read them.
By this time even I've started to forget
I don't speak Mandarin,
as smiles are seamlessly translated
and names tell their own story.

They don't think about the missiles pointed at them,
she explains, at least not much.
Even though there is no direct connection
and to get a visa she would have to say
she is someone she is not,
so she avoids the mainland.

Our island tragedies share unlikely echoes.
How much are we prepared
to lay claim to ourselves
and whether it's really worth dying over?
These choices have eaten up my country too.

We swap tales of other cities,
Paris, Berlin, New York.
Being shouted at in the street.
How Europeans hate each other,
how Americans are too arrogant for that.

How mothers always think the world
so much smaller and more dangerous than it is.
The glass violence of the television.
There is I realise something universal about fear,
and as I slide into the yellow taxi
thinking of you,
perhaps love too, perhaps love too.

Aoife Mannix

HALLOWEEN IN STOCKHOLM

Coming back to where I was born,
a city I have no memory of.
Crossing the bridges arm in arm,
you take another photograph in the rain.
The shadows of a medieval mist cling to my eyes.
I had lost my family in a fruit market.
You frame the mountains of pumpkins.
A giant paper ghost hanging above the street of lions,
painted witches and goblins laughing behind glass,
the trick of foreign words instantly translated.

I struggle to remember snow.
A young couple sliding in the ice,
a green pram bouncing on the path,
crashing through the years,
I lie blinded by white,
cold and lost.
The blue vastness of the midnight sun.
Surprised by responsibility,
my mother wrapping me tight.
Your fear of car crashes.
Sailing through the air.
My breath of snowflakes.
I had forgotten how to walk,
now my feet dance under water.

I have been here before,
a polaroid birth,
instant memory pasted in a book.
All that newly wed hope,
shot guns fired from a balcony.
Like stepping ten years into the future,
moving forward a generation.

The best part going through customs at the airport.
This is for all your adventures.
They were so young and they knew nothing.
My mother scared because I didn't laugh enough.
Too quiet,
too deeply buried in winter.
The past is just another disguise,
I don't recognise myself

Aoife Mannix

## THE LAST BORROWER

Battered, water damaged,
the cover greenish grey,
one corner dog eared,
I'm about to throw it away
when inside I discover –
*please return this book*
*by the date stamped last below,*
followed by the faded columns of years.

The final entry gives me pause,
*22 November 1978,*
and underneath the address –
*British Council Library, Tehran.*
Due back just a couple of weeks
after rioters sack the British Embassy,
after the outbreak of a revolution
in which such a title and such an author
will no longer be tolerated.

And I try to imagine the last borrower
of *Edna O'Brien's A Pagan Place*
reading quietly in some corner
while in the streets history
prepares to interrupt.

Aoife Mannix

SEARCHED

I'm twenty two years old and four months after
the IRA launch three unsuccessful mortar attacks on
Heathrow airport,
I emigrate to London via Stansted.
The customs officer waves everyone else through
but puts his hand up when it gets to me.
'Irish?' he asks, only it comes out more like an accusation
than a question.
I want to tell him that I'm not a card carrying member of
any paramilitary group,
that I've no idea what exactly I want to do with my life,
but none of my ambitions include blowing people up,
but he doesn't give me a chance. 'What is the purpose of
     your visit?'
Should I point out that technically it's not a visit
when you haven't got a return ticket?
Or explain about the latest unemployment statistics,
the depressing hopelessness of my country's economy,
the mass desertion of my friends, the confusion of my
     identity,
the complications of my own heart?
I know he doesn't really want my life story but
simultaneously it hits me
that I've actually no idea what I'm doing here. All I really
want is to go home.

It turns out his question is rhetorical or he knows the
answer just by looking at me
because he turns away to unzip my bag. He quickly
removes all my underwear,
knickers, bras, some grubby t-shirts, unmatched socks,
lipstick, mascara, a battered novel,

then reaching deeper stares at me and demands what's
    this?
I flush bright red, guilt is written all over my face
even though I've no idea what he's found.
He slowly pulls out the incriminating evidence
a small plastic figure of Donald Duck that I have carefully
assembled myself.
It sits bright and cheerful in the palm of his hand.

'It's a Kinder Surprise,' I stammer.
'A what?'
'You know the chocolate eggs with the toys inside. You
put them together like a puzzle ...'
I'm babbling as he carefully, painstakingly, removes one
    by one,
Mickey Mouse, Minnie Mouse, Asterix, Obelix, a mini
scooter, Goofy, a racing car,
a skate boarding squirrel, all four of the teenage mutant
    ninja turtles ...
He lines them up in a row on the security belt
as the people behind me forget they might miss their
    flight
and become oddly fascinated by the growing collection.

I struggle to explain 'my little brother wanted me to take
them with me for luck ...'
With one sweeping gesture, the customs officer gathers
them all up
and drops them back in the bag. 'The luck of the Irish ...
well you people are certainly full of surprises.'
And it hangs there for a second, all the murderous
    intentions
of my fellow countrymen,
the letter bombs, knee capping, assassinations, fertilizer
    explosions,
alcoholic Republican fanaticism mixed with Catholic post
    colonial fervour.

Then suddenly he smiles at me, like a promise of better
   days to come,
'welcome to the United Kingdom of Great Britain and
Northern Ireland'
and he waves me through.

## Bobby McDonagh

Original Sin in a Brave New World *(extract)*

How can we know the dancer from the dance?
(W.B. Yeats, *Among School Children*)

*The Human Factor*

Negotiations involve people. The issues addressed, the positions taken and the solutions reached are not free-floating notions in an elaborate mindgame. A negotiation, such as that leading to the Treaty of Amsterdam, consists as much of the people involved as of the ideas they bring to the negotiating table.

The dancer and the dance are, in a sense, inseparable. In the European Union, of course, it takes 15 to tango.

A summary account of the IGC [Intergovernmental Conference] negotiations, which is all that is possible in this book, tends inevitably to focus on underlying ideas and trends. It tends to present the wide-lens shot of the emerging pyramid rather than zooming in on the army of workers who are labouring on its construction. For someone involved in the construction, however, it is the people that are at the forefront. It is the people that constitute the sights and the sounds, the conflicts and the friendships, the reality of the experience. When I look back at the two years of negotiations I see people, not paper.

Apart from confidentiality considerations, there is an obvious constraint in describing individuals involved in the negotiations. The singling out of some for admiration could wrongly be interpreted as implicit criticism of others. The present book would, however, represent a quite incomplete picture were I not to say something about the people involved in the IGC.

The human factor, of course, had many dimensions reaching deep into each national administration and, indeed, the media. I will, however, focus my brief comments on the negotiators themselves.

## The IGC Representatives

The IGC Representatives Group was the pivot around which the negotiations turned. At the outset there had been much discussion as to what category of people should be appointed to the Group. The choice was rightly left to each Member State, since the appointment in each case had to respond to different pressures and to meet a different set of requirements. The appointment of a mixture of Ministers of State, Permanent Representatives and others worked smoothly. [...]

The Representatives Group brought together, and was seen to bring together, an effective mixture of technical expertise and political nous. No apartheid was practiced between different classes of Representative. Indeed, Ministers demonstrated a grasp of a level of detail which is usually left to officials, and the officials were capable of being every bit as political as the Ministers.

It takes all types, of course. Some Representatives took a broader view of the issues at stake and defined and presented their specific concerns accordingly. Others tended to focus on more narrowly defined national concerns. While some had a relatively straightforward job, for others it was trickier. One in particular, with a general election in prospect, had to cope with the possibility of being required to switch horses in midstream.

Some Representatives were content to remain in the lowlands of ambition. Others on occasion wandered so high up the moral high ground that, if they stood on their tiptoes, they could just about catch a glimpse of cloud-cuckoo-land. Some based their interventions on carefully prepared speaking points. Others didn't have a note in sight. Some were kept on a tighter rein by their capitals than others. The succinct and the long-winded. Graduates of the various schools of international diplomacy, including the distinguished Mike Tyson academy.

Every single intervention involved its own tactical choices. Intervene early to set the tone for the discussion (or because there was an early plane to catch). Intervene later to make it possible to take the temperature before speaking or to provide cover – it's sometimes more comfortable to intervene in support of a previously enunciated position. Intervene comprehensively on every aspect or focus on key concerns only? Low-key or tough? Whether to risk a joke?

It is fair to say that the Representatives brought an exceptional array of talents to the negotiations. Some of the Representatives were *outstanding intellects* – individuals as bright, razor-sharp and articulate as one could meet. Another category, overlapping with the first, is what I would call the particularly *effective negotiators*. Effective negotiation requires a subtle mix of skills.

Although the Representatives had strong and distinctive personalities, they also had a great deal in common: an ability to explain, a willingness (usually) to listen, an exceptional capacity for hard work. Each Representative brought to bear a mastery of complex detail on a vast array of issues, an ability to present in a coherent way evolving and sometimes internally incoherent national positions, and indeed a commitment to the process above any obvious call of duty.

The camaraderie between negotiators may, just on occasion, reflect a little touch of what one might imagine was the mixture of profound empathy and edgy respect between gladiators of old, girding up for a mortal combat not of their making.

Together, the Representatives, applying their skills as much to persuasion and presentation at home as to the bargaining and huxtering in Brussels, managed to do the difficult business of transforming the dogged pursuit of conflicting national interests into something which could serve the collective interests of Europe.

I cannot pass without brief comment on my own opposite numbers, the deputies to the IGC Representatives from other Member States and the Commission. Breach-fillers, Foible-handlers, Human Filofaxes, Creatures of the Shadows – thanks for the help, the understanding and especially the humour. See you at the next *Jeux sans Frontières*!

## The political level

The human factor was, of course, important at every level, and much of what I have said about the IGC Representatives Group applies to other levels also.

The negotiation was a political one. The 15 Heads of State or Government, in addition to their preparatory discussions and to their involvement in the launch of the IGC at Turin, met to advance the work of the Conference no fewer than five times in 15 months. It was they who eventually struck the key deals at Amsterdam.

Perhaps unsurprisingly, the personal relations between individual members of the European Council seem to count for more in negotiation terms than such personal relations at any other level. To an extent this may reflect the fact that, at the highest level, there is greater scope for adapting or even abandoning national positions with a view to an overall deal or indeed with an eye on some ideal picture beyond the scope of the particular negotiation. Personal sympathy or irritation as well as the negotiating skills of individuals can play a very significant part in determining the outcome of a European Council.

Foreign Ministers devoted great amounts of time and skill to advancing the work of the IGC at their monthly Ministerial meetings. At that level, which involved the refinement of the emerging package rather than the striking of deals, what mattered most was the coherent, constructive presentation of national positions. Of course, the relations between personalities counts at Ministerial level as at every level, but personality at that level is often to an extent indivisible from the presentation of firm and detailed national positions. Although many of the Ministers are particularly colourful and humorous individuals, the interplay of character at formal Ministerial sessions is at times somewhat akin to the profound but stylized dialogue of Greek tragedy.

## The interplay between different levels

One sometimes hears it suggested about a European negotiation that the level of ambition has been dampened by bureaucrats. If only the politicians had been allowed to act 'politically', we are told, the story would have been very different. If only the real negotiations had been conducted at the level of Head of State or Government instead of at Ministerial level. If only they had been conducted at full Ministerial level instead of at the more technical level of IGC Representatives (which brought together officials as well as politicians).

This sort of wishful thinking portrays a misleading, or at best a very partial, picture.

Those negotiating at a more technical level do not operate in a vacuum. They act under the political guidance and control of their Governments. If anything, their instinct, if given a freer hand, would probably be to go further than the political level. Whatever their starting point may be, they are at the daily interface in Brussels of competing ideas. The ideas which they hear from others are often convincing and sensible. They can come quickly to see the weaknesses in their own positions and the strengths in those of others.

At the same time, Ministers are in their own way guided by those working at a more technical level. Ministers cannot decide their approach in a vacuum. They must be given the facts. The options and their consequences, the possibilities and the constraints, must be explained to them. In our democratic system it is the politicians who must face their electorates and who must sell the deals. It is therefore they who must call the shots. When the European Union is perceived by some to lack ambition, it is likely to say more about what the public at large wants (or what politicians think it wants) than about the hesitations of insiders.

The relationship between the political and official levels in the European Union is necessarily a symbiotic one.

Of course, politicians – unlike officials – may on rare occasions decide to throw caution to the wind. They can opt to take a significant leap forward. If they do, it is not their officials they have to bring with them, but their voters. That's democracy. Politicians know it. They are all too conscious of the human factor.

*The accommodation of difference*
It should be recalled that the collective ethos in the European Union combines the pursuit of interests with the accommodation of difference. It is not an ethos according to which the race is always to the swift, the battle to the strong; or where the weak are expected to go to the wall (although you should never turn your back for too long).

Of course, by definition, the eventual agreement at the IGC – which required unanimity – would have to be acceptable to every delegation. However, the ethos of accommodation goes much deeper in the European Union than any formal unanimity requirement. The spirit of attempting to reconcile difference applies even where decisions do not have to be agreed unanimously. This reflects the wider interest of every Member State in obtaining the understanding of others. It is a question of 'there but for the grace of God'. More profoundly, the ethos of accommodation reflects also the tentative flowering in individuals of a sense of being European. The surest thing one could do to nip such flowering in the bud would be to overestimate the depth of its roots.

Negotiators in the European Union are the human shock-absorbers between strongly and naturally competing views. They are the reconcilers of contradictory wish-lists, the fudgers of incompatible bottom lines. Their work constitutes the decompression chamber between Original Sin and the Brave New World, the paradox at the heart of this book.

'O brave new world / That has such people in't!'

Philip McDonagh

## A Visit to Loker Hospice Cemetery

"Well done, lads," writes Fitzpatrick, ninety-four,
veteran, in script like barbed wire all these years
on, rain cavorting down as we ignore
the one the other. Thus, at Armenteers,
Pop, Wipers, Shelltrap Farm, one could dispense
with names and packdrill for a soldier's far
intimacy, the enabling reticence
of those about to die, whose graves these are.

Redmond, I find, is buried separately.
The lives lost here would help us to agree,
he dreamt, in Ireland, North with South, and win
Englishmen's trust. The Ulsters brought him in,
grey-haired, soon after dawn. In this mute space,
his one man's no-man's land, he rests his case.

Philip McDonagh

THE MAUSOLEUM OF THE SAMANIDS

Out of the misty morning comes the proud
householder, a white-and-orange cat, to run
before us on the low precinct wall;
the carvings open up to a chaste sun.

This basket-woven look in layers of stone
is placid as we are, a down-to-earth technique,
until a rhythm picks up that veers towards heaven.
The pillars of the Parthenon still speak

for Pericles, this quiet *mazaar* brings back
a Persian dynasty: great Avicenna,
on fire with learning in his library,
hunger in each traversal of his pen,

is one with the engineers whose intricate
channeling of scarce water by the art
of *qanat* eases burdens – old Bukhara,
learning and ingenuity both part

of prayer; 'and to this day,' our guide goes on,
'they make *ziyárat*, a local pilgrimage,
here to the mausoleum.' She points: a man
whose battered bicycle is on the edge

of the sparse lawn will tour the tombs on foot.
'A private thing, a child-birth it could be,
they bring to other saints. But when their need
falls in the sphere of civil society,

they turn still to the Samanids. For us,
a problem-solving justice is a sign

of holiness.' We see him now, our pilgrim,
statue-like, solitary in the shrine.

Those old school notes of half-a-century
ago come back to me, the teaching plan
of Father Redmond, his 'Avicenna, boys'
a shiver in the silk of Transoxiana,

preface to all-encompassing Aquinas
dropping the *Summa theologica*
because a sudden joy caused his life's work
'to seem, boys, in comparison, mere straw.'

Our pilgrim raises fingers to his forehead.
It's more than words. The trusting supplication
that we now share invites the stones to speak:
the whole *mazaar* an arrow in translation.

Peter McIvor

## St. Stephen's Day, 20th August 2006

If it were his, the Chain Bridge would be hers,
Not brick by brick, of course, because the view
From Margit Bridge would surely be enough
To show her what he means: the scale of it,
From parliament, past clusters of light to
The Citadel they looked at on Stephen's Day,
Before a storm from Balaton crashed down
And took away what had been given her.

And months later, she'd speak about it still,
That sudden change: the cold, the driving rain,
The screaming, fleeing crowds – and marvel that
Just hours before he'd said the river view
Had been gifted: the bulbs on the bridge just
Fairy lights on a summer's evening fair.

Peter McIvor

## THE MOST OF IT

Though night had come, the mist on Buda
Brightened up the window pane,
And when he pulled the shutters down,
Something stayed that wasn't there.

Though on his own, he thought it right
That God be thanked for it, as when,
Across the bridges, once he saw
The moon arise above the big

Basilica, as bright and clear
As bells that sound across the square.
Well, even lovers live alone.
They learn to make the most of it.

# Seosaimhín Bean Mhic Néill *d'aistrigh* [Josephine McNeill]

## FINNSGÉALTA Ó INDIA (*sliocht*)

*Editors' note: the original text was published in Gaelic type, as was common until the 1950s. Here, the text is presented in roman type, but the original spelling has been retained, with the exception of the letter 'h' being substituted for the* buailte.

Bhí Raja agus Rání uair agus ní raibh aon leanbhaí aca. Thárla lá gur tugadh a lán iasg isteach 'sa chistín ríoghdha agus bhí aon iasg beag amháin ortha ná raibh marbh. Do thug cailín aimsire 'sa chaisleán fé ndeara ga raibh an t-iasg beag beó agus do chuir sí isteach i n-árthach uisge é. Ba ghearr 'na dhiaidh sin go bhfaca an bhainríoghan é agus nuair a chonnaic sí a áilneacht a bhí sé, do cheap sí é a choimeád mar pheata aice féin. Do thug sí grádh mór do'n iasg toisg gan aon leanbhaí a bheith aice agus bhí sé mar a bheadh mac aice as san amach. Sé ainm a tugadh air ná Mochí Rája (.i. iasg-rí). Ní fada go raibh Mochí Raája ag eirighe ro-mhór don árthach go raibh sé ann agus annsan, cuireadh isteach i n-árthach ní ba mhó ná an chéad cheann é agus nuair a bhí sé ró mhór do'n tarna ceann, cuireadh isteach i ndabhaigh mhóir é. Tar éis tamaill bhí sé ró mhór do'n dabhaigh agus annsan cuireadh isteach i loch beag i n-aice an chaisleáin é agus bhí sé lán-tsásta ann. Thugadh an Rání lón agus biadh dó dhá uair 'sa lá.

Anois níorbh' iasg i n-aonchor Mochí Rája, cé gur dhóigh le gach éinne gurbh eadh. Prionnsa óg a bhí ann a bhí tar éis fearg do chur ar na déithidh agus do dheineadar iasg de agus do chaitheadar 'san abhainn é mar phíonós. Lá dá raibh an Rání ag tabhairt a chuid bidh dó, do ghlaoidh Mochí Rája amach.

'A mhathair ríoghdha, a mhathair ríoghdha,' ar seisean, 'táim an-uaigneach annso liom féin. Nárbh' fhéidir leat bean a d'fháil dom?'

Do gheall an Rání dhó go ndéanfadh sí iarracht ar bhean a d'fháil dó agus do chuir sí teachtaí amach chun gach éinne d'á lucht aitheantais féachaint an dtabharfadh éinne aca a inghean le pósadh d'á mac. Acht do thug gach éinne an freagra céadhna.

'Gabh mo leathsgéal a Rání uasal. Ní féidir liom m'inghean bheag díl a thabhairt d'iasg mór le n'ithe, má's é peata an Rání féin é.'

Ar n-a chloisint sin do'n Rání ní raibh fhios aice cad a dheanfadh sí. Acht, ó bhí grádh thar bárr aice do Mhochí Rája, do cheap sí bean a d'fháil dó ar ais nó ar éigin.

Do chuir sí na teachtaí amach arís acht do thug sí mála mór óir dóibh an uair sin agus dubhairt sí leó.

'Imthighidh i ngach tír de'n domhain mór go bhfaighidh sibh bean do Mhochí Rája agus bíodh an mála so óir ag an nduine a thabharfaidh inghean uaidh chun bheith 'na mnaoi dom' mhaicín.'

Do ghluais na teachtaí leó ar an dturus san acht níor éirigh leó ar feadh tamaill. Níorbh' fheidir na bacaigh féin a mhealladh chun inghean a thabhairt ar eagla go n-íosfadh an t-iasg mór í. Fé dheire, do tháinig na teachtaí go dtí sráidbhaile mar a raibh comhnuí ar ghréasaidhe bocht a bhí pósta ath-uair. 'Seadh, bhí inghean ag an gcéad mhnaoi agus tharla go raibh inghean eile ag an tarna mnaoi. Bhí fuath 's gráin aice sin d'inghin na céad mhná agus thugadh sí an obair ba chruaidhe le déanamh di agus do bheireadh sí an píosa ba lugha le n'ithe di agus do dhein sí a dícheall ar gach aon chuma í do chur as an slí i dtreó ná béadh sí i gcomórtas le n-a h-inghin féin. Nuair a chuala sí trácht ar an rud a bhí ag teastáil ó na teachtaí, do chuir sí fios ortha lá dá raibh an gréasaidhe as baile agus dubhairt sí leó.

'Tabhair dom an mála óir agus bíodh m'inghean agaibh chun bheith 'na mnaoi ag Mochí Rája.'

'Sé rud a bhí 'na h-aigne ná go n-íosadh ag t-iasg mór an cailín agus mar sin ná bhéadh sí ag cur isteach ortha as san amach.

Annsan, d'iompuigh sí chun inghine na céad mhná agus dubhairt sí léi. 'Imigh síos go dtí an abhainn agus nigh do ghúna ann i dtreo go mbeidh tú glan slachtmhar ag dul i bhfochair na ndaoine uaisle seo go dtí caisleán an Ráni.'

Ar n-a chloisint sin do'n chailín bhocht, do chuaidh sí síos ag dtí an abhainn agus brón an domhain uirthi mar do thuig sí ná raibh aon dul as aice sa sgéal ó dí a h-athair as baile. Do chuaidh sí síos as a glúinidh ar bhruach na h-abhann agus do thosnuigh sí as a gúna do nighe agus í ag gol go fuidheach. Do thuit cuid d'á deora isteach i bpluais sean-Athar nimhe na Seacht gCeann a bhí 'na chomhnuí annsan ar bhruach na h-abhann. Do bhí an t-athair nimhe sin an-chríonna agus nuair a chonnaic sé an mhaighdean, do shín sé chúichi ceann leis as an bpoll agus dubhairt sé léi.

'Cad 'na thaobh go bhfuilir ag gol, a ghearrchaile bheag?' ar seisean.

'Ó, 'dhuine uasail, 'táim an-bhrónach mar 'tá m'athair as baile agus 'tá a bhean tar éis mé a diol le lucht na Rání chun bheith im mhnaoi ag an iasg mór úd, Mochi Rája, agus 'tá 's agam go n-íosfaidh sé mé,' ar sise leis.

'Ná bíodh eagla ort, a inghean ó,' ars' an t-athair nimhe, 'acht tóg na trí clocha so agus cuir i bhfolach i n-áit éigin id' ghúna iad.'

Agus do thug sé trí clocha, mar bheadh trí liathróidí beaga, di.

'Ní iasg i n-aonchor Mochí Rája. Rája óg isead é gur imreadh draoidheacht air.

'Tá seomra beag tógtha ag an Rání 'sa bhfalla atá timcheall an locha, 'chun bheith 'na tigh agat. Nuair a bheidh tú annsan istigh, caithfidh tú fanacht id' dúiseacht mar is fíor go dtiocfaidh Mochí Rája chun tú ithe má théigheann tú a chodla. Nuair a chloisfidh tú chughat tríd an uisge é, caithfir bheith ullamh agus chomh luath 's a chífir é, caith an chéad chloch leis. Tuitfidh sé annsan go dtí bun an locha. Nuair a thiocfaidh sé an tarna h-uair, caith an tarna cloch leis agus tuitfidh an rud céadna amach. An tríomhadh uair a thiocfaidh sé, caith an tríomhadh cloch leis is annsan, cuirfid sé crot duine air féin arís.'

Tar éis na focail sin do rádh, do chuaidh an t-athair nimhe isteach 'na pholl arís.

Máire Mhac an tSaoi

## A FHIR DAR FHULAINGEAS

A fhir dar fhulaingeas grá faoi rún,
Feasta fograím an clabhsúr:
Dóthanach den damhsa táim,
Leor mo bhabhta mar bhantráill.

Tuig gur toil liom éirí as,
Comhraím eadrainn an costas:
Fhaid atáim gan codladh oíche
Daorphráinn orchra mh'ósnaíle.

Goin mo chroí, gad mo gháire,
Cuimhnigh, a mhic mhínáire,
An phian, an phláigh, a chráigh mé,
Mo dhíol gan ádh gan áille.

Conas a d'agróinnse ort
Claochló gréine ach t'amharc,
Duí gach lae fé scailp dhaoirse –
Malairt bhaoth an bhréagshaoirse!

Cruaidh an cás a bheith let ais,
Measa arís bheith it éagmais;
Margadh bocht ó thaobh ar bith
Mo chaidreamh ortsa, a ógfhir.

Máire Mhac an tSaoi

AR THRIALL DO DHUINE ÁIRITHE CHUN NA HAIFRICE

Ní chreidfear é, a chara na gcarad,
Ach ó tán tú arís as baile
Ní dom is folláin –

Bia ná an deoch is mian liom,
Greim an ocrais, braon a' liathaithe,
Ní chucu 'táim.

Ná fan rófhada ar siúl uaim,
Ná trost insa bhá giúnach,
Fill, a ghrá!

Máire Mhac an tSaoi

CODLADH AN GHAISCÍGH

Ceannín mogallach milis mar sméar –
A mhaicín iasachta, a chuid den tsaoil,
Dé do bheathasa is neadaigh im chroí,
Dé do bheathasa fé fhrathacha an tí,
A réilthín maidine 'tháinig i gcéin.

Is maith folaíocht isteach!
Féach mo bhullán beag d'fhear;
Sáraigh sa doras é nó ceap
I dtubán – Chomh folláin le breac
Gabhaimse orm! Is gach ball fé rath,
An áilleacht mar bharr ar an neart –

Do thugais ón bhfómhar do dhath
Is ón rós crón. Is deas
Gach buí óna chóngas leat,
Féach, a Chonchúir, ár mac,
Ní mar bheartaigh ach mar cheap
Na cumhachta in airde é 'theacht.

Tar go dtím 'bhachlainn, a chircín earnan,
Tá an lampa ar lasadh is an oíche ag tórmach,
Tá an madra rua ag siúl an bóthar,
Nár sheola aon chat mara ag snapadh é id threosa,
Nuair gur coinneal an teaghlaigh ar choinnleoirín óir tú.

Id shuan duit fém' borlach
Is fál umat mo ghean –
Ar do chamachuaird má sea
Fuar agam bheith dhed' bhrath.
Cén chosaint a bhéarfair leat?
Artha? Leabharúin? Nó geas?

'Ná taobhaigh choíche an geal,'
Paidir do chine le ceart.

Ar nós gach máthar seal
Deinim mo mhachnamh thart
Is le linn an mheabhraithe
Siúd spíonóig mhaide id ghlaic!
Taibhrítear dom go pras
An luan láich os do chneas
I leith is gur chugham a bheadh,
Garsúinín Eamnha, Cú na gCleas!

Máire Mhac an tSaoi

## JACK

Strapaire fionn sé troithe ar airde,
Mac fheirméora ó iarthar tíre,
Ná cuimhneoidh feasta go rabhas-sa oíche
Ar urlár soimint aige ag rince,

Ach ní dhearúdfaidh a ghéaga i thimpeall,
A gháire ciúin ná a chaint shibhialta –
Ina léine bhán, is a ghruaig nuachíortha
Buí fén lampa ar bheagán íle...

Fágfaidh a athair talamh ina dhiaidh aige,
Pósfaidh bean agus tógfaidh síolbhach,
Ach mar conachtas domhsa é, arís ní cífear,
Beagbheann ar chách mar 'gheal lem chroí é.

Barr dá réir go raibh air choíche!
Rath is séan san áit ina mbíonn sé!
Mar atá tréitheach go dté crích air –
Dob é an samhradh seo mo rogha 'pháirtí é.

Máire Mhac an tSaoi

SEA NEVER DRY

I gcuimhne an Ghinearáil Khotoka as Ghana

É d'éag d'fhág trom mo chroíse,
An saighdiúir gorm,
I bhfad ó fhód a shínte,
    An saighdiúir gorm –
Mo chreach an treabhchas coillte
'Chíonn lao na bléine á ídeadh
Is an t-ál beag tá gan tíosach –
    An saighdiúir gorm!

Gan smál ar chlár 'onóra,
    An saighdiúir gorm,
Is nár dhearúd an trócaire,
    An saighdiúir gorm –
A mháigh os chomhair na ndaoine
Nár dhual don neart an díoltas
Is nár chliamhain an tslad don tsaoirse –
    An saighdiúir gorm!

B'fhearrde é é mo shuan istoíche,
    An saighdiúir gorm,
Ach a phearsa 'chur ó chuimhne,
    An saighdiúir gorm –
Ciúinbhriathra na cúirtéisí
Is an t-iompar 'oir don éide
Is an mheabhair – bladhm obann déadgheal!
    An saighdiúir gorm.

An t-urchar san a chloighh thú,
    A shaighdiúir ghoirm,
Arbh eolach don té a scaoil é,
    A shaighdiúir ghoirm,

214

Cé d'fhág i gcósair chróluí
Cois leaitirít an bhóthair?
Plúr laochra chósta an óir seo –
    An saighdiúir gorm –
    An saighdiúir, an leifteanant, an
captaen, an *major*, an coirnéal, an
    ginearál –
    An saighdiúir gorm!

Is é an bás an geocach,
    A cheann na bhfian.
Nár theip and tuathal fós air
    Le pór na gciníoch;
Nach mar sin atá scríte
Is ag teacht mar sin dó choíche?
Go dté muir i ndíse is
    Ar mhuir ní thriomaíonn!

Máire Mhac an tSaoi

SLÁN

Má fhágaimse slán fada leat
A ghleann a chonaic mo dhaltachas,
Led mhuintir is led thailte, féach,
Ná bíse bristechroíoch.

Dá thréigean, dá mba mhian liom san,
Nach léir go raghadh ródhian orm
Nuair táim anois chomh cloíte sin –
Is go bhfillfead ort arís?

Pé bóithre atá i ndán dom,
Pé ceantar ina dtarlód,
Pé treibh thar toinn a ghlacfaidh liom,
Pé cúram atá romham –

Ní ar shráideanna Bhleá Cliath,
Airíonn mé ar a clainn,
Thriallfaidh mo smaointe scaipithe
I ndiamhaireacht na hoích'

Ach ar dhúthaigh i bhfad siar
I raon na gréine buí,
Dúthaigh chnoc is farraige
Ná bhféadaim cur óm chroí.

Máire Mhac an tSaoi

Codail, a laoch dár thugas grá,
Codail go sámh im bhánbhaclainn,
Tusa mo rogha thar togha fear Fáil,
Thar rí na bhFian is a chóir fairis –
    Codail, codail, a chúl na lún,
    Le faobhar na hoíche, codail, a rún.

Is mór rí tíre is ceannaire cúige
A luifeadh le fonn anocht id leaba;
B'fhearr leatsa síneadh saor scópúil
Gan céile id chlúid is measc an aitinn –
    Ach codail, óir fós ní baol duit san,
    Codail gan ceo, a mhuirnín ban.

Seachain, a sheanabhroic liath ón gcnoc,
Seachain, a shionnaigh chríonna an fhill,
Fágaidhdse fúinne an áit seo anocht,
A shluaite a mhaireann faoi scairt i gcoill –
    Is codail go fóill, a chroí im chléibh,
    Go héirí gréine de dhroim sléibhe.

Codail, a laoich dar thugas grá,
Codail go sámh is do cheann lem ucht,
Mise a thug ort dianseachrán,
Mise a fhairfidh do shuan anocht –
    Codail, codail, a mhian gach mná,
    Codail, a mhaoin, roimh theacht don lá.

Máire Cruise O'Brien

THE SAME AGE AS THE STATE *(extract)*

The international organisation that had outsourced the
humdrum International Organisations section and had a
new section all to itself was the United Nations. Already
that section was seen – at least to itself – as the most
important section in the Department. The Irish delegation
to the eleventh session of the General Assembly of the
United Nations in September 1956 was Ireland's first. It
was led by the then Minister for External Affairs, Liam
Cosgrave and Conor [Cruise O'Brien] (not yet mine), who
had returned from his post as Counsellor in Paris to head
the new UN section at headquarters in Iveagh House,
accompanied the Minister; in New York, Ambassador
Freddie Boland, formerly Secretary of the Department at
Iveagh House, was our Permanent Representative. It was
something of a baptism of fire for Ireland – the year of
Suez and Hungary – but, under a Fine Gael-led coalition
government, our delegation remained safely, if in no way
necessarily disgracefully, in the camp of the United States.
Conor, who took to the heady atmosphere of international
politics as to his native element, was nevertheless
frustrated by the subservient line that his country was
content to follow, and also by a degree of duplicity, almost
for its own sake, with which that line became attended. He
had other reasons for depression nearer home: his
marriage of sixteen years to Christine Foster, a beautiful
and talented young woman of liberal Northern stock – her
mother was a Lynd – had broken up and the strain of
maintaining a domestic façade 'for the sake of the
children', not to mention his career, was almost intolerable.
I had always known Conor and Christine as a couple,
slightly. Because, in part, of the Lynd connection, my
parents were fond of her, as was my Uncle Paddy. Now
Conor had come back from New York for the Christmas

holidays, but by the Thursday after Christmas – I have reason to remember the day – he had come in to town from Howth in search of some distraction.

It so happened that my own Christmas had not been particularly happy either. I had spent the holiday with my parents as a dutiful daughter. We were, all three, desperately missing Barbara's two boys, who, after a year in our care while their mother was so ill, had rejoined their parents, on her recovery, in London, where their father had been posted, something which left us disconcertingly bereaved. I have always loved small children, not sentimentally but with a deep – and I hope clear-sighted – abiding interest, as some people love dogs, or horses. Up to this, minding my two small nephews had, to some extent, masked the emotional waste my life had become. Now, with Christmas over and the need for a show of seasonal good heart past, I had taken myself into the Department on the pretext of having arrears of work to clear. As I remember my then working habits now, I am pretty sure there were arrears, but I was certainly not engaged in clearing them. I sat at my desk and tried to confront the reality that my all-consuming love affair was over, and that only habit now disguised the fact that it was ending, for me, in rejection. Some lines of GK Chesterton's went round and round in my head: 'Nor stretch the folly of our youth to be the shame of age,' and I felt that I was both very foolish and no longer young. It was at this point that I heard click, click, click, an electric snapping of fingers along the corridors outside. This had always been a warning of Conor's approach; he had that habit of shedding surplus energy like static, as he walked briskly and purposefully about some activity, as like as not some mischief. I felt a pang of envy of people who obviously had interesting and entertaining uses for their Christmas leave, and then my door opened, and Conor said something like, 'What exemplary industry! Chuck it and come and have a drink.' It was all as simple as that.

I had always affected to have no time for Conor, in spite of his dazzling intelligence and charm and his meteoric success in his career; he was also slim, black-haired and handsome. Anyone who had found favour with Seán MacBride was discredited in my eyes. It did not matter whether they espoused the Minister's new, IRA-backed republicanism from conviction or self-interest – one was as bad as the other. My mother was not fooled; in her day such a display of hostility by a young woman for a young man was always an index of attraction. We never discussed any of my affairs of the heart as such, but she always knew.

I had indeed proclaimed, during a truth or dare party, way back when I first joined the Department, that there were only two men in Ireland I would be bothered marrying, and that both of them were already married. I had to name the two, and one of them was, of course, the object of my continuing adolescent passion. The other, perhaps for purposes of camouflage, to distract the company from the first mentioned name, was Conor. The Spanish have a proverb that fits the case: 'Toma lo que quieres', dice Dios, 'y pagalo' ('Take what you want,' says God, 'and pay for it'). Now I was absurdly flattered by the invitation. The Department was hierarchical, and a counsellor was always a counsellor, and this was not just a counsellor, but the Department's white hope; the government's policy had been to meet the demands of UN membership by keeping 'more of our stronger men' at home. At the very least, going out for a drink beat sitting alone in an empty building working up a suicidal gloom. We went to Davy Byrne's on Duke Street.

We had a wonderful evening talking shop. The dramas of Hungary and Suez were played over at first-hand: it was as you might say, the view from the corridors of the

UN. People familiar with Conor's writings will realise how fascinatingly this differed from the official accounts. For my part I had an inside track on home affairs to share with him. It was 1956, the year of Seán South's funeral (the IRA man killed in an attack on Brookeborough police station in Northern Ireland), and there was a general election coming up. I had told Conor that Fianna Fáil expected to be the next government, specifically thanks to the plank in their platform that promised to bring back internment for the IRA. I bet him a good dinner, when next he returned from New York, on this outcome. I hope he laid off his bet, because I won mine, and he paid me a very good dinner indeed on losing. By the spring of that year we knew we loved each other, and that it was a committed relationship. He brought his two small girls, Kathleen (later called Kate) and Fedelma, in their smart Irish tweed overcoats and their smart French haircuts, to see me (his eldest, his son Dónal, was away at boarding school), and I knew that their happiness, no less than their father's, would preoccupy me the rest of my life.

## Daniel Mulhall

## A NEW DAY DAWNING (extract)

Perched on top of Killiney Hill overlooking Dublin Bay, there is an eighteenth-century obelisk that is visible from many of the southern suburbs of Dublin. This stark monument, erected in 1742 as part of a famine relief scheme, stands at the highest point of a public park that carries in its name a reminder of Ireland as it was the last time a century came to a close. In 1900 this amenity was known as Victoria Park and this was the year when Queen Victoria made only the third visit to Ireland of her very long reign. Victoria Park had been acquired in 1887 by the Queen's Jubilee Memorials Association to commemorate the 50th year of her reign. In April 1900, as the recently-commissioned royal yacht, *Victoria and Albert,* sailed into Dublin Bay for the start of the Queen's three-week stay in Ireland, the obelisk in Victoria Park could be seen from the deck of the monarch's vessel. Someone in her party may well have pointed the monument out to the ageing monarch, and recalled its connection with her. There was a fireworks display on Killiney Hill on the evening of her arrival while the Queen was still on board the vessel docked at Kingstown.

For many in turn-of-the-century Ireland, this rare Royal visit was a huge highlight, the year's undoubted centrepiece. For others, the aged Queen's presence in Dublin served as an uncomfortable reminder of the painful calamities that had befallen the Irish people during her reign. It was essential for the British establishment to tread warily between the competing forces of nationalism and unionism. In a burst of doggerel, the popular poet, Percy French, imagines the Queen's after-dinner speech as overheard by Jamesy Murphy, the fictional Deputy-

Assistant-Waiter at the Vice-Regal Lodge. The Queen recalls advice she received not to travel to Ireland:

> 'They was greatly in dread,' sez she,
> 'I'd be murthered or shot,' sez she,
> 'As like as not,' sez she.[1]

French's lines manage to conjure up the atmosphere of the period and the political squabbles generated by the Queen's Irish sojourn. He visualises the advice she might have given Lord Zetland before they set out for Ireland:

> 'Remember and steer,' sez she,
> 'Uncommonly clear,' sez she,
> 'I know what you mean,' sez he,
> 'Up wid the green,' sez he,
> 'And 'God Save the Queen,'' sez he.[2] [...]

The Royal visit's immediate political purpose was to stem the tide of anti-British feeling generated by the outbreak of the Boer War. As the Marquis of Salisbury remarked, 'no one can suppose that she goes to Ireland for pleasure.'[3] Cadogan, the Lord Lieutenant, assured the Queen, who was known to have had no great warmth of feeling for Ireland, that she would be greeted 'with unbounded loyalty and pleasure,' but this reassuring simplification was not the full story.[4]

In nationalist circles, Dublin Corporation's decision, taken by 30 votes to 22 despite the body's nationalist majority, to deliver a 'loyal address' to the visiting sovereign, caused a considerable stir. The prime mover behind the decision was the Lord Mayor of Dublin, Sir Thomas Devereux Pile. Elected as a home ruler, and having been a member of the Wolfe Tone and '98 Martyrs Memorial Committee, Mayor Pile, an English-born fish merchant about whose political views Dublin Castle initially had strong misgivings on account of his association with Fred Allen, a Lancashire man with a Fenian background,[5] had already broken the conventions of nationalist politics by making an official call on the Lord

Lieutenant and by failing to keep himself sufficiently aloof from the British administration.

Pile's unpopularity marred Dublin's first ever St Patrick's Day Parade which was 'favoured with charming weather'. The Mayor was hissed by sections of the crowd and had stones thrown at his carriage. There were pro-Boer cheers from sections of the crowd and when a Boer flag was flown it was seized by a mounted policeman and the crowd was baton charged.[6] On the eve of the Queen's arrival, dissenting members of the Corporation provoked renewed political debate, this time about the Act of Union, whose centenary was the ostensible rationale for the visit. They declared that the Union had been 'obtained by fraud and shameful corruption', and that there would be 'neither contentment nor loyalty in this country until our national parliament is restored.'[7] The public gallery was crowded for the debate and those who condemned the Act of Union were loudly cheered. After heated exchanges, the nationalist motion was carried by 42 votes to nine. Taunts of 'flunkeyism' were levelled at the motion's opponents who complained of its extreme language. As a result, the Royal visit, though meant as an opportunity to acknowledge Ireland's English connection, was turned into an occasion for underlining nationalist Ireland's undying opposition to the Union between the two islands. Local authorities had become an important new arena within which nationalists could air their political grievances and vaunt their identity. Later in the year, Dublin Corporation moved to confer the freedom of the City on the Boer leader, President Kruger, who was then in exile in Paris. While this bid was ruled out of order on procedural grounds, it further highlighted the Corporation's anti-establishment credentials. Other local authorities did succeed in honouring Kruger. There were frequent disputes because of decisions by local authorities to fly nationalist flags on public buildings in defiance of local unionist opinion.

The Royal visit posed a dilemma for nationalist parliamentarians who could hardly warm to it. At the same time, they had no desire to give offence to the aged monarch. To mark the visit, there were a number of Royal pronouncements designed to please Irish opinion, including the creation of a new regiment, the Irish Guards, to be based at Buckingham Palace. After consulting with Tim Healy, John Redmond decided to adopt a conciliatory line. Alluding to another recently-announced Royal gesture, he predicted that the Irish people:

> would receive with gratification the announcement that Her Majesty has directed that for the future the shamrock shall be worn by Irish regiments on March 17th to commemorate the gallantry of Irish soldiers in South Africa.

Parnell's sister, Anna, was decidedly unimpressed by the Queen's 'cruel little insult' to the shamrock, and wrote that:

> those who cannot refrain from wearing the shamrock should dip it in ink until its dishonour has been wiped out either by the final triumph of the Boers or in some other way.[8]

The issue divided the Parnell family. Her brother, John, distanced himself from his sister's defence of the shamrock's honour and took part in the ceremonies marking the Queen's arrival in Dublin. On St Patrick's Day 1900, many English people took their cue from the Queen and decided to wear the shamrock. On arrival at Kingstown, the Queen was careful to display the emblem prominently on her lapel.

NOTES

1    'The Queen's After-Dinner Speech', in Mrs De Burgh Daly (ed.), *Prose, Poems and Parodies of Percy French* (Dublin, Talbot Press, 1962 [1st edition, 1929]), pp. 55–8.

2   'The Queen's Advice to Lord Zetland before Starting for Ireland', in *ibid.*, pp. 53–4.

3   Letter from Salisbury to Balfour, 7 March 1900, quoted in L.P. Curtis, *Coercion and Conciliation in Ireland, 1880–1892: a study in conservative unionism* (Princeton, Princeton University Press, 1963), p. 419.

4   *The Letters of Queen Victoria,* third series, Vol. 3, p. 501.

5   DMP Crime Special Branch memorandum 20996S on the Dublin Municipal Elections, 24/1/1900 (NAI).

6   *Irish Daily Independent,* 19 March 1900.

7   *Irish Daily Independent,* 2 April 1900.

8   *The Northern Whig,* 17 March 1900.

Daniel Murray

SLOANE SQUARE

Through the school's corridor
   with pictures of Field Day
followed by smells of
   teachers' cooking, we go
through the door to
   the Whole Wide World

The marble floor, the
   iron railings, the
rough bricks, the
   scream of glee from
children, the big school
   buses and the signs

Through the car-mending building
   with broken and smashed cars,
past Peter Jones and his
   necklace of roads, we enter
the long streets

Taxis charge, cars rush,
   buses march, vans walk by,
"Say It With Flowers" is on
   the island next to
the useful Smiths,
   Peter Jones sells hats,
chairs, tables, toys and gear

Across the road; when
   the man's red with
anger, he stops you but
   when he's green with
joy he lets you go

The ice-cold water
    in the middle of
the island; the water stings
    your hand like an angry
wasp. Pigeons have a refreshing
    bath while trees hover you.

Like skinny trees the
    lampposts stand.
The great trees are
    rough. The Great
World War statue guards
    while pigeons drop bombs
like Hitler's deadly
    Stuka dive bombers

The air smells of
    fumes and dirt,
Old fogies sit down
    on the benches,
gargoyles glare at you

Health shops stand in
    the polluted London air as
well as clothes and shoes
    and yummy food shops

In the army base, the Duke
    of York's, boys run
while spies come in
    but not out.

Paul Murray

FROM THE SHADOW OF DRACULA *(extract)*

A widely held belief in Dracula commentary is that the
character of the Count was modelled on Henry Irving.
Some go further and see the cast of the novel as reflecting
the personalities of the Lyceum Company. While there are
some obvious similarities, there are also emphatic
differences between the Count and Irving, who, among
other things, did not share the werewolf characteristics
which Stoker so obviously attributed to his vampire
(although Ellen Terry did compare Irving playing Macbeth
to a great famished wolf). The case for seeing Irving as
Dracula, apart from any physical resemblance (they were
both tall) and dramatic personality, is based largely on his
nocturnal habits (although these are inevitable in the
acting profession) and an alleged feeling on Stoker's part
(for which there is no supporting evidence) that he was
exploited by the actor; this is a variation on the Marxist
identification of vampirism with economic exploitation.
Dracula's reinvention of himself as an English gentleman
does parallel Irving's recasting of his unpromising
attributes to become a great actor through a supreme effort
of will. However, Stoker's descriptions of Irving do not
generally suggest the supernatural; by contrast, the
drugged appearance of Sarah Bernhardt's husband,
Jacques Damala, who frequented the Lyceum, made Stoker
think that he was a living dead man. Other aspects of
Dracula recur in Stoker's fiction without any obvious link
to Irving; the furious cat in his short story, 'The Squaw', for
example, bears more than a passing resemblance to the
Count: the very incarnation of hate, her green eyes blaze
with lurid fire and her sharp white teeth shine through the
blood around her mouth.

Some at least of Dracula's characteristics may have come from contemporaries other than Irving, Sir Richard Burton being an obvious example. Stoker first encountered Burton in Dublin and maintained contact with him at the Lyceum. They first met when Burton visited Ireland in 1878 to lecture in Dublin on ogham, the early Irish alphabet, at a time when his star was very much in the ascendant. Irving was in Dublin at the same time, on his way to give a reading at the Samaritan Hospital in Belfast and he introduced Burton when Stoker met him off the train at Westland Row Station. Stoker's attention was riveted by the explorer's air of dark, forceful ruthlessness. In January 1879, Stoker met him again at the Green Room Club, where he sat between Burton and James Knowles, editor of the *Nineteenth Century* magazine.

In the following few weeks, Stoker met Burton and his wife at supper several times. His first impression of Burton as a man of steel was confirmed. He also noticed that, when Burton laughed, his face seemed to lengthen, with the upper lip rising, showing the right canine tooth, just like Count Dracula. Burton enthralled Stoker with his tales of the East: 'As he talked, fancy seemed to run riot in its alluring power, and the whole world of thought seemed to flame with gorgeous colour.'[1] There is a reference in *Dracula* to the *Arabian Nights*, which Burton had translated and which he had, indeed, suggested might provide the material for a play at the Lyceum. Like Dracula himself, Burton arrogated to himself the power of life and death with a casual imperiousness. He told Stoker of how he had murdered an Arab lad who had recognised him as a foreigner in Mecca, without being troubled; as he recounted the tale, his canine tooth gleamed like a dagger.

Burton was a generation older than Stoker, having been born in Torquay, in the west of England, in 1821. He had family roots in Tuam, County Galway, where his paternal grandfather had been the Church of Ireland rector and owner of an estate. Like Stoker, Burton had definite ideas on the issue of Home Rule and advocated the adoption of the Austro-Hungarian constitution as a model for Ireland. He wrote on the parallels between the Irish and the Magyars and was familiar with the life and work of Arminius Vambery, the Hungarian writer and traveller who some believe first interested Stoker in Vlad the Impaler, the historical Dracula. When Stoker met Burton in London in 1879, the explorer told him of a planned expedition to reopen the old Midian gold mines in Arabia; Stoker asked him to take his adventurous brother, George, with him as a doctor to the party and Burton was agreeable but Arabi Pasha's 1882 revolt led to the indefinite postponement of the project.

Stoker shared an interest in the supernatural with Burton, whose analysis of 'The Preternatural in Fiction' featured in Justin McCarthy's ten-volume *Irish Literature* (1904). Stoker and Irving subscribed to the private publication of Burton's five-volume *Persian Tales* but the most interesting of Burton's literary efforts from the perspective of *Dracula* is his *Vikram and the Vampire or Tales of Hindu Devilry* (1870). It is fair to assume that Stoker read it and while the evildoer of the tale is the character, Jogi, not the vampire (who saves the King's life), the concept of the vampire and the horrific descriptions in the book may well have influenced Stoker. It features blood-sucking demons among a ghastly crew and the manner in which Jogi raises his hand to silence nature anticipates Dracula's ability to control the wolves by a similar gesture. The decapitation of Jogi also resembles the fate met by the Count.

Another man of action who inspired Stoker was the explorer, Henry Morton Stanley, for whom Irving gave a dinner at the Garrick Club in October 1882. Stanley had just returned from the experiences he would later chronicle in *In Darkest Africa* and had been in close consultation with the King of the Belgians about the foundation of the Congo Free State. He held his audience at the Garrick spellbound and Stoker sat up until 4 a.m., enthralled by the traveller's tales. At the same time, Stoker recognised a darker side in Stanley: in 1882, he saw horror ingrained on Stanley's face, feeling that there were times when he looked less like a living than a dead man, a real-life example of the living dead. Stanley returned Stoker's admiration, telling him in 1890 that he had mistaken his vocation and should devote himself to literature. Stanley's opinion was based on Stoker's least significant work from a literary perspective; his pamphlet on the United States, *A Glimpse of America*, was one of very few books the explorer had taken with him to Africa. They shared the same publisher around this time: Edward Marston published *Under the Sunset* and *A Glimpse of America*, as well as Stanley's *Through the Dark Continent*.

In some respects, Stoker himself is closer to the Count than Irving. Like Dracula, and in marked contrast to the actor, Stoker was a man of many parts, willing to turn his hand to more or less anything. Just as Stoker tackled a multiplicity of roles for Irving, so the Count made himself generally useful, acting as a coachman, cook and domestic servant. He also arranges travel and transport (his boxes of earth resembling the theatrical baggage which Stoker looked after), reading reference works and dabbling in the law. Like Stoker, too, he is immensely strong physically. If Stoker did contract syphilis, it might reflect a dualistic nocturnal existence on his part not entirely dissimilar to the Count's sexual adventures which are cloaked in darkness.

NOTE

1    Bram Stoker, *Permanent Reminiscences of Henry Irving* (William Heinemann, 1906), vol. 1, pp. 360–1.

# Sinéad Nic Coitir

## FLICK

As she opens the car door she sees mud caked in ridges on the road. She levers herself and the bump around awkwardly until she is perched on the edge of the seat, and waits for him to come around the car to help her. He's there now, leaning over and offering his hand.

'Need a shoehorn to get you out.'

He makes this joke every time, ever since the bump got big. At the beginning she asked him not to because it annoyed her, but he didn't seem to hear. He keeps on saying it, anyway. She reaches out, places her foot on a clean patch of concrete, and half-pushes, half-pulls herself upright. He closes the car door behind her and they look at the row of half-built houses before them. Only one, the show-house, has been finished. Sunday afternoon. A married couple looking at new houses. A show-couple, she thinks.

Everything about the road, except this one house, is half-finished, unkempt. The show-house is like a healthy tooth in a mouth full of decrepit stumps. Or else it is the front door which is like an open mouth; the path leading to it, smooth concrete streaked with mud, is like a tongue extended in welcome. This doesn't make much sense, though nothing does, these days.

'The horny-handed sons of toil are off today,' he notes. This is another of his jokes. There is a building site near his office, and when he comes home most evenings he complains of how the sons of toil have blocked someone's car, or are holding up service in the local newsagent's, buying elaborate sandwiches and cheap newspapers, standing about in their rough overalls and heavy boots. She had said to him that he was being snobbish. 'No, I'm not,' he said, affronted, and that was that. His 'nos' are facts, brick walls. There's no arguing with them. Her 'nos' are tentative, plasterboard you could put your fist through.

Inside, other couples are moving around, looking at cupboards and running their hands over work surfaces. They murmur to each other, private consultations that emphasise their companionship. The smell of paint is making her head swim. Her shoulders, her jaw, her teeth are tense; they ache with tension, with the strain of holding things in.

He hands her a floor plan of the house and she looks at it stupidly. All she wants is to go off somewhere quiet by herself. The floor plan reminds her of photos she saw once of rats in a maze, running from one box to another.

'We're here,' he says, pointing to one of the boxes. He has begun pointing out the simplest things to her recently. He says he has to, that her pregnancy has made her addled and slow. 'You know this,' he said to her. 'I don't like doing it, but one of us has to keep this show on the road.' She does not contradict him anymore. She has given up, out of exhaustion. Her words, like her 'nos', have no substance; they make no mark on the walls of his certainty. She senses that these walls have been put up out of fear rather than a conscious desire to dominate or keep her out, but it's all the same if you're outside them.

'I'm going upstairs,' she says. 'You look around down here.' She drags herself up the stairs, talking to the baby whom she calls 'baba'. Look, baba, we're going upstairs. Maybe this is the house where you're going to live. Maybe this will be your bedroom, baba. She goes into a small box room and pushes the door closed. There is a small bed under the window and she sits on it. Oh, the relief, she thinks, the relief to sit down, to feel the bed's softness sag beneath you, to feel the pressure on your legs ease. To be alone. Despite herself, she cannot resist lying back on the bed.

Anyone could come in! Anyone could see you! Can I not take you anywhere? This last has never been said, but might as well have been. The ceiling of the room is white stippled plaster. Look at the ceiling, baba. Hello, ceiling. Isn't it nice here; isn't it nice, just for one minute, to be quiet? She turns her head slightly. Look out the window, baba, see the sky? Hello, sky. She has taken recently to addressing inanimate objects. They don't answer back, they don't demand anything of her, and their listening gives her a sense of connection.

But she can't enjoy her solitude. She hears voices on the landing, then footsteps, and she manages to lever herself up just in time. When yet another nice couple appears she is getting to her feet. The woman frowns and says, 'It's a bit small, isn't it?'

She murmurs and edges past them onto the landing. The size of rooms is so far from what concerns her now, what concerns her all the time, that she cannot think of any cliché or commonplace to offer the woman. What she sees and hears around her is a stream of shapes, colours, sounds, as if she were at the bottom of the sea. She is bitter with frustration. She is like a half-formed chick whose shell has been caved in. There is no peace, she thinks. Will I never be left alone? Despair sucks at her but she resists. What good would that do?

But I can't think. At any moment, I could fall over, give way. If you do, she thinks, you're done for. Even now, he's not all wrong. Don't prove him right.

She goes into another bedroom, the master bedroom, and finds him looking out the window. Scenes of married life will be played out in this room for years and years, she thinks, and she feels sick. The baby is a wound inside her since it has brought her to this, but she resists blaming it. It's not the baby's fault.

One of the side windows is open and she goes over to get some air. He glances at her, with his habitual air of harassed concern. 'Are you all right?' he asks, in the confidential, urgent tone that irritates her to the point of screaming. 'I'm fine,' she says. He looks unconvinced. They both know he is right not to believe her. This also makes her want to scream.

The window overlooks the back gardens of another part of the estate where people have already moved in. Someone has tied a dog to a post in one of the gardens. 'That's cruel,' he says, nodding at it. 'People shouldn't keep dogs if they can't treat them properly.' She shrugs. She has very little sympathy to spare for the dog.

'It's probably sensible,' she says. 'He'd only ruin the shrubs otherwise. I'm sure they let him out for a run now and again.' She has tears in her eyes. 'What's the matter?' he says, trying not to show his impatience and what lies behind it. She shakes her head. Again she is threatened by despair, because she can think of nothing to say, nothing that would satisfy him.

Downstairs they talk for a few minutes to the woman who is showing the house. She nods at the bump and says pleasantly, 'Is it your first?'

'What?' she asks, muddled, because she has been going through the motions until they can get out and has not been paying attention. Then she says 'Yes,' brusquely, because she can take no more.

When they go outside he upbraids her. 'You were rude to that woman. She must have thought you were odd.'

She snaps at him. 'You can be sharp enough yourself.'

He goes silent. This is usually a bad sign.


In the car she too sits silent, her face towards the window. He drives away. She thinks about the scene with the woman, re-playing it as an onlooker, or the woman herself, would have seen it. People make allowances for pregnant women, don't they? And anyway, so what? But there is no point in discussing it. It would be like her accusation of snobbery. At the time she had accepted his 'no', but now she thinks, I was right. He *was* being snobbish. How many other false 'nos' have I deferred to? She feels she is drowning, and struggles to keep afloat. Every part of her goes into that struggle. Nothing she sees or hears is real, compared to that.

He says, desperately, 'What's wrong?', and she says, 'Nothing.' He pulls the car over suddenly, stops, strikes the steering wheel and screams, 'What's going on? What's happening?' She flinches. She hates it when he screams. He doesn't do it often, so he must be bad now. His face shows panic, terror. She takes his hand. The truth is too big for them as they are now, and she does not know what the truth is. All she can do is stop things getting too bad.

'It'll be all right.' She tries to calm him.

His words come in gasps. 'I can't take much more of this.'

She feels sorry for him in a numb, impersonal sort of way. He is suffering too.

When he becomes calm he asks, 'Will it be all right?' and she says, 'Yes'. What else can she say? He frowns, breathes deeply, drives on. She looks out the window.

After a while he says, 'It'll be better when the baby is born,' and she agrees. What else can she do? It helps to behave as if things will be all right, and she tries not to think. All she can do is notice things, although she cannot take them in. Noticing things is her way of keeping faith with life beyond, her way of getting outside her misery.

Right now, they are driving on a motorway. There is the road. Hello, road. There is the concrete underside of a flyover. It flicks past, gone before she can take it in. There is a grass verge, banks of shrubs, more grass. Flick, and they're gone. Cement walls, a bridge. Flick, flick. Gone, gone.

She knew before that things were wrong but she thought: they will get better. Getting pregnant was a way of testing and proving this. Now she is weak, ill and even more demoralized. Things would not get better. She resisted knowing this until the slow, insistent erosion of misery wore away her resistance. There was no sudden moment of insight. She simply noted one day, in the course of the conversation in her head, that if things were bad now they would be worse after the birth. There would be a thousand new ways in which they would rub against each other, and the small space she had clawed out for herself between them would vanish.

She is ill and emotional, but that does not make her wrong.

I could feel sorry for myself, she thinks, but where would that get me? What I have, all I have, is this road, this grass, that petrol station. Flick. That roundabout. She thinks about the dog in the garden behind the show house. It'll never get out. Poor dog.

The thought comes to her: I'll never get out.

He is a good man in many ways, but he has shrunk her existence. He is considerate and generous and all he asks in return is the air she breathes. Nothing she says or thinks is quite real to him. He would deny this if she put it to him, so she does not. She hasn't the strength to insist. She has almost come to believe that she is too weak to exist without him.

They are in the suburbs now. They drive through estates of gardens and houses and cars and trees. She sees people, children, families. She thinks: the two of us, in this car, look like a family. They pass a couple standing on a corner. She sees their faces for a second, then they are gone. They look normal, she thinks. But so do we.

A few months ago she said to him, 'Couldn't we go and talk to someone?' and he had reared back, as though she had just confessed an infidelity, and said, 'I'm not discussing my business with a stranger.' Then, trying to be conciliatory, he added, 'But can't you talk to me?'

Now she finds comfort in looking at things, but they go by so quickly. If I felt better – if I could think more clearly – I might be able to hold on to something. There's a bus stop, railings, a park. Look, baba. Look at the trees. What am I going to do when you're born, baba? She goes under, lashes out and breaks the surface, gasping for air. Treading water, she finds balance again. I'll never get out, baba. She feels the slow, deep, drag of despair. No.

They reach the coast road. Look at those shops, baba. A butcher's. A newsagent's. Flick. I'll never get out. No. Look at the sky, baba. Look at it. She feels herself going under again and struggles. Look at those birds, look at the sea.

Look at that ship going out.

It is a container ship, so large and so far out that it does not flick by. It seems hardly to move yet its progress is steady, determined, and it surmounts the sea.

'Look at the ship,' she says.

'What?' He glances over. 'I can't. I'm watching the road.'

He is right, of course. He is responsible for her safety and cannot indulge her in trivialities. She sees his point of view so clearly, better than her own. She looks back at the ship. Other things flick by, but she can keep the ship in sight.


Later, at home, she runs a bath and wallows, sensing weightlessness and warmth, release from her body's discomfort. He brings in her book and a cup of tea and leaves to watch television. Once she would have asked him to stay and talk, and despair seizes her again. I'll never get out. No. It's harder to come back up than to resist going down. Think about the ship.

The water of the bath calms her. She cannot think clearly, but impressions and conjectures emerge and she muses on them. The ship's deliberation, its intentness, its certainty of reaching its destination. It could be going halfway around the world, yet it must still pass the battered ranks of stacked containers lining the port, and the pleasure craft in the waters off Clontarf. It must plough along the deep channel and pass the North Bull and Poolbeg lighthouses before reaching open water. The arms of Howth Head and the Dublin mountains fall behind, recede as the ship progresses towards the featureless horizon.

She soaps herself, dimly aware of some enjoyment of scent and sensations. Featureless, but not uncharted. Navigable. There are maps, measurements, guiding lights. Others have sailed this way before and left markers. You might not know the way, but you could find it.

She cries weakly.

What keeps the ship on course in the black ocean? Nothing as fanciful as hope. Something more basic. Survival.

I'm not without resources, all the same. I used to cope.

This thought floats up suddenly, as if misery has finally worn through numbness into a kind of clarity.

Through the bathroom window she sees that night has fallen. She turns a tap, feels the hot current surge through tepid water, wonders how far the ship has got on its journey. Maybe, she thinks, maybe I could get out.

This is not hope, merely the recognition of a possibility. In the meantime, she is being left alone. She lingers as the water cools, postponing her re-emergence.

Helena Nolan

AT FIRST SIGHT
*im Wisława* Szymborska
*(2 July 1923–1 February 2012)*

You have seen someone like me, once
And I have met you too, perhaps
At the curve of an iron stairway
A junction with lights, some pause
On a railway platform, a meeting of eyes
The passing, steamed up window of a bus
We are all of us only each other's
Shadows, foretelling of future's past
Walking in familiar footsteps
On the city's Google maps, watched
By the same dark satellite, I wonder
How we missed each other for so long
The years will pass, the only thing
That's definite is time, shaping our passage
We move between the lanes
Like careful liners, watchful for the rocks
The threat of secret icebergs, we are trained
To call for help but do not like to shout
Don't make a fuss, the days are growing longer
Spring will soon pull hope out of the earth
Do not regret the dark shroud of winter
You will forget again what was forgotten once
I will remember only the silhouette of one
Once glimpsed, the one who smiles like you did

Helena Nolan

THE BONE HOUSE
*'I think you will like the pictures from Dublin Zoo*
*… did you know they raised lions there?'*
– Elizabeth Bishop to Marianne Moore, August 1937

These places are reminders, exposing how, after such acts,
we share the scent of animals – eating, sex and death.
Our language tells us we are similar – brave as, mean as –
how we are lions, weasels, or we have our *heads in the sand.*
Like forced comparisons, emotions pace in cages, for
    display.
Here, in this one room, it is different; there are creatures
    here
whose scent we'll never smell, the colour of whose eyes
we'll never see, never hear their whimper or their roar.

I think nothing could be better than to be a skull
in a glass case, picked and pickled clean; all that gleaming
    whiteness,
the clear edges of things, emerging from the mess that
    was before,
the open eye sockets, polished nasal bones, the silent
    yawn of jaw
all appearing as plain and unreadable as words on a page;
skulls may keep their secrets, even in glass graves.

Helena Nolan

## MAKING THE BED

Unfold me,
Spread me like a sheet
Across the vacant bed.
They are sleeping
In New Zealand.
We should lie down too,
See what can be salvaged
From our tiredness.
All day long I have been folded
Like a concertina,
Or that paper game
We played as kids.
So spread me out now
But tuck me under.
No one should see what's written
Beneath any of my corners

Helena Nolan

PLATFORM

The embarrassed backs of houses
Showing us more than we are meant to see
Like girls with their skirts caught up
Defiant only in numbers, blushed by dusk
We stare at them through the flashing window
Until night draws a curtain on their shame
I look across at you who reveal so little
Your eyes like small battlements
From where tears might fall
Your fingers steepled
Elbows buttressed on formica
Your lonely stare giving nothing away
Even after I left the carriage
And stood on the platform
You did not look out
And if you had, what would you have seen?
Just me, vanishing backwards into the distance
Like an exercise in perspective

Helena Nolan

## THINGS YOU LEARNED IN THE ICE HOTEL

Everything in the Ice Hotel is made from ice –
The bar, the stool you sit on,
The vodka and the glass, melting together
As you drink them both,
Until your hands are empty, wet and cold.

The bed you sleep on is frozen too,
Like a glass bed in a story.
Covered in furs,
You lie buried in it,
Snow White in her coffin, waiting for the Prince.

When he comes to bed, he tells you of
The snow safari, what you missed.
Though what most delights him
Is that every year, they let the hotel melt
And cut a new one from the ice.

# Donat O'Donnel [Conor Cruise O'Brien]

## CAREY BLOOM

On his native soil the Kerry blue is a shaggy blue-black animal, a little short on leg, purposeful and reticent, and a fierce fighter. So was our Kerry blue in Paris, above all shaggy, and we were very proud. The Parisians are exceptionally fond of dogs; they are also inexhaustibly curious about the diversity of the creations of God, or the Supreme Being. For both those reasons our Kerry blue attracted a good deal of attention. It was therefore nothing exceptional when the stout lady, proprietress of the restaurant in the Place Notre-Dame-des-Victoires, came over and asked what it was, as a dog. I told her it was an Irish dog, of a race unknown in France. To this she replied that she had an Irish dog herself, and went and got it. She produced with pride a rather impressive beast, trim and tufted, resembling an exceptionally tough poodle and having about it that suggestion of the sinister which the combination of physical strength and marked elegance always seems to evoke. As the two dogs were introduced I admired the stranger. He was, I confessed, superb as an Irish dog but, I was ashamed to say, I did not recognize the breed. The reply was crushing:

*'Mais, mon pauvre monsieur, c'est une des races les mieux connues de chiens irlandais! C'est un Carey Bloom!'*

There were, she revealed, only three 'Carey Blooms' in all Paris: her dog, a bitch in the Avenue Henri Martin, and another dog in the Boulevard Raspail; but in the last case she thought the district cast doubt upon the pedigree. I could have added to the list, but found it too hard to explain that my own dog was also striving, in his woolly way, to be a Carey Bloom.

I got two things out of this encounter: a new name for my dog and a new place to take Irish visitors in Paris. Irish people in Paris, like other visitors, want to plumb the depths of French wickedness and perversity, but it is by no means sure that they all know a depth when they plumb one. The dog of the Place Notre-Dame-des-Victoires was a good answer to this sort of thing. He constituted visible and tangible evidence of French perversity, in a form which any Irish person could understand. 'When I look at that dog,' said one of the Irish visitors, 'I understand the Fall of France.' His cup was full when I revealed that the dog had belonged to André Gide, when he lived in the Rue Vaneau. As the beast sneered at them across the café table, my friends found it easy to believe themselves in the presence of a disciple of Gide's. Only that diabolical brain, surely, could have conceived the project of tonsuring a Kerry blue into the semblance of a poodle.

I always meant to survey the field completely, to visit the pedigree bitch of the Avenue Henri Martin and the attainted dog of the Boulevard Raspail, but my newspaper decided otherwise. My new editor felt that the Irish people were not interested in what was happening in Paris; they were interested in what was happening in Donny-carney: I was to come home, quickly.

This raised a difficulty: what about Carey Bloom? It is very easy to bring a dog from Ireland (or England) to France: you just bring it. But to bring a dog back from France to Ireland or England is quite a different matter. You must, to begin with, obtain a license to import a Canine. If you get this you must, on arrival in Ireland, hand over the Canine, in an approved Nose-and Paw-proof Receptacle, to an approved place of Quarantine, there to be confined for Six Calendar Months, at a cost to owner of £2 a week. Then, if the dog is still alive, you can have him. All this is understood to be required to keep the scourge of rabies out of Ireland and, of course, England. The French, however, have a different story.

It became clear that there were three courses possible:

1 To leave Carey Bloom in France.
2 To bring him to Ireland complying with the Regulations.
3 To bring him to Ireland without complying with the
  Regulations.

The first course I should have favoured myself, but it was ruled out by my two small daughters. The second course found no supporters: it would probably kill or at least disable the dog, and it would also cost us more than £50; the sentimentalists and the realists united in rejecting any such policy. It was therefore decided, by elimination, that Course 3 was to be adopted. Carey Bloom was to be smuggled, and I was to do the smuggling.

This was a more formidable and dangerous task than at first appears. In Ireland it is the Department of Agriculture that administers these laws. And it has been said that there are only two forces worth mentioning in Ireland: the Church and the Department of Agriculture. I risked not merely a heavy fine and a jail sentence, but also the loss of my job. Then hope dawned. I didn't have to smuggle Carey Bloom into Ireland at all. England would do. England and Ireland, politically, are fractured, but to the veterinarian they are still one and indivisible. If Carey Bloom were once in England, he could be brought to Ireland without fuss or formality. And even if I were caught smuggling into England, it would be by Englishmen, having broken an English regulation, and possessing therefore a sacred claim on the sympathy of my own countrymen. Even my newspaper would have to back me up; my friends could see to that. If it failed me it would be accused of playing England's game, and then let it look to its circulation!

In good spirits, then, I prepared for the attack. My family went ahead by air, leaving me with the car and Carey Bloom. My last dinner in Paris I took in the Place Notre-Dame-des-Victoires. The stout lady, pleased at what I had done for the reputation of her dog and house, gave me photographs of both. The picture of the dog had been taken at one of our evening gatherings. The dog was seated at a café table, with a hideous expression of intelligence, in the middle of a lively group; he had a glass of Pernod in front of him and four saucers – a surprising number, for he drank very little. On the wall behind, someone had taken care to hang a portrait of M. Gide. To a man facing, perhaps, an English prison on the morrow, it all seemed a little childish, and yet endearing. They put me to bed on the premises.

My start on the following morning was not as early as it should have been, nor my head as clear. It was eight o'clock when, with Carey Bloom upright in the seat beside me, I left Paris by the Porte de Neuilly, on the road to Dieppe. I stopped at Pontoise to consult the local vet. My plans involved putting Carey Bloom in a case, and the case in the boot of the car; anyone who knew Carey Bloom realized that this could hardly be done without assistance, much noise, and perhaps even bloodshed, unless the patient were unconscious.

The vet of Pontoise was large, *sportif*, and *très gentleman* – with crew cut. He was also in full sympathy with my project. The English quarantine laws were a piece of cynical hypocrisy. *La rage canine* was, without doubt, a very terrible disease, but did I know when the last case of it had been notified in France? No? *Eh bien, mon pauvre monsieur*, the last case of *la rage canine* in France occurred in 1910! *Dix ... neuf ... cent ... dix!* Under President Fallières! Had I so much as met anyone who had even heard of President Fallières? No? Well, then!

The vet of Pontoise was striding up and down the room, breathing heavily. I tried to bring him back to the immediate practical aspects of the problem: I had a boat to catch, needed instructions on dog-doping, and the dope itself. 'None of that,' said the vet, 'presents any difficulty.

Do you know the real reason for the quarantine regulations? It is that the dog breeders of England fear the French competition – and Dutch competition perhaps a little too –'

'My boat goes,' I said, 'at 12:30, and if you could give me some pills, something that would work quickly –'

The vet stopped walking and looked me sternly in the eye. 'Of course I will give you the pills,' he said. '*Ne vous affolez pas. Vous avez largement le temps.*'

I looked at my watch, with gathering hopelessness.

'It is admirably simple,' said the vet of Pontoise. 'Suppose there is a minister who is an honest man and who says, "You are breaking my feet with your silly regulations about quarantine for dogs: I will abolish them!" *Vlan*! So what happens? One dog breeder rings up his brother, the governor of the BBC. Another calls his uncle, the editor of the *Times*. A third takes up the phone and says, "Give me Canterbury 1."'

'So all the hysterical old women of England – that is 40 million out of a total population of 50 million – get together and make some *brou-haha*. They say: Keep out French Diseases! They say: A Vote for Labor Is a Vote for Rabies! Then one day the minister gets up in the House and says the question needs further study, and he sets up a commission of dog breeders' brothers to study it! As for you monsieur, here are four tablets of Gardenal. Give the animal one not more than half an hour before embarkation; give him the other three on the boat – just put them in his mouth, he'll swallow them. You've nothing at all to worry about – he'll sleep like a woodcutter, and the customs people in England are the same as our own, they never look at anything.'

Out in the yard the vet of Pontoise – who refused any payment – took a good look at Carey Bloom. 'He could be a nice-looking dog,' he said, 'if he were properly trimmed.'

Having no time for this controversy, I got into the car and prepared to turn into the street.

'Of course,' said the vet, 'I know that in England they like dogs to be like that. They have the mania of the natural. It is perhaps,' he added thoughtfully, 'a form of hypocrisy.'

As I drove through the Vexin on the road to Dieppe I felt considerably fortified by the vet's remarks. His exposure of the economic basis of the quarantine regulations was convincing enough – allowing for French hyperbole – and it conferred on my own enterprise an agreeable touch of righteousness. I was encouraged, furthermore, by what he had said about the laxity of the customs examination.

It was only in Dieppe itself, driving down to the port, at noon, that the brightness of this vision began to fade. I realized that I was a half an hour late, and that the doping of Carey Bloom was going to present certain difficulties. At the port I had two simultaneous problems to solve rapidly: to get the car on board, and to dope Carey Bloom. *En principe*, cars are not accepted at all, unless presented an hour before departure. And it was now – successive officials pointed out – thirty minutes … twenty minutes … ten minutes before departure. French officials, once they have logically established the utter impossibility of some course of action, usually like to show that they, being *élite* personalities, can none the less do it, this impossible thing, and the formalities in this case were pushed through with surprising speed. This involved, however, running up many steps and gangways, and the frequent assumption of that air of harassed and apologetic helplessness that, for the French official, is the mark of a deserving member of the public.

In between these interviews I had repeatedly to get back to the car for an even more difficult argument, with Carey Bloom. Carey Bloom is a patient dog, and he did not at all object to my trying to feed him Gardenal. I could put the tablet in his mouth and hold his massive jaws together. He would look at me sadly but uncomplainingly, his eyes deep violet pools under the blue shadow of his shaggy brows. Then, when I let go my hold, Carey Bloom would deposit a white and glistening object on the seat of the car. The ultimate official, who came to the car with the cleared papers, seven minutes before departure time, found me still clutching Carey Bloom's head, the two of us staring at each other fixedly. The official mistook this for a display of Anglo-Saxon sentimentality and disapproved. 'You had better get your car on board immediately,' he said. 'You need not fear seasickness, either for yourself or your dog. The sea is perfectly calm. But hurry in the name of God.'

There was clearly now no question of putting Carey Bloom into a suitcase and the suitcase into the boot of the car. That, and the doping, would have to be done on board, at leisure as I hoped. I pushed Carey Bloom onto the floor in front of the seat and covered him with a rug. The result looked depressingly like a dog covered with a rug. I drove to the ship's side and sat in the car waiting to be hauled aboard. But a face, covered with soft coal, appeared at the window, and spoke:

'You are not, monsieur, by any chance a member of the Union of French Stevedores and Port Workers, affiliated to the CGT? No? In that case, monsieur, perhaps you would be good enough to hand me the key of your car, and proceed, yourself, on foot, on board the boat. I will take your place at the wheel and will occupy myself with the loading of your car. You can be tranquil.'

I got out, as tranquilly as I could, but did not proceed on board the boat. I waited. In a remarkably short time the stevedore was out again, jumping up and down and waving long blue-bloused arms. He was not, it seemed, paid to be bitten by dogs.

It was not the Queen of England who ruled in France, and French workers had rights, for which, through their syndicates, they knew how to enforce respect. Other members of the Union of French Stevedores and Port Workers, gathered round, agreed with these views. I was not impressed, because I knew the man had not been bitten. Persons who had been bitten by Carey Bloom stayed bitten; they did not jump up and down in this frivolous manner, conversing about the Rights of Man and of the Citizen. I explained, and demonstrated, that the dog was sage and gentle. As for myself I owed no more allegiance to the Queen of England than they did, being a good Irish Republican. In fact, the dog was there in defiance of an English regulation – a regulation, moreover, which was unfairly aimed at French exports and was devised to protect the private interests of the English four hundred families, including Sir Eden himself. The stevedore, to whom I gave a thousand francs, saw my point of view. He would put car and dog aboard: 'Once there you are in England. The sailors are all English and capable of anything. They are all little bourgeois, Calvinists, and police spies.'

How right he was I found in a very few minutes, aboard the S.S. *Black Prince*. It was a fine clear day with a dead calm sea, but no sooner had my car been hoisted onto the lower deck, and the French stevedore departed, than a company of Calvinists descended with a huge tarpaulin. Silently, with grim efficiency, they lashed this covering into position over the car, securing it tightly. A small gap remained between the lower edges of the tarpaulin and the deck; as a window of the car was open, air could still penetrate to Carey Bloom. But only air; no question now of the leisurely administration of drugs, no question of a doped dog sleeping quietly in the boot. No possibility of tampering with that tarpaulin without detection, even if I were a skilled tarpaulin-tamperer, which I was not. The seamen might not all be Tory police spies, as the French stevedore claimed, but they had a look about them of belonging to that class of men who are described as 'law-abiding' because they like to see other people getting into trouble.

I made my way to the bar, for a Guinness. The barman, I found with pleasure, was an Irishman, even a Kerryman – Mahoney by name – and therefore by definition indifferent to the law, 'our pets,' and the public health of England. He heard my story gravely. No, nothing to be done with those seamen. All non-Catholics, mostly Methodists, don't smoke and don't drink, would inform on their own mother. The only help he could give, the Kerryman said, was with the Newhaven dockers. These were a decent crowd, that is to say, mostly Irish, who could be trusted to keep quiet if it was made worth their while. With the help of the dockers I should be able to get the car and dog quietly off the boat and as far as the customs shed. After that I was on my own. He thought the chances were about five to one against my getting through. You would be better off in England poisoning old women, the barman thought, than to be caught smuggling a dog. However, he would do his best for me, and wished me luck.

At Newhaven, the dockers did their part, as arranged through the barman. I drove slowly along the quayside, using one hand to pull the rug back over Carey Bloom. Cary Bloom, normally a very quiet dog, growled and shook the rug off. I pulled it back again, wishing I were in some quiet English watering place, respected by all, happily poisoning old women. Carey Bloom stayed under the rug this time, but shivering and sniffling. I reached the customs shed.

The customs shed (motor vehicles) at Newhaven is a building I now know rather well. It is open at both ends, full of wind and echoes. There are a few officials there, but it is difficult to make them out at first, so still are they in the uncertain light of the great windowless hall. You make them out, however, as you go along. One of them now came forward: the Automobile Association, a gingerhaired man with that touch of slightly furtive affability that marks the man who has one leg in the official world and another in that of private enterprise. He would clear the car papers while the other customs formalities went through; it would only take a few minutes. He took my triptyque and disappeared into the shadows.

Several minutes passed in a silence broken only by an occasional whimper. Then suddenly H.M. Customs was beside me: a friendly fresh-faced man with an outdoor look about him and a perfunctory sort of expression which I liked even better.

'Anything to declare?'

'No, I'm in transit to Ireland – going on to Holyhead tonight.'

'Nothing intended for the United Kingdom? No brandy, wine, cigarettes, or perfume?'

'Nothing at all.'

'All right, sir, you can carry on.'

My car began to move forward as on its own initiative toward the exit of the cavern, toward freedom and success. Its lights shone on a gingerhaired man: the Automobile Association. He waved; I stopped. They were a little slow clearing the papers – the usual man was away – would I mind waiting where I was for a few minutes? By this time H.M. Customs had strolled up, benevolently, a man with time on this hands. I wanted to say that I would like to wait anywhere except where I was, but I had some difficulty in finding suitable words for this thought. I said I would wait. H.M. Customs decided to keep me company. He was a fisherman, and it was his opinion that the best fishing in the world was to be found in Connemara. Or perhaps Donegal. Though Lough Derg, in Limerick, at dapping time was hard to beat.

Bored, Carey Bloom stretched himself under his rug. At least I hoped it was under his rug. I had a hideous feeling that the rug by now had slipped off. But it was impossible to look around. All I could do was to trust to the dim light and try to make intelligent answers about dry-fly fishing in the west of Ireland.

A figure appeared, moving briskly from the direction of the exit. The Automobile Association! The figure came closer. It was not the Automobile Association. It was more of H.M. Customs. More, and older, and nastier.

'Have you cleared this car?' he asked my fisherman friend.

There was a slight Scots edge on his voice, and a singularly unpleasant inflection to it. The remark had an unfortunate effect on Fisherman. He dropped the subject of the May fly on Lough Derg and took a quick look inside the car.

Then his manner changed. 'I'm afraid, sir,' he said quietly, 'I'll have to ask you one further question.'

Something told me what that question was going to be.

'Are you carrying any animals in this car, sir?'

'No,' I replied firmly.

'Since you declare you are carrying no animals, sir, perhaps you would tell me what that is?'

I looked around, for the first time. Carey Bloom's muzzle and two front paws were resting on the front seat. His shoulders were covered with a tartan rug. He was asleep.

'That,' I said, 'is my dog.'

'Since you admit that it is your dog, sir,' said the Scot, 'how do you explain your previous declaration that you were carrying no animals?'

Clearly he felt that this was a telling piece of cross-examination. Privately I agreed with him, but I decided to go down fighting.

'This dog is being conveyed to Ireland,' I said. 'In Ireland he will be put in quarantine immediately. I am taking him direct to Holyhead. He will not be let out of the car in England at all. All your previous questions were about what I had in the car for the United Kingdom. I took it that this question was the same. As I had no animals intended for the United Kingdom I thought it was right to answer the question in the negative.'

Fisherman's mouth hung open, like that of a Lough Derg trout in dapping time. He was obviously dazzled by this unexpected piece of dialectic. There was a silence.

I was weak enough to break the silence by a conciliatory remark. I should have known better than to make a conciliatory remark to a Scot, but my nerves had been under a strain for some time. 'I should prefer to take him to Ireland for quarantine,' I said, 'but of course, if that would be contrary to your regulations I'm perfectly prepared to put him into quarantine here.'

I thought this a fair offer, but it brought out the worst in the Scot.

'You don't seem to r-realize your position,' he said grindingly. 'It's not a question of what you are *prepared* or not prepared to do. The animal of course, will be impounded, and *may* be committed to quarantine if the authorities are satisfied as to your willingness and ability to pay for his upkeep. Otherwise he will be dest-r-royed. The fact is that you yourself have already committed two very serious offences: first by importing a dog without a license and second by falsely declaring that you were not carrying animals. On either count you are liable on summary conviction both to a heavy fine and to a p-r-rison sentence of not more than Six Months. I shall now have to report the matter both to the police and to my own superiors. You, sir, will please remain where you are and ensure that the animal does not leave the car until he is officially impounded.'

The program for the evening was faithfully observed. The police arrived and took a statement. And later came an overalled contingent with a handcart on which stood a large crate. They looked like something out of Defoe's *Journal of the Plague Year*. To them, not without a twinge, I handed over Carey Bloom. He licked my hand in farewell, but otherwise made no sign. As they wheeled him away, toward imprisonment or death, I saw on the back of his crate a huge sign in yellow characters:

DANGER!

RABIES!

I thought bitterly of President Fallières. I became aware at the same time that a new character, and one having authority, had come on the scene. This was an elderly man, not in uniform but in sports coat and flannels. The old gentleman's general appearance was kindly and paternal, but I could see from his expression that he had Very Little Sympathy for Certain Classes of Offender and that I belonged to one such class.

'I'm afraid,' he said, 'that in view of what's happened we'll have to put some further questions to you formally. After that we'll have to search your car thoroughly. You see you've already made one false declaration, so you can't expect to receive normal tourist treatment.'

He left a moment for this insult to sink in. Then: 'Are you carrying any Narcotic Drugs?'

'No.'

'Any Plants or Parrots?'

'No.'

'Any Arms or Ammunition?'

'No.'

'Any *more* animals?'

This was too much.

'Look,' I said, 'I'm not a professional dog smuggler, or any other kind of smuggler. That dog belongs to my daughters, who are very fond of it. If it had to go into quarantine I wanted to bring it to Ireland. If it were quarantined there they could visit it every day. As it is they won't be able to visit it at all. I'm sorry if I infringed your regulations, and you can go ahead and search my car. You won't find anything.'

For the first time since coming to Newhaven I had managed to strike the right note. The old gentleman's manner perceptibly softened. He made no reply, however, until the car had been searched and been found, as I had said, to be free from Narcotic Drugs, Arms, Ammunition, Plants, Parrots, and Other Animals. He addressed me now as a fellow human being, rather than as an individual engaged in a Vile Traffic.

'I can understand your feeling for your Pet,' he said. 'I have three dogs of my own. But, believe me, it's in the interests of Our Pets themselves to see that these regulations are observed.'

He lit a cigarette, for effect. Then quietly: 'Have you ever seen a case of rabies?'

'No, I said. 'I'm afraid I haven't. You see the last case of rabies in France was in 1910. The year of the coronation of King George V. That was before I was born.'

Balked of his dramatic effect, the old gentleman looked at me thoughtfully. 'We don't want to be unnecessarily severe about this,' he said. 'We should prefer not to have to prosecute, if we can avoid it. I'm quite prepared to accept your story, send the dog to an approved place of quarantine in England, and let you go on your way, without further formality. So if you'll just show me the license from the Eire Department of Agriculture to import the dog into Ireland, we can regard the matter as closed.'

The Scot, who had looked depressed during the earlier part of this speech, cheered up at the end perceptibly and unpleasantly. He could obviously see, merely by looking at me, that I possessed no licenses of any kind. He was quite right.

'I didn't have time to get a license,' I said. 'I was ordered by my employers to come home at very short notice indeed. My first idea was to leave the dog with some French people, who would give it a home for a time, while I made the necessary arrangements in Dublin for its importation. Then at the very last moment, the night before I left, I found that the home was quite unsuitable. I couldn't just abandon the dog, so I decided to take him to Ireland and hand him over for quarantine there. I don't think the Irish authorities, in the circumstances, would have made too many difficulties about there being no license.'

The Scot smiled. What *he* thought of my story was quite clear. But his superior, the owner of three dogs, looked puzzled. He could, at least, not condemn me out of hand.

'You say you found this home was unsuitable,' he said. 'Now just what do you mean by that?'

'Well,' I replied, feeling better, 'you see, the man who offered to take care of the dog was a Frenchman, a café proprietor. My dog is a Kerry blue – you know the breed, I expect – and this man said he owned a Kerry blue, too. That made me think he would know how to look after my dog, so I agreed to leave it with him. Then, to be on the safe side, I decided to go and have a look at this dog. This is what I found.'

I handed over the photograph of the dog of Place Notre-Dame-des-Victoires.

The three customs men studied it. The two Englishmen were visibly affected. They seemed like men peering into an abyss. It was the old gentleman who spoke.

'Do you mean that they give this unfortunate dog ... drink?'

'Pernod,' said I quietly. 'Then they make him do tricks for the customers.'

'Do you know,' said the old gentleman, 'I wouldn't have believed it, even of the French.'

One felt that moral condemnation had reached its ultimate. He examined the picture again for some time, then handed it back.

'I can't condone breaking regulations,' he said, 'but I must say that if I had to choose between breaking a regulation and leaving my dog with a man like that – well, I might do what you did. I'll recommend no further action. I wish you good luck and you can be sure your dog will be well looked after.'

It was the Scot who showed me past the police, to the Automobile Association and freedom. The Automobile Association, in an undertone, wanted to know what had happened. The Scot told him:

'The gentleman made a false declaration to the customs and was caught in possession of contraband,' he said. 'He gets off under English law because he once knew a poodle that took to the drink. Good night.'

Conor Cruise O'Brien

KING HEROD EXPLAINS *(extract)*

You can see now what I am trying to say?
Why I have had to talk to you in this manner
At such inordinate length and so deviously?
I am asking you in the name of the little Herods shut up
    in your own bosoms
Only awaiting a suitable opportunity of self-expression;
I am asking you in the name of the permanent need
    which you have as political animals
For some kind of Herod –
A master politician – a man who gets things done;
Things, and people;
I am asking you in the name of a terrible thing –
Our common humanity –
I am asking you because in all of you there is something
    which would like to do what I have done, and be what
    I have been.

[*He falls on his knees*]

I am asking you to give me that which I contemptuously
    withheld from Cassius
In his boring agony before Philippi
I am asking your forgiveness,
Forgiveness for Herod the Great,
The King of the Jews.

CURTAIN

# Kate Cruise O'Brien

## A SUNDAY WALK

It was a sunny French Sunday. Elizabeth felt that life was as near perfect as it had been for a long time. At least it seemed normal. The doors of the house were open and sunlight gleamed on the black and white tiles in the hall. There were no oily barges on the river across the road, for it was Sunday. The river looked clear and calm and a seagull wheeled above the weeping willows which dropped at the edge of the water. She could smell a roast cooking in the kitchen. Her father was reading a newspaper in the sitting room. She looked through the door. His foot was twisting round and round in its plaid carpet slipper but she felt that carpet slippers were suitable on Sundays and surely other people's fathers twisted their feet.

Elizabeth felt it was just possible that the winter weeks of sickness and baked eggs, closed doors and tired voices had passed. She hadn't minded them really. At least while her mother lay in bed, indifferent and ill, she had found it easy to avoid school. She had said firmly that she was too ill and she had taken to her bed with an earache, a cold, a pain in her tummy. She had actually slipped on a banana skin on one of the rare occasions that she *had* gone to school. Everyone had made a great fuss because she refused to move her legs afterwards. Her mother had come, shaken and anxious, and bent over the stretcher lovingly. Like a mother in a book. However, the doctor had discovered that she could move her toes and everyone became less anxious. Still, it had been worth three weeks in bed with sympathetic adult voices reading to her in English about delightful normal children who seemed to live in a perpetual holiday world. When she'd recovered enough to go back to school she pitched herself, somewhat ineffectively, down the stairs. She hadn't hurt her back though.

She was afraid of the school. The children there wore little aprons and spoke very fast. She didn't understand French anyway and she was always afraid that they were laughing at her. Even coming home from school was difficult. There was a long narrow tunnel leading towards their house and sometimes there was a man there in a large grey overcoat. He often pulled back the overcoat and then Elizabeth could see that he wasn't properly dressed. He'd giggle then and try to pat her head and she never knew whether she should run away fast or just smile and walk on. It seemed rude to run away. It might make the man embarrassed about not being properly dressed. She never talked to him though, because she knew she shouldn't talk to strange men. On the other hand, she never told anyone about him either because it would be difficult to talk about him not being properly dressed.

When she got home and was sitting in the warm kitchen eating greasy Irish chips cooked by the fat Wexford maid, she sometimes felt like crying because everything was so different and difficult. The cold school playground with its chilly row of latrines lining one side. The tunnel with its embarrassments. The big chilly house with its hard tiles and the warm kitchen with its steamy windows. Upstairs her mother's room smelt softly powdery, the room off it where her father sometimes slept was rather dark and didn't really smell of anything. Perhaps it smelt as if no one really lived there. Her mother's room had a balcony off it. It was a bright room when the curtains were drawn back but often during the winter her mother had lain in bed in the dark. The balcony had vines growing around the little pillars at the edge. Last September before the winter came, Elizabeth had found bunches of grapes. When she picked a little bunch she found that the grapes were hard and dry and bitter as if they'd died before they were ripe. She'd often thought about the fuschia at home. It was purple and red and if you broke off the rounded bit near the stem, sweet sticky stuff oozed out and you could lick that.

Still, perhaps the grapes would ripen this year, and in the meantime it was sunny and Sunday and there was a big sandpit in the garden where she could play all morning. It had been too cold all winter to play there. She walked out through the front door into the sun and walked towards the sandpit. As she passed the sitting room window her father called her.

'Elizabeth, would you like to go for a walk?'

'Yes. Well, where to?'

'To the piscine. You could have an orange there or an ice cream.'

Last summer they'd gone to the piscine. Elizabeth had tried to swim there but the only way she could swim at all was partly submerged, which alarmed people. She looked as if she was drowning. It was nice there though, and there were tables with big umbrellas which had fringed tasselly ends. All the same, she felt like crying because her father wanted to take her there. She felt it was so kind of him but somehow rare and strange.

Her mother had departed a few days ago in a flurry of tissue paper. She'd looked well and pretty and her hair had shone with a reddish shine as if it was well again too. Elizabeth had been sorry that her mother was going away when she was well and pretty but she'd felt that if her mother had stayed, she just might have gone back to bed and felt ill again. Elizabeth admired, with a sort of breathless admiration, the kind of comforting sensible things that adults said to each other, so, when her mother told her that she'd miss her, Elizabeth said, 'It will do you good to get out and have a change of air.' She didn't know why air should change in different places but maybe it had something to do with different places smelling differently.

Home smelt of sea and in the summer of the coconut smell of gorse in the sun. And here smelt of oil from the barges and sometimes of very fresh bread and garlic. Her mother had laughed when Elizabeth had mentioned the change of air and hugged her, but her face had looked stretched and glassy and her eyes shone as if she might cry.

And now her father wanted to go for a walk and it seemed strange to go for a walk just with her father though her father had taken her for walks during the winter when her mother was ill. She supposed it seemed strange now because her mother was away and not at home in bed.

Elizabeth felt nervous as she and her father walked along the quiet road by the river. The road was dusty and rutted and it reminded her of the lane at home which was rutted too, but muddy and lined with prickly gorse. She noticed that the spindly green bushes at the edge of this road were covered now with hanging flowers in white and purple and mauve.

'What's that flower?' she asked her father. It was an offering, for she could tell lilac when she saw it, but her father liked telling her the names of plants and trees.

'It's lilac of course,' he said. 'Did you never see lilac at home?'

'No, I didn't. I don't think we have it at home,' she said, getting her own back for that 'of course'.

'Well, we do,' he passed his hand over his eyes in a gesture that Elizabeth envied. It was so adult. Weary annoyance, she called it.

'I'm sorry,' she said. She wished she'd stayed in the sandpit safe and warm with something to feel and touch and pour through her fingers.

'No, I'm sorry,' said her father. 'I'm just tired. Would you like to take my stick?'

The stick was beautiful. It was blackthorn, strong and knobbly with a surprising smooth warm handle. Her father used to use it walking home. He used to swing it over the ruts in the lane and thrash it through the ferns on the headland. He always walked with a straight back, his chin high in the air, and Elizabeth liked the way the stick swung out from his tall straight body.

'I'd love to take the stick, thank you.'

He smiled at her as he gave her the stick and she felt like crying again. When she smiled he looked as if he'd been thinking of something else and had just remembered her, was surprised to find her there. She wished she could give him something to comfort him and as soon as she wished that, she knew that he needed comfort and she knew that she'd known this for a long time.

She'd known it on the nights that he hadn't come home before her bedtime. On those nights she'd leave an orange beside his bed in his strangely smelless room. It was something to do with her mother being away but she knew it wasn't just that. It had something to do with the fact that she'd known since her mother went away that she mustn't mention her mother to her father. Not even ask normal questions about her coming back. She'd never thought about this before. She'd never just asked about her mother and now that she had thought about it she wished her mother was here holding her, soft and safe, and she felt guilty that she wanted her mother when her father was here and sad.

# Gearóid Ó Clérigh

## Barra Trá *(sliocht)*

Gluaiseacht an ghrá chúirtéise, leath sí ar fud na hEorpa sa Luath-Mheánaois. [...]

Arae bhí an saghas sin seanbhunaithe i litríocht na nArabach, riamh sin sarar thánagadar chun na Spáinne, agus sa leithinis féin bhí an cleachtadh ann le fada. Tá cur síos ar mhalartú véarsaí idir file éigin anaithnid agus Al-Ballūti, a rugadh i gCórdoba sa bhliain 886, is é sin, Mundir Ibn Sa'id ibn 'Abdillah ibn 'Abd ar-Rachmán, Abú 'I-Hakam. Dúirt an file leis:

> Seo ceist le réiteach duitse,
> a fhir léinn is feasaí fáth,
> a mbíonn tóir ar do thuigse
> 's do chomhairle eagnaí ag cách:
> cén fáth go scéitheann deirge
> an rún seirce in éadan mná
> fhaid fheicfear gur glas leimhe
> 's dath d'fhireann i bpéin ón ghrá?

D'fhreagair Al-Ballūti é:

> Ní deacair: 'n aighthe bruinneall
> is claíomh gach súil mhalldubh
> a tharraingíos fuil i sruithibh
> ón chroí dar tadhall banrosc,
> ach dath deireadh lae 's glaise
> ar dhul don ghréin as amharc
> in aghaidh fireann searclag.

Seo mar atá ag Yehudà ha-Levi:

> *Gazelle*
> A eitilt an ghrásta ar mo bhréagadh ag d'áille
> chas do chruálacht im dhaor me;
> an scaradh ba dhán dár mbeirt-ne táite
> is ní fhaca conách do scéimhe.
> Suífead faoi scáth na hubhaille ar scáil í
> ar d'óige a hanáil, ós craorac

a torthaí fásta mar do ghrua in airde
's iad i gcrut do dhá chíc caomha.

Eimar O'Duffy

KING GOSHAWK AND THE BIRDS *(extracts)*

*Cuanduine Reads a Newspaper*

The Philosopher's attic had not changed much in the years that had passed, save that it was grown older and the rent higher. The old man had a new suit of clothes waiting for Cuanduine, of a nice pattern of tweed, and fashionably cut, with snow white shirt and tie of poplin. When he was dressed in these the Philosopher served them a breakfast of milk and bread and cheese, as he had done before when Cuchulain came to Earth; after which he offered the young man a newspaper, and himself opened another.

'What is this?' asked Cuanduine.

'That,' said the Philosopher, 'is one of the marvels of human civilisation.'

Cuanduine turned the newspaper over in his hands; looked at it right way up, wrong way up, and sideways; opened it and counted pages; and finally looked at the Philosopher with an expression of bewilderment on his godlike countenance.

'It is called a newspaper,' the Philosopher explained. 'In it is written down the news of all things that happened yesterday in the world; and tomorrow I shall get another which will relate all that happened today.'

'But how,' asked Cuanduine, 'can the truth be ascertained in so short a time?'

'I did not say that it told the truth,' replied the Philosopher. 'I only said it told the news.'

Then Cuanduine began to read aloud from the newspaper: '"Social and Personal. King Goshawk gave a garden party at Tuscaloosa yesterday …. The Duke of Dudborough is fifty-one today." Who is the Duke of Dudborough?'

'I don't know,' said the Philosopher.

Cuanduine held his peace after that. These are some of the things he read:

## A STRAIGHT ISSUE

Once again it becomes our duty to tell the Government in plain and unmistakable language what the best elements in the country – and we speak in no undemocratic sense – think of the way it is handling the present situation. This is a time for plain speaking; a time to search men's souls; and to apply to every word and action the acid test of Truth and Justice. We do not count ourselves among those – if there are any such – who would deny that there is never an occasion when the cause of true Justice might not be less disadvantageously served by a not overinflexible adhesion to the strict *litera verecundiae* than by a too inopportune application of those solemn precepts which are the concrete foundation on which morality and true civilisation subsist. But nevertheless there are occasions such as the present, when the whole fabric of Society... [...]

## A GREAT SPORTSMAN

Lord Puddlehead, who died last Monday, was almost as distinguished in the field of sport as in that of politics. His greatest kill was on his own estate at Puddlington about five years ago, when he shot 850 brace of pheasants in a day. But his performance in Scotland last year runs it close. On that occasion he shot 3600 head of grouse in five days, an average of 690 per day. Altogether over one million birds and beasts have fallen to his gun during his amazingly active life. [...]

## CENSORS' GOOD WORK
## IMMODEST WOMEN PENALISED

In Wolfe Tone Street yesterday two young women wearing immodest dresses, which revealed their throats and ankles, were arrested by the Censors, stripped, and taken before the District Court. They were sentenced to a year's hard labour. We hope this will be a lesson to those young persons that the world-wide reputation of Irish womanhood for modesty and chastity is not a thing to be lightly imperilled. [...]

## PROVINCIAL NEWS

The Ballycatandog Urban District Council met yesterday to discuss the resolution forwarded by the Ballymess Council, condemning the proposal of the Government to establish the metric system in Ireland.

Mr Brady, proposing the motion, said that it was the duty of every Irishman worthy of the name to denounce the most tyrannous piece of legislation ever introduced into a democratic country. The action of the Government made the deeds of Nero, Queen Elizabeth, and Oliver Cromwell look mild and benignant in comparison.

Mr Grady: Where was your grandfather in 1916?

Mr Thady: Under the bed.

Mr Brady: I defy any man here to say my grandfather was a funk.

Mr Grady: The Bradys were always great heroes.

Mr Brady: They're every bit as good as the Gradys anyhow.

Mr Grady: You old fool.

The Chairman: Order! Order!

Mr Grady: Don't start putting in your oar.

The Chairman: I will if I like. And who has a better right? My grandfather was out in 1916.

Mr Grady: Yes. Right out of it.

The Chairman: No. That's where yours was.

Mr Grady: Do you call my grandfather a funk?

The meeting broke up in disorder.


## HOUSES TO LET

A five-roomed house to let. South suburbs. Moderate rent. No children.

Cosy house. Two bedrooms, sitting-room, kitchen, bath. £150 and taxes. No dogs. No children.

Delightful house. Five miles from city. Six bed, four reception rooms. Billiard room, conservatory, stables, garage, kennels, garden and kitchen garden. No children.

Fine house, beautifully situated in own ground ten miles from city. Children objected.

Gate lodge to let. Five rooms. No dogs, no poultry, no children. Suit married couple.

Perfect house. Situated in own grounds. Beautiful scenery. Healthy climate. Five bedrooms, four reception. Day and night nursery. School-room. Large flower garden. Playing field, with goal-posts, etc. Tennis-court. Suit married couple. No children.

Pigstye to let. 10s. weekly. Suit large family.

Victorian mansion. Beyond repair. Situated in formerly fashionable quarter in heart of city. Reasonable rent. No objection to dogs, cats, poultry, canaries, tortoises, goldfish, axolotls, or even children. [...]


### Cuanduine Meets Divers Strange Persons

Having shaken off his guide, Cuanduine passed out of the city and came presently to a grove not far off, wherein an army of workmen had just finished erecting a huge pyre of logs over tar-barrels. A hundred and fifty feet square it was at the base, and forty feet high, and it was overtopped by an earthern ramp over a mile in length. Just as Cuanduine arrived torches were put to the tar, and flames two hundred feet high shot up into the sky. Then up the ramp came a motor lorry heavily laden, which, when it reached the summit, was tilted back until there tumbled upon the flaming pyre an avalanche of hams and gammons of bacon, to the amount of nearly three and a half tones. What a sizzling there was as the flames fastened on this succulent feast, and what a divine odour. It was as if a fifteen-acre rasher were being fried for the breakfast of Zeus Olympicus, which, had he smelt it, would have provoked his mouth to watering the world with a second deluge. Then came a second lorry and emptied into the fire ten thousand or so long hundreds of eggs. But that sent forth a different savour, not quite so appetising: indeed, you would have thought the Plutonian cook was brewing a hell-broth of asafoetida for the supper of the legions of the damned. This was followed straight by other lorries, more than I can count, which shovelled on to the leaping flames a goodly holocaust of meat, butter, vegetables, groceries, wheats, oats, barley, flour, fruit (both fresh and preserved), fish, poultry, game, sweetmeats, biscuits, cheeses, and a thousand other sorts of provender, some packed in bales and boxes, but much of it loose and au naturel, until the mixture of smells was so foul that the stomach of Cuanduine could stand no more of it, and he was about to withdraw in search of a more salubrious climate, when he noticed a workman standing near, whom he approached and asked the meaning of this incineration.

'This is the Regional Destructor, sir,' said the workman, 'where we destroy the surplus food, sir, to keep the prices up.'

'Why do you keep the prices up?' asked Cuanduine.

The workman took a handbook from his pocket and read: '"Low prices depend on mass production. Mass production depends on unlimited capital. Capital requires a reasonable rate of return for its outlay. Therefore the prices must be kept up. Q.E.D. Socialism is an economic fallacy."'

'This,' said Cuanduine, 'seems to me the very sublimate of criminal folly.'

The workman gave him a look of incredulity not unmingled with horror. 'What, sir?' said the honest fellow. 'Do you speak like that of the inevitable laws of political economy? – you who are so well fed. Look at me. My children are all crippled with rickets because I cannot afford to give them butter, yet I see all this butter burned without complaint. Why? Because I know that if it wasn't for the good Capitalists there'd be no food, nor money, nor nothing. Besides, this destructor gives employment to hundreds of men who would otherwise have none.' So saying the honest fellow picked up a firkin of butter that happened to have fallen from one of the lorries, and hove it into the fire. Then, 'Thank God,' said he, 'I have done my duty,' and walked away, whistling very resolutely the tune of 'Blue Bananas.' Soon afterwards men came with eighty big hosepipes and quenched the embers of the fire with a deluge of milk.

# Eimar O'Duffy

## ASSES IN CLOVER (extract)

*Why Economists Are So Impressive; and Why Some Have Longer Necks than Others*

'That speech will go down,' said Mr Robinson to Cuanduine. 'I know the public. That sort of stuff impresses them no end.'

'I do not know the public' said Cuanduine, 'but I fear you are right, though why I cannot tell. An economist is not interesting, like a scientist, nor elevating, like an artist, nor stimulating, like an original thinker, nor informing, like a traveller, nor suggestive to those who read between the lines, like a politician, nor authoritative, like a priest; yet he impresses more than any of them. No matter what dull nonsense he talks, it is swallowed without straining. No matter how many of his prophecies have proved false, they are not remembered against him. 'Sdeath, but when I see one of these shallow pompous asses mouthing it on a platform, and mark his dreary ditherings of a sham science whose premises anyone in whom common sense has not been destroyed by text-books and newspapers can see to be false, whose logic any first year student could pick to pieces, and whose conclusions are not only what you might expect from such antecedents, but can be clearly seen to have landed the world in the filthy mess from which they have the impudence to pretend to be saving it, I marvel that such blitherers and such blitherings can be listened to without shrieks of derision.'

'Steady on, old chap,' replied Mr Robinson. 'Aren't you drawing it a bit strong? I don't know what premises are, I never learned any logic, and, as for conclusions, I've got to draw the sort that Lord Cumbersome pays me to draw. So you see, I'm not in a position to say whether these fellows are right or wrong; but if they're such fools as you say they are, how the deuce do they get away with it?'

'It can only be by this magic power of impressiveness that the Devil seems to have dowered them with,' said Cuanduine. 'Tell me this my friend, suppose I were to give a lecture on the art of growing cabbages, and to deliver myself in this fashion: "Gentlemen, the purpose of growing cabbages is to wear away the edge of spades. To begin with, therefore, you choose the hardest and stoniest ground you can find, and on the coldest day in midwinter, you begin to dig. When the ground is fully prepared, you sow it, but not with cabbage seed, for this is an extremely scarce commodity, and, if placed in the ground, might rot, so that there would be danger of a future scarcity of cabbage seed, with a consequent danger of a loss of opportunity to wear down spades. Instead, you sow dandelions, and while living on this plain but wholesome fare, you proceed to wear away some more of your spade by preparing another bed for next year's crop." Who, if I were to speak thus, would be impressed?'

'None but a congenital idiot,' said Mr Robinson.

'Therein lies the solution of the mystery' said Cuanduine. 'For the economists' stuff impresses idiots that are not congenital, but made so by education. This puts me in mind of a dinner to which I was invited when I was a lion in London; whereat an economist held forth after his usual fashion. Well, I thought to myself when he was finished, and the whole company sat agape at his learning, this fellow has neck enough for anything; which put it into my head to ask out loud: "Why have some people longer necks than others?"'

'I suppose' said a priest who was present, seeking to improve the occasion, 'because God made us in what shape conforms in each case to his divine will.'

A scientist sitting opposite took him up, saying: 'Does it not rather show that God – or the Life Force – like every other artificer, proceeds by the method of trial and error?'

'Doesn't it mean' said another guest 'that Nature, like a true artist, aims at variety?'

'You are all wrong' declared the Economist. 'The variations in the length of the neck are Nature's method for increasing employment. The purpose of the neck is evidently to give employment to collar-makers, and the more it varies in size, the greater the employment they get.'

J.L. de Belder; translated from the Flemish 'DE SCARABEE' by Una O'Dwyer

## THE SCARAB

It has fallen
The small scarab beetle
That you gave me,
Fallen into the sands
Of the immense desert
And escaped.

This small scarab
Was our love
Given to us
To last forever
And it too has gone.

But come what may
Do not forget
That a scarab does not die
But is forever reborn.

J.L. de Belder; translated from the Flemish
'GARDEROBE' by Una O'Dwyer

WARDROBE

So snug and warm in nappies
And a baby's pinafore
And then a pretty little frock,
The first you wore;
Next skirts in rainbow colours
And blouses gay in style
(as hand in hand with friends you went
to school, dancing all the while);
Then later, fashionable with hat
And bodice of red sateen
When going out with your young man
Dressed up to be seen.
And then a long white bridal gown
No clothes but hair your only cape
Or the silken dress of his kisses
Around you like a drape.
And then a wide concealing smock
(around your sweetest loads)
And many other different clothes,
A dress with stripes, a collar edged with lace,
A scarf, some buttons made of brass,
And then a long white burial gown.

And then your shroud of grass.

J.L. de Belder; translated from the Flemish
'WINTERNACHT' by Una O'Dwyer

WINTER'S NIGHT

From the creaking
Of the bamboos
All at once I know
That outdoors
It snows.

# Jacqueline O'Halloran Bernstein

## ELIZA LYNCH IN CONTEXT

The story of Eliza Lynch, uncrowned Queen of Paraguay in the mid-nineteenth century has become better known in Ireland in recent times. This is partly thanks to the work of Michael Lillis and Ronan Fanning with their interesting and readable book, *Eliza Lynch: Queen of Paraguay* as well as the documentary film by Alan Gilsenan based on their work. Her story as the partner of Paraguay's ruler Francisco Solano Lopez, and de facto 'First Lady' of Paraguay, from 1862 to 1870 was of course always well known in Paraguay and to Paraguayan people and historians.

In my own case I first came upon the story of Eliza when, on my first posting in Buenos Aires in the early 1990s, I met a young female Paraguayan diplomat who told me that in her country Ireland was well known, both for our national symbol, the harp, which we share with Paraguay, and also because of Eliza Lynch whose story she told me. While fascinated by this unexpected Irish link with a country with which we did not at that time even have diplomatic relations, it was many years later, as Deputy Director for the Department's Latin America and Caribbean Unit in 2014 that she crossed my path again, this time in the form of a request for background material for President Higgins as he was going to attend and launch the Irish premiere of the film about her life as part of the Dublin International Film Festival of that year.

Many will be familiar with the outlines of Eliza Lynch's life to the extent that it has been possible to trace it, as well as with the more lurid stories and scandals which were attributed to her and her contested personal history. This was particularly the case in Paraguay but also in the countries that formed the Triple Alliance with which

Paraguay fatefully went to war in 1864, Argentina, Brazil and Uruguay. We know this from Eliza's attempts to respond to and refute the many calumnies which were spread about her, both in the years before the war as Solano Lopez's partner and also after his death. As well described in Michael Lillis and Ronan Fanning's book, Eliza could well be described as one of the first victims of what today we would, undoubtedly, call 'fake news'.

So what do we actually know?

She was born in Charleville, Co. Cork in 1833, though only ever admitted, in time honoured fashion for an Irishwoman, to having been born in 1835. She married at 16 a French chemist and officer in the French Army in a marriage which, while legal in England where it was performed, would not have been recognized in France. That marriage, for reasons we do not know, failed within a few years, leaving a now 19-year-old Eliza free to become the lover of the then 26-year-old Solano Lopez.

For his part Solano Lopez had been sent to Europe in June 1853 by his father, President Carlos Antonio, Dictator of Paraguay, to establish and develop relations with the French, Spanish and the Italian States, including the Vatican. Another major objective was to purchase weapons, rolling stock and rails as well as to hire professionals in engineering and medicine. In England, Lopez commissioned the gunship Tacuari from the shipbuilder Blythe and by late December had moved to Paris. In England he had been received by Queen Victoria and now in France by Louis Napoleon. It was at this time that he met Eliza, who seems to have been living in Paris with her mother, following the breakup of her brief marriage.

Subsequent stories that Eliza was living as a courtesan or even a prostitute and tales of Russian noblemen and other lovers have never been substantiated. As Eliza herself says in her *Declaration and Protest* many years after these events, there would not in fact have been time following the failure of her marriage, for her to have established herself in the Parisian demi-monde of the time or to have had the numerous sexual relationships attributed to her by her enemies. What seems far more likely is that, at 19, and with a failed marriage which was in any case of dubious legality behind her, this beautiful, educated and attractive young woman sought and found the next best means to financial security for herself, the protection of a wealthy and well-connected man.

In the context of the times, which is what I want to reflect on, this choice was a rational one. More than that, it was one of the few remaining to a woman of her background and education following the failure of her marriage.

Eliza Lynch came from a respectable professional background, from a class whose young women were brought up to marry young men of similar background and standing. Her father was a doctor and came from an old professional clerical family. It seems likely that he died during or just after the Irish famine, possibly from one of the epidemic diseases which were rife at that time. Her mother came from a family of naval officers and, after her father's death, the young Eliza and her mother went to live with her uncle, a retired naval officer living in Boulogne sur Mer in France.

As we know from the literature of the period, and increasingly from historical and social studies, there were very few opportunities open to women in these classes if they did not marry. The family described in the pages of Michael Lillis and Ronan Fanning's book, though a generation later, is very similar to that of Fanny Price, the poor relation and heroine of Jane Austen's *Mansfield Park*. Fanny, destined to be an unpaid upper servant and companion to her richer relations, was also the daughter and sister of junior naval officers. She was saved from her fate by the love of the youngest son of the wealthy family, Edmund. By contrast the favourite daughter of the family, following a loveless marriage with a wealthy neighbour, throws it all away to elope with a lover who then in turn deserts her. With her respectability gone, this character is doomed to live out her days on her father's charity, seeing no-one and sharing a cottage with a maiden aunt.

More contemporaneously, if we look at the lives of Anthony Trollope's female characters from this minor gentry, educated but poor professional class, we see how limited the possibilities were for young educated females with no money of their own. Looks and respectability were the passport to security in this world. Otherwise the options were few, poorly paid teaching or companionship posts, or living on sufferance as a poor relation with better off relatives.

Once the respectability was gone, in Eliza's case represented by her possibly illegal and in any event failed first marriage, with only her youth, charm and beauty to offer, the liaison with Lopez, for whom she appears to have felt a genuine attraction, must have looked very attractive indeed.

In this she was part of a strong tradition of nineteenth-century Irishwomen who, refusing to accept lives of unparalleled narrowness, dullness and poverty, instead chose to live differently for which they were both condemned and envied by their peers. Women like 'Lola Montez', another Eliza, born in Sligo as Eliza Gilbert in 1821. When her marriage also failed at a young age, Eliza took to the stage and, in the persona of Spanish dancer Lola Montez, captured the heart of the Duke Ludwig of Bavaria, became a Countess and eventually, following the 1848 revolution for which she was partly responsible, was forced to emigrate to the US where, following various adventures, she became a worker and lecturer with an organization which rescued 'fallen women'.

Dorothy Jordan was yet another Irishwoman who was able to use her unique talents to carve out a singular destiny. A truly talented actress, Jordan, whose family had originally been from a similar class to Eliza, but had sunk well beneath this by the time of her birth, went on the stage early, and following a series of love affairs and great professional success on the London stage, eventually became the lover of the Duke of Clarence, later King William IV of England. She had ten children with the Duke and, though she died in poverty as was sadly the eventual fate of many of these startlingly able women, many noble houses today count her among their ancestors.

Returning to Eliza Lynch, having secured a release from any claims on any future property she might acquire from her ex-husband, Eliza sailed for Paraguay and for 10 years lived the life of the favourite mistress and de facto 'First Lady' of Paraguay. Though not accepted by the ruling elite of Paraguay which was attempting to impose a 'moral' order on Paraguay's notoriously relaxed social codes, she nevertheless acquired great wealth and social standing among visitors to the city and, from contemporary accounts, appears to have been popular with ordinary people.

She remained with Solano Lopez, throughout the terrible war of the Triple Alliance, until the bitter end when he, and her eldest son, the 15-year-old Pancho, were finally run to ground and killed by Brazilian forces. The story of her insistence on a proper burial and her assisting with her bare hands in the digging of the grave, remains emblematic of the story of this most terrible of Latin American wars.

More serious to a modern sensibility than the allegations of sexual misconduct and of living with Lopez outside of marriage, are the accusations that she was also implicated in, and responsible for, not just the war itself, by encouraging Lopez to it, but also for the terrible atrocities, including the cruel tortures and executions, carried out by Lopez in his final years as conspiracies and military defeat closed in around him. Again there is no evidence for her encouraging Lopez in his fateful decision to go to war, or that anyone other than himself and his small coterie of singularly poor advisors took that decision. Neither is there evidence of her complicity in the other horrors, other than in her choice to remain with him, if at that stage, there was any choice. In later years her daughter in law recalls her as:

> A warm hearted, sentimental, early Victorian Irishwoman with a ready sympathy for anyone in trouble. In later times of stress the families of political prisoners would beg her to use her influence in favour of their people and on more than one occasion she did so at the risk of her own life – for her influence with Lopez was very limited.

Given the evidence of her later life, much of which was spent in futile attempts to retrieve what was left of her fortune from the victors in the war, it would seem that, like many women and probably all mothers, her actions were driven by concern for her own and her children's lives, and their future security and prosperity.

Eliza died in Paris in poverty in 1886. Her remains were subsequently repatriated to Paraguay and she was declared a national heroine of Paraguay in 1961. Her tomb is in the Recoleta cemetery in Asuncion.

Seán Ó Riain a d'aistrigh ó bhundán Esperanto Leen Deij

## DON GHIÚDACH A D'IMIGH

Dhún sé a mhála, chroith lámh liom, d'fhág slán!
Gan aon agóid a d'imigh sé … Inniu
A thuigim san; caithfidh gurbh ionadh leis
Gur mise, an Críostaí, a lig dó imeacht.

A cheann cromtha, an mála aige á iompar,
Chuaigh sé an bealach go hAuschwitz, don bhás,
Gan aon agóid … caithfidh gurbh ionadh leis
Gur mise, an Críostaí, a lig dó imeacht.

Is lá éigin labharfaidh a mhac lem mhacsa,
Cuirfidh sé ceisteanna, an fhírinne lorgóidh.
Tostfaidh mo mhacsa … is ní bheidh air ach ionadh
Gur mise, an Críostaí, a lig dó imeacht.

Mhothaíomar trua, bhailíomar airgead,
Is cuid againn a dhein na páistí a chosaint.
Ach bhí **Auschwitz** ann! Sea, cad eile 'tá le rá?
Ach gur mise is tusa … a lig dó imeacht.

# Tadhg O'Sullivan

## GOODLY BARROW *(extract)*

'Rivers are highways,' wrote Pascal in one of his *Pensées*, 'moving highways that carry us where we wish to go.' Where was it, then, that I wished to go? Or did it matter? Robert Louis Stevenson, who knew many a highway, maintained that travel for travel's sake was enough. 'For my part, I travel not to go anywhere, but to go,' he declared in *Travels with a Donkey*. 'The great affair is to move.' And indeed there is a singular freedom and exhilaration about the open road. But few of us would embark on a journey for the pure pleasure of locomotion. There is usually some destination, some reason for going from here to there, even if it is only the green of far-off hills. The great affair is not so much to move as to be elsewhere.

Mobility is a phenomenon of our times. Whether for business or for pleasure, to broaden the mind or to relax the nerves or simply for a temporary change of environment, enormous numbers of people have themselves transported from one place to another, and back again, at least once a year. No holiday is regarded as complete unless it includes this element of displacement. People willingly abandon their familiar surroundings and subsist for a time elsewhere, often in conditions of purgatorial discomfort, in the belief that they are enjoying themselves. It is not exclusively a twentieth-century phenomenon. Chaucer's pilgrims suffered from the same urge: 'so pricketh hem nature in hir corages, than longon folk to goon on pilgrimages.' But by the time Auden and Isherwood came to write *The Ascent of F.6*, it was very much a part of twentieth-century behaviour:

> ... the fortnight in August or early September,
> The boarding house food, the boarding house faces,

The rain-spoilt picnics in the windswept places;
The camera lost, and the suspicion,
The failure in the putting competition ...

That was in the 1930s. Nowadays it would be the package tour to Benidorm or Torremolinos, or Greek tummy or rapacious Brussels taxi-drivers or getting bilked by a Vienna tax-free shop. Affluence and the jet engine have created a more peripatetic flagellation, but the constant factor is that one's penance is inflicted at some distance from home. Such is the need of urbanized man for a change of scene that people annually return in droves to submit themselves to further tortures, heedless of what happened to them the year before. We all have our dreamlands and our fantasies, and they are indestructible.

Dream and fantasy are the stuff of the romantic imagination, something we share with the great poets. It matters little whether one travels in the physical sense or not: one can set forth on a voyage around one's room; one can go sailing to Byzantium. Even the most prosaic of us preserves a certain balance between reality and illusion, if only in self-defence. 'No man can drink of the whole wine' was how Yeats put it. He himself lived in the restless borderland between reality and dream, and it was his struggle to resolve the conflict between the two that produced his greatest work. He believed in the occult; as a young man he practised magic and learned some quite peculiar lore from people like MacGregor Mathers and that strange Russian lady, Madame Blavatsky. In later life he invented an elaborate and esoteric metaphysical system which it would be easy to dismiss as absurd had it not nourished some of the noblest poetry of our age. He explored many dream countries, one of which was Ireland, an enchanted land peopled by invisible deities. His deep love for the Irish countryside – lake and mountain, stream and strand, yellow pool and old brown thorn tree – was accompanied by a belief, which he shared with the ancient tribal Irish, in the identity of the race with the soil, expressed for instance in *Autobiographies* when he asks: 'Have not all races their first unity from a polytheism which marries them to rock and hill?'

Sean G. Ronan

THE HORROR AND GHOSTLY WRITINGS OF LAFCADIO HEARN
(*extract*)

Living in a world that accepts the supernatural as an integral part of its daily life and having explored the Buddhist theory of Karma in terms of Spencerian evolution, Hearn was convinced that the ghostly is at the very centre and not just at the periphery of human existence. His concern now is with the domain of ghosts. Everything he sets out to recreate is weird or ghostly whether it be horror, beauty or laughter.

He gives us a large number of stories romantic, heroic and horrible, all of them with a fascination of strangeness yet perfectly intelligible to Western readers. They read like the most delicate and modest of translations whether he is translating or not. The tales scattered through his books and almost filling *Kwaidan*, which means strange or weird tales, make up one of the greatest treasures ever found by a translator in an entirely foreign land. Their beauty, splendour, tenderness or horror is not to be denied. His great achievement is harmony of tone with a plain lucid style leaving the reader free to listen to the characters and watch events.

Among the best known of his Japanese tales is 'The Story of Mimi-Nashi-Hoichi' or 'Hoichi-the Earless', the opening piece in *Kwaidan*, which was Hearn's own favourite. A blind biwa player is a renowned reciter of a medieval battle between famous clans. His chanting is so magnificent that even the goblins weep. Trouble begins when Hoichi is led away nighty by a ghostly voice to appease the souls of the ancient warriors. The patron-priest writes down the holy sutra text all over the body of Hoichi – except his ears. That night Hoichi is for the first time free from the ghostly power, but the angry spirit tears off his ears, which boost his professional success all the more!

The artist theme appears again in 'The Boy Who Drew Cats', one of Hearn's few fairy-tales. It is about an acolyte of a village temple who is dismissed because of his excessive fondness for drawing cats on walls, screens and holy scriptures. That night, when he takes shelter at a deserted temple, he cannot resist drawing cats before falling asleep. Ironically, the cats he has drawn save his life from 'a goblin rat bigger than a cow'.

A very beautiful tale with a Tír na nÓg or sort of Rip Van Winkle theme is 'The Dream of a Summer Day' (*Out of the East*). It is the story of Urashima, perhaps the most famous of all Japanese legends. For releasing a turtle sacred to the Dragon God of the Sea, a fisher-boy was brought by the Sea God's daughter to an enchanted island where summer never dies. They married and eventually he insisted on returning to see his parents but it was four hundred years later. Recklessly he broke a promise he made to his flower-wife by opening a lacquered box she gave him. Suddenly, he began to change and fell down lifeless on the sand like Óisín.

This tale relates to another one 'Hi-Mawari' (*Kwaidan*) meaning 'sunflower' which has an Irish setting. 'The dearest and fairest being in his little world' referred to in both stories was his aunt Mrs Catherine Elwood.

The young samurai in 'The Story of Ito Norisuke' (*The Romance of the Milky Way*) represents the archetype of all Hearn's ideal lovers. He is led to wed a beautiful ghost but they are destined to meet only once in ten years. When morning dawns they exchange gifts in remembrance – a little *suzuri* or ink-stone for the *kogai* of his sword. He departs from the ghostly region, dreaming of their reunion ten years ahead. His health gradually fails and he dies just as the tenth year comes around asking that the ink-stone be placed in his coffin.

Other famous tales are 'The Story of O-Tei' (*Kwaidan*) about a girl who is reborn in another human being to be finally wedded to her lonely betrothed, thanks to their mutual pledge; 'Of a Promise Broken' (*A Japanese Miscellany*) where the dead wife's ghost returns as soon as her samurai husband breaks his promise to remain faithful to her memory and tears off the new bride's head; 'The Story of Chūgorō' (*Kottō*) about a poor retainer who dies in love with a beautiful woman at the bridge, actually a great and ugly frog; 'Yuki-Onna' (*Kwaidan*) the Snow Woman who melts into a bright white mist as soon as her human husband reveals their secret; 'The Story of Aoyagi' (*Kwaidan*) about the spirit of a tree which marries a young samurai only to return to its own world; 'Jikininki' (*Kwaidan*) the man-eating goblin who in awful Shape entered the death chamber to devour the corpse and indeed the offerings possibly for dessert! and so forth.

Professor Basil Hall Chamberlain has said that noone could understand Hearn who did not take into account his belief in ghosts. His ghostly tales and legends have indeed earned him an honoured place in the supernatural literary tradition.

Apart from that he stands out not merely as a writer who has revealed an idealized Japan to the Western world but one whose thought and wide range of interests have rendered him universally appealing. His nomadic and mental destinies have been followed with both joy and anguish. A century after his time his aesthetic standards and the charm of his art survive. This shows him to be a man of genius and a very great writer.

Richard Ryan

That ragged
leaking raft held
between sea and sea

its long
forgotten cable melting
into deeper darkness where,

at the root
of it, the slow
sea circles and chews.

Nightly the dark-
ness lands like hands
to mine downward, springing

tiny leaks
till dawn finds
field is bog, bog lake.

Richard Ryan

THE LAKE OF THE WOODS

Winter began with
The birches turning to glass
And the wild geese

Over the lake nightly,
Evacuating in their loud squadrons.
For weeks still there

Were roads, light
And the repeating moons; but
Slowly, through the sunk woods

Snow is climbing toward
The cabins now and
Twice our cemetery

Has opened its
mouth and closed it again.
Nothing lives in the woods

Any longer, only
A crumbling moon and the stars
Above the lake

Collapsing, one by one.
It is getting worse, and
We will survive

As we are able. Out
On the lake a man has chopped
A hole in the ice

To fish through; his

Son is snapping twigs from
The pines, it

Sounds like pistols,
But suddenly there is a fish on the ice.
Daily it worsens

But somehow they know,
The fish and the trees
And the men, that it is temporary,

That some bright
Morning the geese will return
Singing down the

Runways of sunlight and lake water.
We are sure of this,
Or we have no memory,

Any of us, of the ice
Like an iron giant
Stalking the earth, that

Deep beneath the
Snow, the buried bottles
And the wrecked boots, beyond

All further thaw
A lost world of lizards
And leaves lies frozen in stone.

Richard Ryan

MASTER PLAN

I will not travel tonight.
Toward dawn a star
In Andromeda will abruptly

Die, but the world and his wife,
Tonight shrouded in snow
Where they live, will see

Nothing of this, instead will marvel
With drinks through glass
At a slow lace of snow slipping

Down the dark limbs of trees
Or, when that bores them, may
Number together as they drift

Toward sleep the thin
Skins of heat like leaves
Slipping from little hands

And little feet, feeling
Their warm houses with leaves
And snow filling, the children's rooms

Softly into dark drifts
Tilting, will take at dawn
What small comfort they may need

From the high spars
Of trees returning safely
Home on a grey tide and,

Under the trees, a few

Calm stars straying down
Over the rim of the planet

Of the living where each brain
In its pit stirs again
For me only, a waking world

Recollects its purpose
And I – abroad I will go once more,
Savouring my choices

As there, and there again, life
Whistles from a clutch of thorn,
Spawns bone in the humming ponds.

Richard Ryan

No sound but snow
falling, the sunken city

of the world drifting
silently under its crosses.

In far darkness
a siren begins to moan

softly, for this
is the world of the living

and everywhere here
punctual odd clocks are

whirring and striking.
Yes, tonight again it seems

I must climb the dark
spidery stair and again

at the top wait
shivering, staring at nothing.

Thus to return
as now, knowing nothing,

blind with belief
as a dream of winter roses

to find you waiting
in the simple firelight

soundlessly opening
your skin, bringing me in.

Richard Ryan

From my high window I can watch
The freeways coiling on their strange
Stilts to where the city glows
Through rain like a new planet.

Tonight the radio speaks
Of snow and in the waste plots
Below trees stiffen,
Frost wrinkles the pools.

Through high dark air
The apartment buildings,
Like computer panels, begin
Again to transmit their faint signals —

For they are there now, freed one and all
From the far windy towns, the thin
Bright girls compounded of heat,
Movement, and a few portable needs.

But I have no calls to make tonight,
For we are all strangers here
Who have only the night to share —
Stereos, soft lights, and small alarm clocks.

Of our photograph albums, our far
Towns, and our silences we do not speak,
Wisely we have learned to respect
The locked door and unanswered telephone.

I turn from my window and pause a moment
In darkness. My bed and desk
Barely visible, clean paper
Waits in its neat circle of light ...

I wait; and slowly they appear, singly,
Like apparitions. They stand all round me,
On metal bridges and in the wet streets,
Their long hair blowing, and they will not go.

# C.M. Rafferty [Kate Slattery]

## MARMALADE

She had been reading her paper in the booth when she recognised the voice, the clipped inflected accent punching through the air.

Alice, he shouted, Alice! What a lovely surprising!

Alice looked up from her newspaper and nodded.

Well hello, she said, how are you?

He gestured to the seat beside her, was it free?

She moved across and put her newspaper away, of course.

Well, well. How *are* you, he balanced his cup and saucer as he sat, how *are* you?

Alice was fine, fine. And you?

He was okay, he frowned a bit and gestured to the table, had she eaten?

Alice was just having a little breakfast, she pointed at the pastry plates cheerfully, pigging out a bit, she laughed.

They sat in one of the deep red booths to the left of the café, a warm cushion of velvet between them, condensation rolling up in coils from their saturated coats. All around them the noise and clatter of cutlery and china, interrupted across the space by silent women who had left their fur hats on against the cold and were checking their lips for smudges. Steam rose between greetings, men with gleaming umbrellas moved to one side, starched waitresses flitted along the matching tablecloths, pencils behind their ears, 'Gruetzi' and 'Wie geht's', glissando, delivering shining silver jugs and trays of pastries, tiny white porcelain dumpling-pots of jam. Outside the snow was full of yellow puddles and footprints and men in heavy coats leaning like dancers into the wind.

He moved a casual elbow up on the tablecloth and looked in her eyes. Now, he said, settling down, I want to hear *all* about you. Alice began to butter a croissant and smiled, there was nothing to tell really, everything was the same.

You moved house, he said, I heard you moved.

She nodded and scooped up a spoonful of marmalade, that's right, I did.

Still this cravings for your funny orange jam he said, smiling towards her plate. Alice tipped a crumb from the corner of her mouth and laughed.

So where are you living now?

Oh, Alice ran her tongue across her teeth, not far.

Where are you living he persisted, tapping his finger slowly on the table, I want to know *everything*.

Alice smiled and heaped a spoon of blackberry jam on to her croissant. he wagged a conspiratorial finger at her and winked, I think you are exaggeratory with your hidings Alice, and he leaned forward lifting his finger from the table, and tapped her lightly on the nose.

Maybe, she said.

He begged her pardon, straining to hear, his face in a spout of steam.

I said maybe, she repeated, smiling, and turned the pastry plate around.

She suggested he eat something, pushing the plate towards him gingerly, dabbing her lips with the pink serviette. She offered some cheese, fruit. Croissant? Jam?

But he wasn't hungry really, his eyes stayed fixed on her face.

Really?

No, he wasn't hungry he said.

Oh I know I'm a glutton she said, it's just that it's all so delicious.

He laughed and kept his eyes on her.

You always had such lovely hairs, he said and reached a hand towards her, stroking her head. She swallowed a mouthful of coffee and said thank you, and a moment later, I do my best.

He sat back against the padded bench and smiled.

So, he took his hand away and spread it out over the tablecloth, how have you been?

And she had been fine, fine, just fine, she examined the pastries again while he watched her. Fine really, very busy, you know, here and there, this and that. She chose a Danish one, with three concentric swirls of nutmeg and cinnamon.

*Eat* something, please do, she said, I really can't finish it myself.

Fine, he repeated, fine, crinkling his deep grey eyes, fine?

Absolutely, she said, fine.

He pout-sulked against the corner of the booth, he made a pretend face with his eyes, he blew his cheeks out in mock exasperation, *fine.*

How have you been yourself, she wondered?

Actually, he lit a cigarette, searching the stucco work on the ceiling, the patterns on the floor, the faces locked together all around him, actually, he said, removing some tobacco from his tongue, I have been up a bit of bad shape lately.

Really?

Well, yes, actually I have, he snapped his fingers lightly for more coffee.

And where, she ventured, exactly up the bad shape was he?

He leaned over and borrowed an ashtray from the next table, slipping back into his seat. After a moment he shrugged, looking up at her quickly and then casting his eyes around again.

Claudia has left me, he said.

Oh.

She raised her eyebrows and cleaned the edge of her knife against her plate, cutting another piece from her pastry.

Yes, he stubbed the cigarette out, she took her things away and said she was moving to Damascus.

A bit extreme surely, Alice said, the last word muffled by icing.

No. No. She is doing a researcher thesis for arabesques in Islamic architecturals.

Interesting.

Yes, but, my relations with her were faltered anyway, I think she makes this journey as an excuse.

An excuse for what?

She needed some breaks, he waved a listless hand.

Alice pronounced the pastry very delicious and licked her fingers.

You miss her?

He cocked his head to one side and pouted. He thought for a while, looking around and after a few moments he said that he did. Yes. He took some cheese.

Alice nodded.

Some time I am quite isolate in fact he said. The flat is empty. Yes, he rubbed his chin, his voice quiet, I miss her. Alice gathered the crumbs into a corner of her plate and rounded them into a ball, well, the flat *would* be empty if she's gone, she said brightly.

He looked away and shrugged.

After a moment Alice rolled her arm in an exaggerated arc, well goodness me she said laughing, and tapped the face of her watch, is that the time already? She collected her newspaper from the table and began to get ready to leave.

He leaned over the table, ignoring her, and took the tiny porcelain pot of marmalade between his hands. He tipped it over against the light, examining it.

Now *that*, he said, concentrating, is something that has always been a puzzle with me.

Hm? She was already standing up.

This marmalade, he said, holding it towards her, this word.

This is quite typical actually, his nostrils stiffened over the tablecloth, so unnecessary. Why does English have one word for marmalade, and then all the other confections are just jam?

She didn't know but thought the blackberry one was particularly tasty and opened her mouth wide, rolling out her blackened tongue. He waved a hand dismissively and put the marmalade pot back on the table.

Maybe we could have dinner one evening he said. He put his hands in his pockets, leaning back.

Maybe, she said, slipping her arms into her sleeves, fine.

I don't have your number he said, sitting forward again, wait, I'll get a pen and some paper.

Oh that's okay, she slipped the last button of her collar into place, smiling at him as she brushed past, I'll call you.

He watched her make her way to the till, standing in line while it chimed out, ornate, glinting, dappled under the light. She waited for a moment, apologising, searching her purse for change, the right notes, and the chignoned head of the cashier smiled back at her, bowing as she walked to the door.


Suddenly she turned around and looked back at him, beaming from ear to ear. She walked over to the booth and leaned her face over the edge, tossing her scarf around her neck. Isn't it French, she said, tucking her hair into place, I think it's from French.

He looked up at her, puzzled.

It's after Marie Antoinette, she said. She got sick and they made her a special jam from oranges. She cocked her head to one side, 'Marie est malade', you see, marmalade.

She rubbed her fingers into her gloves and smiled at him again, then she was gone.

# Catherine [Kate] Slattery

## MOVING

'Bastard! Bastard!'

Cliona had taken all the biscuits, all that was left of the torn crinkly packet, and a few chewed ends of figroll, glutted onto the table, on her nightdress. Her face had got redder and redder and she rose up on the seat and glared at him.

'Dirty! Dirty word!' she screamed 'I'll tell mother!'

He had pushed her off the chair and they were running round and round the table, screaming, the table shook and shook until the milk splattered all over the papers and chairs and slopped into a puddle.

They stopped running and backed away, one either side of the puddle.

'Mummy says bastard.'

'She does *not*!'

'She does so! She does so! I heard her! She said it to Daddy. She did she did she did!'

'I'll tell! I'll tell!'

She kicked him. He kicked back, and they both fell, howling, about the kitchen floor, soggy and scratched, thrusting crumby, sticky fingers all over each other, each in turn the victim, braced to roar when the other made contact.

Their mother, working in the sitting room next door, heard the noise and came in. In a moment she had them, an arm each, and was dragging them up off the floor.

'Stop it. Both of you. *Now*.'

'Mother he …'

'Cliona!'

The carpet out in the corridor was rolled up and spiders were making their way across the damp floorboards.

'She …'

'Shh! Shh! Come on, upstairs. Up!'

They went up the stairs, along the right hand side, avoiding the boxes on the steps, rubbing along the walls. The carpet on the stairs, too, had been taken up and there was a series of marks, almost like stretch marks where the edges had been; and the patter of the feet made imprints in the dark, shallow dust.

'Stephen. Stephen, please be careful of your head. You'll knock the paintings. Stephen!'

'Ow!'

'Oh go on. Get up!'

The night was cool and fragrant, an end of summer night, breathing. From there, at the top of the house, one could smell sweet peas and meadowgrass, fruit – a kaleidoscope of summer smells weaving their way into each other, and through the house. The end of summer – humming, ticking down in the garden, and inside, shimmering, groping shadows dappling white walls, roaming around them, incredulous.

Ten o'clock already.

'Bed.'

The children were on their knees, smelling of toothpaste, flung across the pillow. The two heads bobbed together –

'There are four corners on my bed ...'

The words were breaking across the room, running along, past each other, into each other; crashing.

'Start it again please.'

She stood by the window, watching them, her arms folded around each other, keeping time with the pat-pat of her hands on her shoulders. When she stopped to gather them into bed her arms were full of the perfume of apricot tart.

'Goodnight mummy.'

In a moment they were both around her neck, hugging her. Cliona jumped down and landed on Stephen's foot.

'Ow! *Bastard!*' he howled.

'*Stephen!*'

She dropped him and stared: he had gone suddenly silent and was shuffling his feet along the floor, blushing.

'Stephen!' she slapped him and bundled them both into bed. 'Don't ever, ever say that nasty word again.'

The door clicked shut and she stood outside it, holding the handle behind her back and breathing low. Oh God, she thought, 'I'm tired.' She left the door and strolled across the landing towards her own room. She opened the door and the room was full of lilac light and easy smells, but it was already beginning to be damp, and would soon be musty. There were suitcases and boxes piled high, half labelled, half-closed. She walked towards the bed, her fingers strolling along the table, chest, lamps. Her feet were sore. Children, oh but they remember the most amazing things. But then, it couldn't be helped. Lord, how things had changed. Over a year ago now, another summer, receding.

It had been the night of the fireworks. A nation celebrating its liberation. At home, tired, he had begun to beat her, beating, thrashing out as hard as he could, and she couldn't move. When he had finally fallen asleep she had managed to stumble down the stairs to reach the telephone, the folds of her dress soggy with blood, and vomit. The next morning, her head swathed in bandages, she had made her way through the antiseptic corridors and taken a bus to a solicitor's office. He was dressed in a crumpled linen suit. A little foreigner sitting behind a pile of documents, he had turned off the fan on his desk when she began to speak. Hordes of flies had come in through the blinds and were buzzing around her head and the solicitor had poured her a drink and asked her to sit down. The Irish, they always loved whiskey, yes? He smiled at her, and as he clinked the ice-cubes into the glass her hand loosened on the arms of the chair, and she relaxed. He had been factual, sympathetic, and by late afternoon had managed to draft divorce proceedings, reassure her. He walked her along the corridor and shook her hand, gesticulating, promising her rights in a myriad of paragraphs and quotes. Women have rights in this country, he told her.

When she got home Cliona and Stephen were still playing in the limetrees, down by the river. She pushed the backdoor open quietly and slipped inside, on tiptoes. Across the drawing room she could see his shadow in the porch, drinking, rocking slowly on the canopy. The floorboards creaked and he turned towards her and stood up.

'Elizabeth?'

He was sobbing. 'Elizabeth ...'

He was inside now too, opposite her, and she backed away.

'My God! Look at you. I am so sorry.'

He was moving towards her slowly, groping, hunched.

She moved toward the backdoor –

'Please. Don't.'

'My God. Elizabeth I was drunk. Look. Look Elizabeth will you look at me please. Elizabeth!'

She was going through the door and she pushed it open, slamming it back against the porch.

'I'm so sorry.'

'Yes. And the last time and the time before that too.' Her hands were clenched by her sides.

'Get out!' she said.

Night after night he had called to her, coming all around the windows, unable to get in. Night after night after night he came back, pleading, contrite. It had gone on too long. She never answered. Then, on a very hot night, he had hacked his way through the porch with a hatchet, reeking of whiskey, screaming that he wanted to kill her. She had run into the children's bedroom, bolted the door, and waited behind it, shivering. All the old photographs had been smashed downstairs, the windows broken. In the morning the solicitor had picked his way through the smashed, crinkling glass and told her it would be alright, she had enough to get a court injunction against him. She had. Yes, it would be done as quickly as possible. By the end of the week it would be granted. Nothing in the house, or in any of their property, anywhere, could be touched by him, taken by him. He was not to approach her, nor her children. The injunction would take effect on the following Monday, at noon.

At nine o'clock on the Monday morning she awoke to the sound of lorries on the driveway. She came downstairs in her dressing gown to see her husband supervise the removal from the front hall. Clocks, pictures, lacquered chests, wedding gifts and honeymoon vases, the piano, the carpets, even her Persian rug, beds, silver, wardrobes, garden chairs, linen, everything. Every single blessed thing. He hadn't worked for nothing, had he. It was his. Everything. And the children? They were hers. There was money for them. Everything. Packed. Gone. She stood on the porch watching the last of it being driven away.

'You bastard' she said, and that was all she could say, over and over. Over and over, and he was gone.

By twelve o'clock Cliona was hanging from her belt, asking where Daddy was. Stephen was sitting on a window ledge, wide-eyed, watching. She spent the whole day there, staring. She couldn't move. Everything. Nothing. Hollow.

Ten days later she had arrived in Ireland, complete with three new suitcases full of clothes, and two tired children. They had taken a bus out to Saggart to the old house, and the children had whispered on the landing and played. They climbed up into the attic and began taking down beds and chairs. Gradually the old house grew habitable and at least it was still summer.

If nothing else it was safe. She set about organising a school for the children and some work for herself. She could still type. Her children were happy and each night, as always, she would open the door of their bedroom, and in a shaft of light, would kiss them. They visited her mother, and after the initial sobbing, week by week she would watch relations give her children tenpences and gasp and nod and tuttut until she believed she would burst. She began to understand that the huge anchor of their various sympathies would eventually weigh her down, and she knew that she couldn't come back. Things had changed. She just couldn't.

The news eventually filtered through, as it always will, that he, too, had come back. She felt a pang, a longing to move on. Out. Somewhere bright. Somewhere away from the drizzle and depression, the never-ending run of wellwished afternoon teas. The children had settled happily into school, they had people who were their own age now, playmates. All through the holidays they chattered on, lapping and wriggling, in tales of secret seven gangs climbing rusty, cobweb towers at midnight hours, discovering secret passages.

At least he didn't come near them. That, they had been spared. She wondered how long it would last, but mainly she just rocked in front of the television and thanked God. She had stopped work early in the summer, and organized the ticket and visa, the sale of things she couldn't send on ahead of her, or take with her.

One evening his brother had come to visit. He ran his finger along the mantlepiece and reminisced about the old times, before they left. The summer parties in Saggart, nobody would miss one! After a while she asked him what he wanted. His brother had been hospitalized, he said, dried out, you know? She knew, it had happened before. He shook his head. He wouldn't be released for some time yet. He had no job, of course, nowhere to live. Of course he could stay with his family for a while, that was only natural after all. Of course. And the children, they would be going back to school soon? Yes. Lovely children, lovely children. Yes. His brother had no objection to them living in the house, they had to settle in somewhere, indeed, indeed. She did know that the house was in his brother's name? She did realise that, in fact, it was his house? And she understood that when he was released …

She stood up very slowly and asked him to leave. His solicitors … She knew, she knew and would he please get out. He left and she slammed the door.

It was morning already, and she was lying on the bed, still in her clothes. The sun had come up, but there was a breeze whipping its way about the house. Cliona and Stephen would soon be moving about, chattering. She got up and began sealing the last of the boxes. She had a shower and changed her clothes, wrapping the old ones and stuffing them into the last available corner in her suitcase. She woke the children and watched them wriggle into their school uniforms for the first time since June. They had grown again over the summer, and would soon be needing new ones. As they packed their books and teddy bears she wandered around the house wrapping the last of the paraphernalia, etchings and sheet music, plastic buckets, china.

The taximan was on time, and she thanked him for it. It was almost dark as they left the house, closing out the door with a hollow bang. The taximan was helpful, and strapped Stephen and the suitcases and boxes into the back of the car with equal energy and good humour. The long grass was already beginning to cover the flower beds, the steps, the windows were bolted shut, some cracked, all silent. There was nothing at all left inside but a series of still shadows, stipple on a broad, white canvas. They drove down the road quickly, Stephen and Cliona waving through the back windows.

'Goodbye our house,' they called, sucking toffees.

She sat in the front of the car with her handbag on her knee, open, checking ticket, passport, lipstick. It was beginning to rain. Soon they had arrived at the gates into the school and the children began hopping up and down excitedly. The avenue was long and narrow, shaded on all sides by long, leafy trees and September smoke, trickling through the evening skyline at each new bend. The building was already full of bright, yellow light. The taxi came to a stop and she got out and took the children's suitcases:

'Remember not to fight. Be good now.'

They clambered around the old oak doorway, ringing madly, shouting.

'Stephen. Cliona. Stop!'

'Oh mummy, mummy!'

They ran at her, leaping up, arms flung around her neck, kissing everything they came in contact with, shrieking.

'Shh! Shh ... shh. You'll come out to see me at Christmas.'

'And we'll go swimming?'

'Yes. We'll all go swimming!'

They had buried their heads in her coat. She hugged them and sat down on her heels. She stood them both in front of her and held their hands, speaking very slowly.

'Now remember' she said, 'remember what you have to tell daddy. Tell him that mummy has gone away. Tell daddy that he can go back to his house in Saggart now. Tell him that.' And she kissed them, and left.

John Swift

CRISP

Light breeze, blue sky, bright light, air dry,
Definition sharp and precise,
A day of contrasts, stark and subtly muted.
Taytoed beech leaves neat against bare branches,
Songs of blackbirds and cries of infants
Against susurration of stream over baby weirs.
Yellowish catkins etched on dark-green ivy.
Thrushes, finches, rumors of bramblings and
woodpeckers,
A broken-gaited chaffinch and, at last,
Wild but suburban, the black-legged,long-beaked egret,
Distant and easily mistakeable unless he moves,
Now hunched, brooding, almost motionless,
Persil-white against gray rock and paler reeds.

Mícheál Tierney

CHERRY TIME

Light is coming from nowhere,
peeping into the murky parts of my room,
The Earth is tilting back towards the sun,
And your smile, your smiles – all of you,
Light up the way to Peace;
Your peace, my peace – world peace;
The frail fleece of harmony
With which the pink Cherry blossoms
Try to check the March of Time.

David Toms

## LANGUAGE LEARNING

Somedays I still can't get
my ø's å's or æ's
to fit my mouth
playing the piece
with the embouchure
of a novice

I end up with cheese
when I wanted to go East

David Toms

MILORG GRUPPE 13132

In every wood there's been a war
the memory stone says so
fallen in the fight for the fatherland

at Sarabråten the sun beats down
the lake unfreezing under the weight
of the six-month snow

a memory mark for the names
the men who died on St. Patrick's Day
eight weeks shy of *syttende mai*

David Toms

The first snow falls
little flecks foreshadow

the death and dying that comes annually
annulling the memory

of summer swimming at Sørenga.
*Samhain* approaches, clock hands wound

back manually
the snow builds and builds

tipping first the hedgerows
before getting set into the ground

steeping sweet treats in tea
*bairín breac*

as light disappears
the land of the midnight sun

beckons instead with endless night
we commuters emerge

from the underground.

## Annie Vivanti

### THE DEVOURERS (extract)

### II

A gentle blue February was slipping out when March tore
in with screaming winds and rushing rains. He pushed the
diffident greenness back, and went whistling rudely across
the lands. The chilly drenched season stood still. One
morning Spring peeped round the corner and dropped a
crocus or two and a primrose or two. She whisked off
again, with the wind after her, but looked in later between
two showers. And suddenly, one day, there she was,
enthroned and garlanded. Frost-spangles melted at her
feet, and the larks rose.

Valeria borrowed Edith's garden-hat, tied it under her
chin with a black ribbon, and went out into the young
sunshine across the fields. Around her was the gloss of
recent green, pushing upwards to the immature blue of the
sky. And Tom, her husband, was dead.

Tom lay in the dark, away from it all, under it all, in the
distant little cemetery of Nervi, where the sea that he loved
shone and danced within a stone's-throw of his folded
hands.

Tom's folded hands! That was all she could see of him
when she closed her eyes and tried to recall him. She could
not remember his face. Try as she would, shutting her eyes
with concentrated will, the well-known features wavered
and slipped away; and nothing remained before her but
those dull white hands as she had seen them last – terrible,
unapproachable hands!

Were those the hands Tom was so particular about and
rather vain of – the hands she had patted and laid her
cheek against? Were those hands – fixed, cessated, all-
relinquishing – the hands that had painted the Italian

landscapes she loved, and the other pictures she hated, because in them all stood Carlotta of Trastevere, rippling-haired, bare, and deliberate? Were those the hands that had rowed her and Uncle Giacomo in the little boat *Luisa* on the Lake Maggiore? – the hands that had grasped hers suddenly at the Madonna del Monte the day she had put on her light blue dress, with the sailor collar and scarlet tie? She seemed to hear him say, with his droll English accent: '*Volete essere sposina mia?*' And she had laughed and answered him in the only two English words she knew, and which he himself had taught her across the table d'hôte: 'Please! Thank you!' Then they had both laughed, until Zio Giacomo had said that the Madonna would punish them.

The Madonna had punished them. She had struck him down in his twenty-sixth year, a few months after they were married, shattering his youth like a bubble of glass. Valeria had heard him, day after day, night after night, coughing his life away in little hard coughs and clearings of his throat; then in racking paroxysms that left him breathless and spent; then in a loose, easy cough that he scarcely noticed. They had gone from Florence, where it was too windy, to Nervi, where it was too hot; from Nice, where it was too noisy, to Airolo, where it was too dull; then, with a rush of hope, with hurried packing of coats and shawls, of paint brushes and colours, of skates and snowshoes, they had journeyed up to Davos. And there the sun shone, and the baby was born; and Tom Avory went skating and bob-sleighing, and gained six pounds in eight weeks.

Then one day an American woman, whose son was dying, said to Valeria: 'It is bad for your baby to stay up here. Send her away, or when she is fifteen she will start coughing too.'

'Send her away!' Yes, the baby must be sent away. The deadly swarm of germs from all the stricken lungs seemed to Valeria to envelope her and her child like a cloud—the cloud of death. She could feel it, see it, taste it. The smell of it was on her pillow at night; the sheets and blankets exhaled it; her food was impregnated with it. She herself was full-grown, and strong and sound; but her baby – her fragile, rose-bud baby – was Tom's child, too! All Tom's brothers and sisters, except one little girl called Edith, who was in England, had died in their adolescence – one in Bournemouth; one in Torquay; one in Cannes; one, Tom's favourite sister, Sally, in Nervi – all fleeing from the death they carried within them. Now Davos had saved Tom. But the baby must be sent away.

They consulted three doctors. One said there was no hurry; another said there was no danger; the third said there was no knowing.

Valeria and Tom determined that they would not take risks. One snowy day they travelled down to Landquart. There Tom was to leave them and return to Davos. But the baby was crying, and Valeria was crying; so Tom jumped into the train after them, and said he would see them as far as Zürich, where Uncle Giacomo would be waiting to take them to Italy.

'Then you will be all right, helpless ones,' he said, putting his arm round them both, as the little train carried them down towards the mists. And he gave his baby-girl a finger to clutch.

But Tom never reached Zürich. What reached Zürich was stern and awful, with limp, falling limbs and blood-stained mouth. The baby cried, and Valeria cried, and crowds and officials gathered round them. But Tom could help his helpless ones no more.

His will was found in his breast-pocket. '*Sposina mia,* with all my worldly goods I thee endow. Take our baby to England. Bury me in Nervi, near Sally. I have been very happy. – TOM.'

These things Valeria Avory remembered as she walked in the soft English sunshine, crying under Edith's garden-hat. When she reached a little bridge across an angry stream, she leaned over the parapet to look at the water, and the borrowed hat fell off and floated away.

Valeria ran down the bank after it, but it was in midstream, resting lightly against a protruding stone. She threw sticks and pebbles at it, and it moved off and sailed on, with one black ribbon, like a thin arm, stretched behind it. Valeria ran along the sloping bank, sliding on slippery grass and wet stones; and the hat quivered and curtseyed away buoyantly on the miniature waves. When the stream elbowed off towards the wood, the hat bobbed along with it, and so did Valeria. As she and the stream and the hat turned the corner, she heard an exclamation of surprise, and, raising her flushed face, she saw a young man, in grey tweeds, fishing on the other side of the water.

The young man said: 'Hang it all! Good-bye, trout!' And Valeria said: 'Can you catch my hat?'

He caught it with great difficulty, holding it with the thick end of his rod, and flattering it towards him with patient manœuvres.

'My trout!' he murmured. 'I had been after that fat fellow for three days.' Then he dragged the large splashing hat out of the water and held it up. 'Here's your hat.' It had never been a beautiful hat; it was a dreary-looking thing that Edith had had much wear out of. It had not the appearance of a hat worth fishing three days for.

'Oh, thank you so much! How shall I reach it?' said Valeria, extending a small muddy hand from her side of the stream.

'I suppose I must bring it across,' said the young man, still holding the dripping adornment at arm's length.

'Oh no!' said Valeria. 'Throw it.'

The young man laughed, and said: 'Don't try to catch! It will give you a cold.' He flung the hat across, and it fell flat and sodden at Valeria's feet.

'Oh dear!' she said, picking it up, with puckered brows, while the black tulle ruffles fell from it, soft and soaking. 'What shall I do with it now? I can't put it on. And I don't think I can carry it, walking along these slippery banks.'

'Well, throw it back again,' said the young man, 'and I'll carry it for you.'

So she threw the heavy melancholy thing at him, and they walked along, with the water between them, smiling at each other. On the bridge they met, and shook hands.

'I am sorry about your fishes,' she said.

'My fishes?' He laughed. 'Oh, never mind them. I am sorry about your hat.' Then, noting the damp ringlets on her forehead and the dimple in her cheek, he added: 'What will you put on when you come to-morrow?'

'To-morrow?' she asked, raising simple eyes.

'Yes; will you?' he said, blushing a little, for he was very young. 'At this time' – he looked at his watch – 'about eleven o'clock?'

Valeria blushed, too – a sudden crimson flush that left her face white and waxen. 'Is it eleven o'clock?' she exclaimed. 'Are you sure?'

'Yes; what is the matter?'

'The baby!' gasped Valeria. 'I had forgotten the baby!' And she turned and ran down the bridge and across the fields, her black gown flying, the wet hat flapping at her side.

She reached home breathless. The nurse was on the verandah, waiting. 'Am I late, Wilson?' she panted.

'Yes, madam,' said the nurse, with tight and acid lips.

'How is baby?' gasped Valeria.

'The baby,' said the woman, gazing at her, sphinx-like and severe, 'is hungry.'

# III

The young man went to fish in the little stream every day, but he only caught his fat trout. The dimpled girl in mourning did not come again. His holiday was ended, and he returned to his rooms in London, but he left a love-letter for Valeria on the bank, pinned to the crumpled black ruffle that had fallen off her hat, and with a stone on it to keep it down.

Valeria found the love-letter. She had stayed indoors a week, repenting. Then Spring and her youth joined hands, and drew her out of doors and across the fields again. She went, blushing and faltering, with a bunch of violets pinned at her belt. No one saw her but a tail-flicking, windy-haired pony in a meadow, who frisked suddenly after her and made her shiver.

Close to the stream her eye caught the tattered black ruffle and the note pinned to it. The young man wrote that his name was Frederick Allen; that he was reading for the Bar and writing for newspapers. He said that she had haunting eyes, and that they would probably never meet again. He wondered whether she had found the baby, and where she had forgotten it, and what baby it was. And she *might* have turned round just once to wave him farewell! He hoped she would not be displeased if he said that he loved her, and would never forget her. Would she tell him her name? Only her name! Please, please! He was hers in utter devotion, FREDERICK.

Valeria went back in a dream and looked up the word 'haunting' in her English-Italian Dictionary. She did not remember his eyes: they were blue, she thought, or perhaps brown. But his face was clear and sunburnt, and his smooth-parted hair was bright when he took off his hat on the bridge.

She thought she would simply return his letter. Then she decided that she would add a few words of rebuke.

Finally one rainy day, when everybody had seemed cross, and Edith had answered rudely, and the baby had screamed for Wilson who was not there, Valeria, with qualms and twinges, took a sheet of paper and wrote her name on it. The paper had a black border. Valeria suddenly fell on her knees and kissed the black border, and prayed that Tom might forgive her. Then she burned it, and went to her baby, who was quarrelling with everything and trying to kill an India-rubber sheep.

Yet one day in April – an April swooning with soft suggestions, urging its own evanescence and the fleeting sweetness of life – Mr. Frederick Allen, in his London lodgings, received two letters instead of one. Hannah, the pert maid who brought them to his room, lingered while he opened them. In the first was a cheque for six guineas from a periodical; in the other was a visiting-card:

VALERIA NINA AVORY.

'Who the dickens ...?' he said, turning the card over. 'Here!' and he threw it across to Hannah. 'Here's a French *modiste*, or something, if you want falals!'

Then, as he had received six guineas when he had only expected four, he shut up his law-book, pinched Hannah's cheek *en passant*, and went out for a day up the river with the man next door.

The card was thrown into the coal-box, and the kitchen-maid burnt it. And that is all.

# Sinead Walsh

## GETTING TO ZERO *(extract)*

As 2014 drew to a close, things were looking up, helped by the end of the six-month rainy season. We started to see a reduction in cases as the various parts of the response, such as community behaviour change, safe burials and the availability of beds, finally came together.

There are different theories on what led to this rapid reduction in case numbers. One global health specialist who volunteered with WHO shared his view with me: 'The outbreak stopped because of what happened in little villages. I suspect chiefs and imams and priests ending the body rinse funerals, and people becoming more hygienic and careful.'

There is no question that communities changing behaviour was critical; no amount of beds and burial teams would have made any difference if communities hadn't fought the disease themselves. But in reality, it is impossible to say for certain how significant each of the different elements was in bringing the outbreak under control – what's certain is that, collectively, they helped reduce transmission dramatically.

After so many months of waiting for the response to improve while the situation got worse, it was amazing to me how quickly the improvements took hold. The last week of November had seen 711 new cases in Sierra Leone but, just four weeks later, the figure was down to 337. There was similarly encouraging news from neighbouring Liberia where cases had been declining every week since mid-November. Guinea's epidemic had never reached the same catastrophic levels as Liberia and Sierra Leone, and tended to fluctuate with no discernible upward or downward trend. It was still persisting and reached 114 cases by the last week of December, although this was a drop from the week before.

So, the picture was largely improving in December. Unfortunately, there was a snag.

The snag was pointed out to us by Mike Ryan, a renowned epidemiologist from the West of Ireland who had worked with WHO in twelve previous Ebola outbreaks and who, with his down-to-earth and jovial nature, could communicate as effectively with President Koroma as he could with a district surveillance officer in Kambia. Mike no longer worked for WHO but, when he arrived in December, he made me realise this was exactly the kind of senior but operational leadership we had been lacking from WHO Geneva.

In one coordination meeting at the NERC, I asked Mike to talk about the period after we would have enough beds, known as the 'getting to zero' phase. 'Ah yes,' he said, with a knowing smile and a shake of his head. 'I hope you're all ready for a bumpy landing.' He went on, 'Lads, you shouldn't think that Ebola case numbers will go straight down the way they went straight up. They will go to a low level alright, but they might stay at that level for months, waxing and waning. It will take a ton more work to get to zero.' There was a moment of depressed silence – we had all assumed when we started to see case numbers dropping that we were nearly at the end of the outbreak. It had seemed logical at the time. Then Sonia from the US bit the bullet and asked Mike to go into detail on what this bumpy landing concept would mean for the response. Mike told us that certain elements, like contact tracing and surveillance, would need to come to the fore and become absolutely top class. 'If you want to get to zero, you can't miss a single contact. Not one.'

Sonia and I exchanged an uneasy glance. We were very aware that contact tracing had been one of the weakest links in the response so far, and it was widely believed that there was still a lot of transmission occurring under the radar. The response was routinely taking swabs from corpses, and 20% of these in Freetown and its surrounding rural areas were testing positive for Ebola. These were people who were not reaching ETUs [Ebola Treatment Units], and if surveillance had been working well, we would have known about them.

Back in the beginning of the response, when resources were completely stretched, the UN Population Fund (UNFPA) had gamely volunteered to lead on contact tracing along with the Ministry. But they didn't have any experience in doing this, as they were an organisation that focussed mostly on reproductive and maternal health. Unlike some organisations who managed to take on new roles effectively, UNFPA never managed to get on top of this critical new responsibility. They carried out a lot of activities, like hiring contact tracers and equipping them with mobile phones, but the supervision needed to ensure that the complex work was done properly was often lacking. I remember raising a concern about UNFPA's ability to lead on contact tracing in a meeting back in July 2014, where I was told by WHO that they should really have been the ones doing it as it was a technical role, but they didn't have the capacity. So, it stayed with UNFPA, remaining a weak link throughout the response.

As the epidemic got worse, the number of cases got so overwhelming that contact tracing became next to impossible anyway. It could take as many as ten staff to monitor the contacts of one Ebola case. Given that, for instance, we had sixty-seven new cases in Port Loko district in the second week of December, that would require up to 670 contact tracers in that district alone. But, as Mike pointed out, there was no way to get to zero without excellent contact tracing. WHO were going to need to step up.

In a similar vein, my recent trips to the north of the country and the conversations I'd been having with WHO colleagues in Freetown had made me realise that international WHO technical staff were now the most urgent need. So I decided to try to help this process along by suggesting to the donor group that we could write a joint letter to the heads of WHO and UNMEER, stressing the need for these additional technical staff to be deployed as soon as possible. The UK and the US both thought it was a good plan, so I drafted the letter with their input and sent it off to the head of UNMEER and the Director-General of WHO on Christmas Eve. I knew that WHO were already moving in the right direction on this, but hoped that this letter might give them an extra push.

It seems it did. One senior UN staffer was not too happy with me though, and cornered me shortly after that at the Radisson: 'Oi!' he said. 'I hear I have you to blame for the fact that I got a call from Margaret Chan on 26 December. As if what I need when I'm trying to have a nice Christmas with my family is the DG saying "How soon can you go to Sierra Leone?"' 'Well, you're here aren't you?' I replied. 'Fait accompli!' All of the various efforts to push this meant that, by end of January, we finally had the full complement of WHO technical staff that we needed to get us through the bumpy landing.

## Mary Whelan

### IRELAND'S CAMPAIGN FOR ELECTION IN 2000 TO THE UNITED NATIONS SECURITY COUNCIL (*extract*)

*Background to our Candidacy*

A successful foreign policy depends on the ability of a state to influence its external environment in order to secure support for its international interests and values. The Irish campaign for election to the Security Council of the United Nations for the biennium 2001–2002 provides a classic illustration of a small country effectively applying its resources to achieve a foreign policy objective. In addition, the way in which the campaign was conducted and its outcome have implications for the future conduct of our international relations. […]

*The Final Weeks*

Towards the end of September, the eventual date of the vote – 10 October 2000 – began to firm up. Rumours had both Norway and Italy claiming very high levels of support. We were also hearing that Italy expected to pick up votes in the second ballot. Our interest was in an early election. There were still a number of countries that had to take a final decision. The remaining weeks would be crucial to maintaining and building support. The period broke down into four distinct sections: the Millennium Summit, the Ministerial Week, the final ten days and election day. […]

*The Final Days*

On 1 October the focus of the campaign narrowed to New York. […]

At 8.00am each day I chaired a co-ordination meeting. Responsibility for lobbying over 180 delegations was divided between the members of the group. We looked at the countries to be targeted that day and considered the issues of concern to them; reports on the previous day's contacts were circulated and any items in need of follow-up identified. The strength of our support was getting clearer. Yet we were continuously told that our competitors were mounting strong campaigns and that they had deep pockets. Specific examples of what this might mean were never provided. Our competitors were visible around the UN building. We became aware that Italy was putting pressure on EU applicant countries to support them. The extent of this pressure became clear in the aftermath of the vote when a newspaper carried a copy of a letter that had been sent from Rome to the capital of one of these countries. The King of Norway returned to New York to host a reception.

It was clear that developing countries wanted us to win. They accepted our arguments on equitable rotation. We were told that there was no need to seek reconfirmation of support, but our interlocutors appreciated the fact that we were not taking them for granted. An unexpected issue, which arose at many of our contacts with other delegations, was the problem that had emerged in the African group. Mauritius was contesting Sudan's claim to be the endorsed candidate of the African group. The US was lobbying hard on behalf of Mauritius and many African states resented this intervention. We avoided taking sides in what was becoming a highly charged contest.

A key issue remained the number of votes that we would have to discount (the lie factor) and the eventual size of the electorate. With 152 votes committed to us and with suggestions from many sources that Norway was in the lead we began to think that we might have to discount 25 per cent of the committed support to arrive at a real assessment. This would give us 114 votes in the first ballot, which would put us in good shape for election. On Sunday 8 October, Michael Hoey, Frank Smyth, Paul Kavanagh and I spent the day at the mission going over each commitment and trying to get a sense of the level of our vote.

The Article 19 issue would not be resolved until the night before the vote. In the end only 173 countries could vote. There were indications that all three candidates believed that they had the support of most of the countries who sought unsuccessfully to have their voting rights restored on 9 October. At the morning coordination meeting on 9 October we discussed the floor plan for election day. Later we walked the ground in the Assembly Hall so that each person would know exactly what had to be done the next day. Arrangements were agreed with Dublin for keeping the Taoiseach and the minister informed of the outcome and alternative press releases prepared to cover either victory or defeat. The mission took a call late on the eve of the vote from a delegation that informed us of its decision to renege on its commitment to Ireland.

*Election Day*

We met at the mission early on 10 October and went over the final preparations. Some staff were tasked with distributing our election day leaflet to each delegation. The leaflet, which highlighted our campaign platform, was printed in each of the official languages of the UN and in Portuguese. We had received the final versions from Dublin only two days previously. The Assembly Hall was divided between a number of 'spotters', whose job was to ensure that there was someone present to cast the vote at the desk of each delegation committed to us. If any committed delegation was not present when the meeting commenced, the spotter was to make contact with the mission concerned – each spotter was armed with a mobile phone and a list of names and numbers. Those who had lobbied during the week were to make contact with their targets in the Assembly Hall to reconfirm, yet again, voting positions. Different scenarios were worked out for lobbying between ballots in the event that one of our competitors was elected before us and further lobbying was required.

The meeting was called to order shortly after 10.00am. Our spotters were in action. There were a number of empty seats, which gradually filled up as tributes were being paid to the recently deceased foreign minister of Dominica. The process of voting is laborious with permanent representatives completing the ballot paper and each then being collected by UN officials and one of three scrutineers. No lobbying was allowed during the voting. As soon as the first ballots were collected we set off again to make contact with supporters to ensure that we could continue to rely on their support in any subsequent ballot.

*Announcement of the Vote*

Forty minutes later the Assembly Hall quietened down as Harri Holkeri, President of the 55th Session of the General Assembly, returned to his seat to announce the outcome of the first ballot. Singapore and Colombia were returned unopposed for Asia and Latin America. The vote for the WEOG [Western European and Others Group] seats was read out:

Total number of countries voting: 173

2/3 majority required for election: 116

Results:     Ireland 130

             Italy 94

             Norway 114

Ireland was elected on the first ballot. It was a wonderful feeling to see Ireland not only win but win so decisively. I went outside to the Indonesian lounge to phone Declan Kelly who was in 10 Downing Street where the Taoiseach and the minister were meeting with their British counterparts. Back in the Assembly Hall papers for the second ballot had been distributed. As soon as these were collected a congratulatory line formed at our delegation. Voting continued throughout the morning until the fourth ballot when Norway reached the quota. The outcome of the vote to fill the African seat was likewise resolved on the fourth ballot with Mauritius defeating Sudan. We adjourned to the delegation lounge for a celebratory drink. The minister phoned from Downing Street.

It took days to come back to earth.

*Reflections and Lessons*

The two years in which I was involved in the Security Council campaign are amongst the most intense and ultimately satisfying periods of my career in the Department of Foreign Affairs. In that period I travelled to Africa, America and Europe on numerous occasions. In addition to seeing and hearing at first hand of the concerns of many states, it was extraordinary to see the regard in which Ireland is held and to appreciate the role of so many people in bringing this about.

It was also gratifying to see how a fairly small and hard-pressed foreign ministry can, through its commitment, skill and teamwork, excel in pursuing its objectives. I felt privileged to work with the small campaign team in Dublin made up of Paul Kavanagh, Julian Clare and Elaine Caul; and with Richard Ryan in New York, who played a central role in our success. Trust and respect for each other's very different skills and styles was to characterise the campaign. The intrepid good humour of our envoys exemplified an attribute that is not perhaps given sufficient recognition in modern management jargon, namely a selfless commitment to public service. The final days of the campaign in New York were exhilarating and great fun. That this was the case reflected the generous spirit with which all those engaged in the campaign worked together.

There are many lessons to be learnt relating to both the formulation and implementation of our foreign policy. The conduct and success of our campaign showed that Ireland has a clear identity to which others relate and that there is a constituency for what we represent internationally. Our history leads many developing countries to identify with us. Our recent economic progress is seen as a role model. The issues with which we are associated – peacekeeping, development and disarmament – give us a modern-day leadership role out of proportion to our size. We are seen as providing a bridge between the needs of developing countries and the concerns of the developed world.

Our foreign service is relatively modest and is likely, even with planned development, to remain relatively small. At the same time the process of EU expansion and integration will demand more and more attention and energy. In this scenario it is important that our wider international role continues to be accorded high priority in the future. We have the ability to act as an initiator of change and a negotiator of choice between those who favour global action to serve their foreign policy concerns and those who prefer alliances of the powerful to secure their interests.

We have a wide international engagement in most spheres of human activity, be it diplomacy, trade or simple people-to-people outreach. Yet our international reputation in the wider world cannot be taken for granted, especially as much of it is based on the contribution made by the Irish diaspora. The presence of two significant elements of that diaspora – Irish emigrants and Irish missionaries – is diminishing. While some of us will continue to travel abroad to work and our aid workers will partly fill the gap in our level of representation in the developing world, neither groups are likely to develop the same depth of knowledge or sense of identification with their host countries as those who left in the past to spend most if not all of their working lives abroad.

A strength of our campaign was our reputation as a country of principle, but one that listens to rather than preaches at others. The listening mode, the lack of arrogance and self-righteousness are characteristics that may not sit well with a newly confident and assertive Ireland. They are, however, essential characteristics of skilful negotiators and for those who seek to build international alliances.

The campaign itself identified ways in which we can, in a cost-effective way, develop our relations with those areas of the world where we are under-represented. It did so by ensuring that we used multilateral encounters to develop contacts across large groups of countries. Post-election, we should continue to use such opportunities to inform our own thinking. Some EU meetings with dialogue partners can seem sterile set-piece occasions. Yet if we look beyond the more formal protocol aspects of these meetings and use them to foster administration-to-administration contacts, we will develop relations that could be of longer-term benefit to us and our interlocutors. Such contacts can be enhanced by the establishment of diplomatic relations on both a residential and non-residential basis in a systematic way.

As a foreign ministry, Iveagh House is perhaps too prone to making unfavourable comparisons between itself and other foreign ministries. The Security Council election showed how networking and teamwork across divisions and functions could increase effectiveness. Additional resources were required but these were fairly modest. The establishment of a small focused unit to strategise and carry forward a clearly defined objective offers a model that has been successfully deployed in the past and of which greater use could be made in future. The campaign also showed that key foreign policy objectives must be made whole-of-government and whole-of-administration objectives. Our embassies were a key resource of our campaign. Properly briefed and tasked, they were highly effective.

At the UN, the East European Group is home to most of the EU applicant countries. Given the proposed enlargement of the EU, the composition of the regional groupings in New York will need to be reviewed in the coming years. As the EU approaches a membership of over twenty states, it needs to find a more coherent way of projecting its identity and interests at the UN. Ireland must be at the centre of that effort.

# Denyse Woods

## WALLPAPER

The letters kept coming. She wrote of Bormio, of winter-white hills and Alpine ridges hanging from the skies, of streets busy with get-there skiers and lithe ski instructors in sausage-skin suits. She described the brittle night air so well that you could smell it off the crinkly stationery. Airmail Light. A traditionalist, then, sending missives in the old style, as though there was no way to communicate other than organizing thoughts into sentences and lives into paragraphs. She had fetched up in Bormio, she explained, a resort huddled in a saucer-like basin with thermal springs, baby slopes and a come-again, go-again population. As a chalet chef, she was learning to deliver tajines that soothed aching limbs and desserts that sweetened the pain of spectacular bruises. She fully intended to be as seasonal as her guests, to move on – or move home? – before the hikers came, and the botanists. Not for her, she insisted, the fresh mountain springs or cow-bell summers.

And yet, soon enough, letters came full of wildflowers and walkers. In summertime, you could loll about in the *terme* without icicles forming on your nose, she joked, and the mirror-eyed ski instructors were replaced by leather-skinned climbers ... But still no lover, for her, although a kind of hope wafted about the pages like the smell of thyme drifting around Bormio's trails. Only passing mention was made of yearning and loneliness, but a wistful eye was sometimes cast back – back to this studio apartment, with its too narrow bench-bed, high on the wall, and its backyard view of urban grit.

All this, in a neat hand. A good hand, easily read, one side only.

Marsha came to crave each new delivery – the bulky envelope with Lombardy stamp and, within, the simple, affectionate greeting, *'Dear You,'* the *'xx'* in parting. It was like having a subscription to a monthly travel mag; and it was soap opera too, with chalet romances and sunburn and tantrums, and change – changing faces, languages, allergies – but the mountains, huddled around her and scratched with ski runs, deep with snow or grey with lack of it, these, she wrote, were ever a wall, encircling.

Marsha pinned each letter to the walls – a scripted wallpaper, encircling, ceiling to floor, door to corner. Words surrounded her, parading stories and trip-tripping across the studio like a caravan across the desert. Within this whirl of writing, she ate and slept, suffered and dreamed, and re-read whichever letter best suited her mood. On a hard day, she liked to wander Bormio's old town in springtime, steeples overhead, cobblestones underfoot, unwinding; a giddy day and she took to the snow, sliding between the conifers on the lonely tracks that had taken perilous tumbles to master. This was what kept her there – in the studio and in Bormio: the inky drift through another person's perspective.

She never wrote back. Sometimes, not often, she wondered who the letters were from and for whom they were intended.

# ABOUT THE AUTHORS

NOTE: *The Irish Foreign Service has been known by various names over the years, beginning as the Department of External Affairs. Here, for clarity, it is referred to by its current name, Department of Foreign Affairs (DFA), or simply, 'the Department'.*

ANNE ANDERSON had a forty-five-year career in the Department (1972–2017). Her first posting at Ambassador level was to the United Nations in Geneva (1995–2001). Thereafter she served as Ireland's Permanent Representative to the European Union, Ambassador to France, Permanent Representative to the United Nations in New York, and Ambassador to the United States. She was the first woman to represent Ireland in each role, and the first woman from any EU member State to serve as Permanent Representative in Brussels. In 2020 she published *Thinking With My Pen*.

DANIEL BINCHY (1899–1989) was a historian and diplomat who joined the Department in 1929, having previously been professor of history at University College Dublin (UCD). In 1929, he was appointed the Irish Free State's first representative in Germany. He had excellent German, having completed a D.Phil. in Munich in the early 1920s, and did much to promote Irish literature and culture in Germany. He returned to UCD in 1932, and later worked at University of Oxford and Dublin Institute for Advanced Studies. He held visiting professorships at Harvard and the University of Wales, and was awarded honorary doctorates from Wales, Rennes, Belfast, National University of Ireland (NUI) and Dublin. *With thanks to The Dictionary of Irish Biography online, a project of the Royal Irish Academy. Extracted from an entry by Thomas Charles-Edwards and Michael Kennedy.*

EAVAN BOLAND (1944–2020) was born in Dublin, the daughter of diplomat Frederick Boland and painter Frances Kelly. She lived in London with her parents in 1950–6, when her father was first Irish Ambassador to the Court of St James. She attended secondary school in Dublin, before graduating from

TCD with a degree in English literature. She taught at universities in Ireland and the USA, and was professor of English at Stanford University from 1996. She received many awards for her poetry, and was married with two children.

EDDIE BRANNIGAN was reared in Coolock, Dublin, and joined the Department in 1995. His first posting abroad was as Consul to Greece, and also covering Cyprus, Serbia, Romania and Albania, from 1998 until 2001. He was Deputy Head of Mission at Ireland's Embassy to Bulgaria (2005–08), and Poland (2008–12), before becoming director at the Press Office of Ireland's Permanent Representation to the EU in Brussels from 2014–19. Recently, he was Head of Mission in Finland over 2019–20, and is due to serve as acting Head of Mission at Ireland's Embassy to Belgium in autumn 2021. He rarely writes, and has lately discovered painting.

MAEVE BRENNAN (1917–93) was a Dublin-born fiction writer and *New Yorker* columnist, where she wrote as the 'Long-Winded Lady'. She moved with her family to the USA in 1934, when her father Robert Brennan (*q.v.*) was appointed secretary of the Irish legation in Washington DC. She attended the American University in Washington and the Catholic University of America before working for a short time in New York Public Library. She was recruited as a copy-writer to *Harper's Bazaar* by fellow Irishwoman Carmel Snow in 1943, before joining the *New Yorker* in 1949. Her column was immensely popular with American readers, but remained almost unknown in Ireland until a late reappraisal of her work in the 1990s, most notably through the research of Professor Angela Bourke. *With thanks to The Dictionary of Irish Biography online, a project of the Royal Irish Academy. Extracted from an entry by Angela Bourke.*

ROBERT BRENNAN (1881–1964), writer and diplomat, was born in Co. Wexford and was active in the Gaelic League and Sinn Féin during the Irish revolutionary period. He was the first secretary of the Dáil Éireann Department of Foreign Affairs in

1921–22, leading the organisation and professionalization of the diplomatic service. Resigning in 1922 in opposition to the Anglo-Irish Treaty, he turned to writing and journalism, publishing two novels and two plays for Dublin's Abbey and Olympia theatres. In 1934 he returned to the diplomatic service as secretary of the Irish legation in Washington DC, where he remained until 1947. On his return to Ireland, he became director of broadcasting at Radio Éireann. His daughter, Maeve Brennan (q.v.) was a noted writer. *With thanks to The Dictionary of Irish Biography online, a project of the Royal Irish Academy. Extracted from an entry by Michael Kennedy.*

JOHN CAMPBELL was born in 1936. With a degree in Classics from TCD and an MA from Yale, he joined the Department in 1961. After serving in Washington during the Kennedy years, and a brief spell in Dublin as European correspondent, he served as Minister in London in 1975–1980. He was Ireland's first Ambassador to Beijing and was subsequently Ambassador to Bonn, the European Community, Paris and the UN. He retired from Lisbon in 2001. Married to Nicole who died in 2001, they had two sons, Marc, a psychiatrist in New York and Jonathan, a lawyer and financier in Vietnam. The author of two privately published novels, he and his second wife Amanda divide their time between the US, Ireland and France.

SIOBHÁN CAMPBELL's fourth collection is *Heat Signature*. Recipient of the Oxford Brookes International Prize 2016, Siobhán has also won awards in the Gregory O'Donoghue, National and Troubadour International poetry competitions as well as the Templar Poetry Prize. With Nessa O'Mahony she edited *Eavan Boland: Inside History*. Widely published, her work is anthologised in *The Forward Book of Poetry* (Faber), *Identity Parade: New British and Irish Poets* (Bloodaxe), *The Field Day Anthology of Irish Literature* (NYU Press) and *The Golden Shovel Anthology: Honouring Gwendolyn Brooks* (UAP). On faculty at The Open University, she researches creative writing practice in post-conflict cultural recovery, working most recently in Lebanon. She is married to diplomat Kevin Conmy (*q.v.*).

KEVIN CONMY joined the Department in 1986 and has served in the Permanent Mission to the UN in New York, as Consul-General in San Francisco, and in Embassies in London and Washington DC. His assignments at headquarters in Dublin have been in Political Division, EU Division and Anglo-Irish Division. He is currently Joint Secretary in Belfast. He is married to Siobhán Campbell (*q.v.*) and they have three children together. He attended the Dublin's Writers Workshop in the 1980s.

RAGNAR DEENEY ALMQVIST (b. 1983) joined the Department in 2008 and has since served on post in Stockholm, Chicago and Washington DC, where he is currently based. The son of a Swedish folklorist and an Irish author, he was born in Dublin and studied at UCD and TCD, where he completed Master's Degrees in Economic Policy and Creative Writing. His short stories have been published in *The Stinging Fly* and broadcast on RTÉ radio. He is married and has two children.

EAMON DELANEY is an author and commentator. He worked in the Department from 1987 to 1995 and was posted to New York to the Consulate as well as the Permanent Mission to the United Nations (1990–93) and briefly to Washington DC. He has published *An Accidental Diplomat*, a memoir of these years, as well as *The Casting of Mr O'Shaugnessy*, a novel, and *Breaking the Mould – A Story of Art and Ireland*, about the career and work of his father, the sculptor Edward Delaney RHA. He is currently creating an oral history project around the British military legacy in Ireland.

DENIS DEVLIN (1908–59) was born in Scotland to Irish parents. The family moved to Dublin in around 1918, where he studied English and French at UCD (1927–9), and law at King's Inns (1928–9). After travelling in Europe in 1930–31, he was awarded an MA in French from UCD. In 1934, he resigned from an academic post at UCD to enter the Department. He held postings in Rome, Geneva, New York, Washington (where he met his wife, Marie Caren Radon), London and Ankara. He began his distinguished literary career with his first volume of poetry in 1930 and became a respected writer, reviewer, and translator. *With thanks to The Dictionary of Irish Biography online, a project of the Royal Irish Academy. Extracted from an entry by J.C.C. Mayes.*

NOEL DORR is a retired Irish diplomat. In the course of his career he served as permanent representative to the UN (1980–83) and Irish representative on the UN Security Council (1981–82); Irish Ambassador to the UK (1983–87); and Secretary General of the Department of Foreign Affairs (1987–95). He was Irish representative on the official-level drafting groups for the EU Treaties of Amsterdam (1996–97) and Nice (2000–01). He has written two books on Ireland and the UN. His most recent book, *Sunningdale: The Search for Peace in Northern Ireland,* was published by the Royal Irish Academy in November 2017. A Member of the Academy, he has an honorary doctorate from NUI Galway. He lives in Dublin with his wife, Caitríona Doran.

BRIAN EARLS (d. 2013) was born in Dublin and studied English to PhD level at UCD. He left a teaching position at Dundalk Institute of Technology to enter the Department in 1973. His overseas postings included Athens, the Council of Europe (Strasbourg), Brussels, Moscow, Warsaw, and Ankara. While in Moscow, he travelled widely, collecting folklore and *anekdoti* (jokes). He took early retirement from the Department to focus on his research on nineteenth-century Irish folk traditions. He read six languages and published on Irish and Russian folklore and literature.

JOE HAYES joined the Department in 1972. He was private secretary to Dr Garret FitzGerald (1973) before postings to Bonn, Moscow and London. He served as Ambassador to China (1995–9), the Czech Republic (2001–05), Denmark

(2006–10) and Singapore from 2010 until his retirement in 2014. Home postings included stints as DFA's Press Officer, director of the Foreign Earnings Unit and Joint Secretary of the North South Ministerial Council in Armagh. From Thurles, he writes occasionally for radio and works with his local theatre group in Tipperary, and is currently Chairperson of the National Council for Special Education.

VALENTIN IREMONGER (1918–91) was born in Dublin. After leaving school, he spent a year at the Abbey School of Acting (1938–9) and was a founding member of the New Theatre Group (1937). He began publishing poetry from the age of 20, and his (then unpublished) collection *Reservations* won the 1945 AE Memorial Prize. In 1946, he entered the civil service, moving to the Department a few years later. He held postings in London, Sweden, Finland, India, Luxembourg, and Portugal. In 1948, he married Abbey actor Sheila Manning, with whom he had five children. Iremonger continued to publish original poetry and English translations of writing in Irish throughout his diplomatic career. *With thanks to The Dictionary of Irish Biography online, a project of the Royal Irish Academy. Extracted from an entry by Bridget Hourican.*

BIDDY JENKINSON now lives on a mountain in Wicklow
– Mount Ararat to a wanderer –
grows potatoes, oats and gooseberries
and writes a poem every year on
lá le Bríde.

NIALL KEOGH accompanied his wife, Elizabeth Keogh, on diplomatic postings to Moscow, Beijing, and Ottawa, where he taught Irish Studies. Niall has a PhD in history from UCC and published *Con Cremin: Ireland's Wartime Diplomat* in 2006. He is currently a teacher in Limerick.

GERARD KEOWN joined the Department in 1996. He has had postings in Vienna and Tokyo, a secondment to the OSCE in Bosnia-Herzegovina and an assignment at the Anglo-Irish

Secretariat. He coordinated the foreign policy review and *The Global Island* statement in 2015, followed by a posting as Ambassador to Poland. He has worked on EU and international issues at the Department of Finance and as UN Director in the Department. He takes up post as Ambassador to the OECD and UNESCO in Paris in autumn 2021. He has published a book and a number of articles on the early years of Irish foreign policy.

MICHAEL LILLIS joined the Department in 1966. As Political Counsellor in Washington DC (1976–79), he negotiated President Carter's Initiative on Northern Ireland of 1977 on behalf of the Irish Government. He was Diplomatic Adviser to the Taoiseach Dr Garret FitzGerald in 1981–2, and as Head of Anglo-Irish Division (1983–85) he was one of the negotiators of the Anglo-Irish Agreement of 1985, proceeding to serve as the first Irish Head of the Anglo-Irish Secretariat, Maryfield, Belfast (1985–7).

IRENE DUFFY LYNCH has also published under the names Irene Christina Lynch and Irene Ní Dhubhthaigh. She was born and raised in Claremorrris, Co. Mayo, studied in Coláiste Muire, Tuar Mhic Éada, Co. Mhaigh Eo, Carysfort Teacher Training College, Dublin, UCD and Trinity College, Washington DC. She is an educator, broadcaster, writer, translator, communications consultant and author of four books. She resides in Dublin and is married to retired diplomat, Joseph Lynch (*q.v.*).

JOSEPH LYNCH is from Oldcastle, Co. Meath and joined the Department in 1968, retiring in 2009. He served as Ambassador in Nigeria (1998–2003) and Switzerland (2003–2007), and was member of the board of Culture Ireland in 2007–2009. He is chairman of the Ireland Saudi Arabia Business Council (ISABC) which he founded in 2011. He was chairman of the Royal Dublin Society's Committee of Arts (2014–17) and member of RDS Council. The French government decorated him with Chevalier de l'Ordre national du Merite in 1999. He is married to Irene Duffy Lynch (*q.v.*).

PIARAS MAC ÉINRÍ is from Dublin. He joined the Department in 1976, with postings in the Permanent Representation to the EEC in Brussels, First Secretary in Beirut and Cultural Attaché in Paris. He took a BA in History and English at UCD, wrote a dissertation at Université Paris III on the emerging 1980s Irish community of Paris and defended his PhD, also on Irish migration, at London Metropolitan University. He taught at the Université d'Orléans from 1986, moving to Cork in 1989. He established UCC's International Office before resuming teaching in 1994 at the Department of Geography.

EÓIN MACWHITE (1923–72) was born in Switzerland, the son of diplomat Michael MacWhite (*qv*) and Danish artist Paula Asta Gruttner Hillerod. He was educated in the USA and Ireland, and graduated from the NUI with a BA in Celtic Studies (1943) and an MA in archaeology (1944). Undertaking further postgraduate study at Edinburgh, Oxford, Madrid, and Rome with the support of an NUI Travelling Studentship, he was awarded a D.Phil. from Madrid in 1947. He resigned from an academic position in UCD to enter the Department in 1947, but continued to publish on history, archaeology, and Russian literature, and was elected Member of the Royal Irish Academy and several international learned societies. He held postings in London, Rome, Berne, Paris, Canberra, and the Netherlands. He married Kathleen Kenny in 1952, and they had six children. *With thanks to The Dictionary of Irish Biography online, a project of the Royal Irish Academy. Extracted from an entry by Michael Kennedy.*

AOIFE MANNIX is a poet and writer from Dublin. Her father, Tony Mannix, was in the Irish Foreign Service from 1969 to 2009. She grew up in Dublin, Ottawa and New York before moving to the UK. She read English and Sociology at TCD and has a PhD in creative writing from Goldsmiths, University of London. She has previously worked as a script editor for the BBC. She is the author of four collections of poetry and a novel. She has been poet in residence for the Royal Shakespeare Company and BBC Radio 4's Saturday Live, amongst others. She has toured internationally with the British Council and performed throughout the UK and Ireland.

BOBBY MCDONAGH is the son of Bob and Róisín McDonagh (*q.v.*), both of whom worked in the Department. He was Ireland's Permanent Representative to the EU (2005–09), Ambassador to the United Kingdom (2009–13), Italy (2013–17), and Malaysia (2000–01). He held several posts at Departmental headquarters in Dublin, including EU Director General (2001–05) and Deputy Secretary General (2017–18), and served in the cabinets of two European Commissioners and was an official of the European Parliament. Since retiring in 2018, he has worked as a consultant and an executive coach, and is a public commentator, mostly on EU issues, publishing regularly in the *Irish Times* and the *Guardian*. He was educated at Gonzaga College Dublin and Balliol College Oxford, where he was President of the Oxford Union. He is married with four daughters and ten grandchildren.

PHILIP MCDONAGH is the son of Bob and Róisín McDonagh (*q.v.*), both of whom worked in the Department. He served as Political Counsellor in London during the build-up to the Good Friday Agreement and as Head of Mission in India, the Holy See, Finland, Russia, and the OSCE, retiring in 2017. He has published poetry collections and a verse drama (*Gondla*). Currently, he is adjunct Professor at Dublin City University and Director of the Centre for Religion, Human Values, and International Relations. He is married to Dr Ana Grenfell McDonagh. They have two daughters.

RÓISÍN MCDONAGH (*née* O'DOHERTY, 1921–88) was born in Philadelphia. She attended UCD where she was the first woman auditor of An Cumann Ghaelach and helped to found the publication *Comhar*. In 1947 she joined the Department as a Third Secretary, one of the first women recruited through open competition. After a posting to Stockholm, she resigned on marriage to another diplomat, Bob McDonagh. She continued to serve the State across their many diplomatic postings, passing in New York in 1988 when he was Ambassador to the UN. Two of their four children were diplomats. *With thanks to Bobby and Philip McDonagh.*

PETER MCIVOR is Ambassador to Lithuania. He was educated at TCD and at Leeds University and joined the Department as Third Secretary in 1982. Since then, in addition to service at HQ, he has served in embassies in Bonn, Tokyo, Budapest and New Delhi and was Ambassador to Estonia from 2010 to 2014. He has published widely on Irish literary and historical subjects, including on the life and achievement of Lafcadio Hearn (1850–1904).

JOSEPHINE MCNEILL (1895–1969) was born in Co. Cork. After taking a degree in French and German at UCD, she became a teacher. She was actively involved in Cumann na mBan during the War of Independence. In 1923, she married James McNeill, high commissioner in London in 1923–8 and governor general of the Irish Free State in 1928–32, becoming a noted hostess in London and Dublin. She published on social, cultural, and economic issues and was a member of the Department's Committee on Cultural Relations. In 1950, she was appointed minister to the Netherlands – Ireland's first female diplomat. Appointments to Sweden, Switzerland and Austria followed. She retired from public life in 1960. *With thanks to The Dictionary of Irish Biography online, a project of the Royal Irish Academy. Extracted from an entry by Michael Kennedy.*

MÁIRE MHAC AN TSAOI [MÁIRE CRUISE O'BRIEN] is an Irish language scholar and poet. She was born in Dublin in 1922, daughter of republican and teacher Margaret Browne and politician Seán MacEntee. She graduated with a BA in French and law from UCD before becoming the first woman recruited to the Department as Third Secretary by open competition in 1947. She was posted to Madrid in 1949, and was part of Ireland's delegation to the UN in 1957–61. She was obliged to resign from the Department on her marriage to Conor Cruise O'Brien (*q.v.*) in 1962. She has published several poetry collections and an autobiography, and is widely considered the greatest living Irish language poet.

DANIEL MULHALL is Ambassador to the United States. His previous Ambassadorial postings were in Kuala Lumpur, Berlin and London, with other diplomatic assignments in New Delhi, Vienna, Brussels (EU) and Edinburgh. Born and brought up in Waterford City, he studied history and literature at University College Cork. He has been awarded Honorary Doctorates by the University of Liverpool and Chatham University (Pittsburgh) and has received the Freedom of the cities of London and Waterford. He has lectured and published widely on Irish history and literature, and is Honorary President of the Yeats Society (Sligo). He is married to Greta and has a daughter, Tara, and a son, Jason.

DANIEL MURRAY has lived in London, South Korea and Paris while accompanying his father, Paul Murray (*q.v.*), on postings. A graduate of Edinburgh University and UCD, he has been an avid writer since primary school. Two of his poems were published in in *Electric Full Stops*, the compilation of winning entries in W.H. Smith's Young Writers' Competition, 1995. He was commended in the same competition in 1998. He channels a passion for Irish history into his blog, *Éireann Ascendant*, and was a commentator on *Cogadh Faoi Cheilt – Scéal an IRB*, a documentary about the Irish Republican Brotherhood.

PAUL MURRAY's book, *A Fantastic Journey: The Life and Literature of Lafcadio Hearn* (1993) won the 1995 Koizumi Yakumo Literary Prize in Japan. *From the Shadow of Dracula: A Life of Bram Stoker*, was published in 2004. He edited *Lafcadio Hearn: Japanese Ghost Stories* for Penguin Classics (2019). Recipient of the Gold Medal of the Ireland Japan Association in 1999, Murray's career in the Irish diplomatic service (1972–2012) included postings as Ambassador to South Korea as well as North Korea, and to the OECD and UNESCO in Paris.

SINÉAD NIC COITIR won the Hennessy First Fiction Award (writing as Sinéad McMahon) in 2003. She holds an MA in Creative Writing from Queen's University, Belfast. She worked in the Department of Foreign Affairs in the 1990s and served in Belfast, San Francisco and New York. She currently works for the Department of the Taoiseach. Her award-winning short story was published in the *Sunday Tribune*, and her poems have been published in 'New Irish Writing' in the *Irish Independent*, *Crannóg*, *Skylight 47*, and on the Poetry 24 website.

HELENA NOLAN joined the Department in 1990 after seven years in the Department of Education and has served in Europe, Asia and Africa. She has an MA in Creative Writing from UCD and is a Patrick Kavanagh Award winner, was Featured Poet in *The Stinging Fly* and one of Poetry Ireland's Introductions Series. Her work has appeared in a range of anthologies and journals, as well as *The Irish Times*, *The Telegraph*, *The Guardian*, *New Irish Writing* and online, and has featured in a number of national and international competitions including Fish, Strokestown and the Hennessy Award. A former Disarmament Director, she completes her term as Irish Ambassador to Belgium in summer 2021 to take up post as Consul General in New York.

CONOR CRUISE O'BRIEN (1917–2008) was a Dublin-born diplomat, politician and writer. A graduate of modern languages from TCD, he joined the Department in 1944. His reputation as a literary critic emerged with a flurry of publications in the late 1940s; his lifetime's bibliography extends to hundreds of articles, essays and creative works. He was posted to Paris in 1955–6, and in 1961 was seconded as representative of the UN secretary general in Katanga, resigning his position later that year. He then held academic positions at the University of Ghana and New York University, before returning to Ireland in 1966 and entering politics and journalism. His daughter, Kate Cruise O'Brien (*q.v.*), and his second wife Máire Mhac an tSaoi (*q.v.*), also feature in this volume. *With thanks to The Dictionary of Irish Biography online, a project of the Royal Irish Academy. Extracted from an entry by Frank Callanan.*

KATE CRUISE O'BRIEN (1948–98), writer and editor, was the Dublin-born daughter of Conor Cruise O'Brien (*q.v.*) and his first wife, Christine Foster. She studied at New York University (where her father was teaching at the time) and at TCD. She was the recipient of a Hennessy Award in 1971 for the story 'Henry Died' and a Rooney Prize for her first book, *A Gift Horse* (1978). Her second book, *The Homesick Garden*, was published in 1991. She worked as an editor with Poolbeg Press from 1995, before her untimely passing in 1998. *With thanks to The Dictionary of Irish Biography online, a project of the Royal Irish Academy. Extracted from an entry by Bridget Hourican.*

Rugadh GEARÓID Ó CLÉRIGH i mBaile Átha Cliath Oíche Nollag 1930. Fuair sé bunús a chuid Gaeilge i gCoill Chluana Gabhann, i measc na ndaoine i gCorca Dhuibhne, agus i gColáiste Ollscoile Chorcaí mar ar bronnadh céim BA sna seanchlasaicí air i 1952. Fuair sé céim LLB i gColáiste Ollscoile Bhaile Átha Cliath i 1956, bliain ar dearnadh abhcóide in Óstaí an Rí de. Chaith sé daichead bliain ag obair sa Roinn Gnóthaí Eachtracha. I measc a phostálacha thar lear tá Chicago, Bostún, Nua-Eabhrac, an Hág, Liobáin, an Spáinn, an Bheilg, agus an Eilvéis. Scar sé leis an státseirbhís i 1996, agus rinne sé céim M.Phil. sa tSean-Ghaeilge i gColáiste na Trínóide. Phós sé Máire Ní Bhriain i 1957 agus tá beirt leanaí acu.

EIMAR (ULTAN) O'DUFFY (1893–1935) was born in Dublin and was educated at Stonyhurst, England, before studying dentistry at UCD, where he edited the student magazine, *St Stephens*. He joined the Irish Republican Brotherhood and the

Irish Volunteers, and was a main contributor to the *Irish Volunteer* newspaper. He left teaching to join the Department, but in 1925 left Ireland to work as a journalist in England and Paris. He was a dramatist, novelist, and satirist. He died in Surrey in 1935. He was survived by his wife Kathleen Cruise O'Brien and their two children, Brian and Rosalind. *With thanks to The Dictionary of Irish Biography online, a project of the Royal Irish Academy. Extracted from an entry by James H. Murphy.*

UNA O'DWYER trained and worked as a physicist before joining the Department on the occasion of Ireland's accession to the EEC in 1973. Most of her career has involved working with EU Institutions, firstly as a diplomat, and from 1990 as a Principal Advisor in the Secretariat-General of the European Commission, coordinating legislative decision-making and interinstitutional relations through all the Treaty changes from the Single European Act to the Lisbon Treaty. Her diplomatic postings were to London and the Permanent Representation in Brussels, and her Dublin-based activities included Press and Information, Political Cooperation, and Development Aid.

JACKIE O'HALLORAN BERNSTEIN joined the Department in 1987. After postings in Buenos Aires, Vienna, and New York, she is currently Ireland's Ambassador to Argentina, Bolivia, Paraguay, and Uruguay. From 2014 to 2018 she worked in Disarmament and was a member of Ireland's award-winning negotiating team at the UN Conference which adopted the Treaty on the Prohibition of Nuclear Weapons. She has a lifelong interest in equality issues and in Latin America. She is married to Dr Gustavo Bernstein and has two children. She has an MA in history from UCD.

SEÁN Ó RIAIN is currently Deputy Head of Mission of the Irish Embassy and Permanent Representation to the International Organisations in Vienna. He joined the Department of Foreign Affairs in 1978 and has served in Vienna, Canberra,

Warsaw, Berlin, and the Permanent Representation to the EU in Brussels, in addition to an eight-year term as a seconded national expert in the European Commission. His PhD thesis, from TCD, deals with language planning in Ireland and Québec, and he is particularly interested in strengthening a European identity in harmony with national identities. Married to Natalie Vernick, from France, his two daughters, Aisling and Ciara, are native Irish speakers.

TADHG O'SULLIVAN (1927–99) was born in Co. Galway and studied at University College Galway, where he was active in the local theatre scene and was president of the Inter-University Association of Gaelic Societies. He joined the Department as a Third Secretary in 1949. His overseas postings included Brussels, Berne, the UN, Nigeria, Vienna, Washington, the USSR, and Paris. After retiring in 1991, he was active in the French branch of the International Fund for Ireland. He was married with four children.

SEAN G. RONAN (1924–2000) was born in Cork and studied at UCD. He transferred from the Department of Finance to Foreign Affairs in 1949 and went on to serve at missions in New York, the Council of Europe, Chicago, the UN (New York), Bonn, the European Commission (Brussels), Athens, Tel Aviv, and Tokyo. He made important contributions to UN policy on Northern Ireland in 1969–72, and developed a long-standing interest in Japanese history and culture, becoming an expert on the life and work of Anglo-Irish Greek writer Lafcadio Hearn. *With thanks to The Dictionary of Irish Biography online, a project of the Royal Irish Academy. Extracted from an entry by Gerry McElroy.*

RICHARD RYAN was born in Dublin in 1946. After studying at UCD (BA 1967, MA in Anglo-Irish Literature 1971), he lectured in American universities in 1970–73, before joining the Department. During his posting in London (1983–9) he contributed to the negotiation of the 1985 Anglo-Irish Agreement and its follow-up. He was Ambassador to Korea,

Spain, Algeria, Tunisia, the Netherlands, the Organization for the Prohibition of Chemical Weapons (The Hague), the Czech Republic and Ukraine, and in 1998–2005 was Ambassador to the UN in New York. He represented Ireland on the UN Security Council in 2001–2 and presided over the Council following the events of 11 September 2001.

KATE SLATTERY (1958–2006), the only daughter of Brud and Nora Slattery, grew up competing with her four brothers in Lahinch, Co. Clare. She was educated at FCJ Convent, Limerick, and Lester Pearson College, Vancouver Island, before graduating BA (Hons) from TCD in 1980. She completed an MA in Creative Writing at the University of East Anglia in 1992. Kate joined the Department as a Third Secretary in 1981 and served in Dublin, Brussels, Bern, and Washington before returning to Dublin as Deputy Head of Protocol. She was an adventurous traveller and was fluent in several languages. A friend of Seamus Heaney and Brendan Kennelly, she could dream with poets, be meticulous with politicians and enjoyed playing golf, especially at Lahinch. Sadly, Kate died in 2006, just weeks after her appointment as Irish Ambassador to the OECD in Paris. *With thanks to Michael Slattery*.

JOHN SWIFT joined the Department in 1963. He served abroad in New York and Ottawa, and later as Counsellor and Deputy Permanent Representative to the EU in Brussels, Permanent Representative to the UN in Geneva, and as Ambassador in The Hague and Nicosia. His posts at home included spells as Press and Information Officer, in Anglo-Irish Section and as head of the Development Co-operation, Bilateral Trade/Foreign Earnings, EU and Economic Divisions. He has published numerous articles, essays and book reviews, mainly on historical, political and social subjects, in *Administration*, the *Dublin Review of Books*, *Studies* and elsewhere.

MÍCHEÁL TIERNEY has published poetry and is author of a one-act play, *Sometimes*. His translation from the French of the play *A Family Resemblance* was produced at the Dublin Fringe Festival in 2004. He has performed in the Druid Theatre, the Gate Theatre Dublin, The Royal Court Theatre, Taibhdhearc na Gaillimhe and the Kennedy Centre for the Performing Arts in Washington DC, as well as broadcast performances on TG4 and RTÉ radio and television. In autumn 2021 he takes up post as Deputy Head of Mission at the Irish Embassy in Paris.

DAVID TOMS is Finance and Community Support Officer at Embassy Oslo. Originally from Waterford, he holds a PhD in History from UCC, and his writing has appeared in *The TLS, Poetry Ireland Review, Stinging Fly, Banshee* and elsewhere. His most recent book is *Northly* (Turas Press, 2019).

ANNIE VIVANTI (1866–1942) was born in London to an Italian-German couple, and was raised in Italy, England, Switzerland, and the USA. Her first poetry collection, *Lirica* (1890) won critical acclaim, and was followed by a succession of novels, theatrical works, short stories, and travel accounts in Italian and English. In 1902, she married John Smith Chartres (1862–1927) who quit the British civil service in 1921 to become Dáil Éireann envoy to Berlin. In 1919, Vivanti assisted the Irish delegation to Versailles, writing journalistic pieces to gain international recognition for the new republic.

SINEAD WALSH is Climate Director of the Department of Foreign Affairs, having joined the Department in 2009. She was a Senior Fellow at the Harvard Humanitarian Initiative in 2016–17 while co-writing *Getting to Zero: A Doctor and a Diplomat on the Ebola Frontline* with Oliver Johnson. She previously served as Ambassador of Ireland to Sierra Leone and Liberia and EU Ambassador to South Sudan. Before joining the Department, she spent ten years in the NGO sector, predominantly with Concern Worldwide. She has a BA from Harvard University, an MSc in development studies from UCD, and a PhD in social policy from LSE.

MARY WHELAN joined the Department in 1973, having taken degrees at UCD and NUI. She spent a year with Voluntary Service Overseas in Northern Nigeria. During her career she served in the Department's Anglo-Irish, Trade, Political and Corporate Services Divisions in Dublin, and was posted to Washington DC, the Permanent Mission in Geneva in 1985–1990, and Ambassador to the Netherlands and to Austria. She was Director of Ireland's successful Campaign for Election to the UN Security Council in 2000. She retired in 2016.

DENYSE WOODS (who also publishes as Denyse Devlin) is an Irish writer and the author of six novels, including the critically-acclaimed *Overnight to Innsbruck*, *Of Sea and Sand*, and *The Catalpa Tree*. Daughter of Irish diplomat Gerard Woods, she was born in Boston and grew up abroad. Her peripatetic childhood strongly influenced her work. Amongst numerous honours, she has been awarded an Arts Council Literature Bursary and residencies in Shanghai, Liznjan, Paris and a one-off residency in Hemingway's studio in Key West. She is currently Writer in Residence at Cork County Council. Her work has been translated into six languages and her short stories and articles have been published in various journals, newspapers and magazines.

SOURCE ACKNOWLEDGEMENTS

*The editors and publisher gratefully acknowledge permission to reproduce copyright material in this book.*

Anne Anderson, from *Thinking With My Pen* (2020). Reprinted by permission of the author.

Daniel Binchy, 'Adolf Hitler' from *Studies: An Irish Quarterly Review*, 22: 85 (1933), pp. 29–47. Reprinted by permission of *Studies: An Irish Quarterly Review*.

Eavan Boland, 'Eviction' from *The Historians* by Eavan Boland. Copyright © 2020 by Eavan Boland. Used by permission of W. W. Norton & Company, Inc. and Carcanet Press.

Eavan Boland, from *Object Lessons: The Life of the Woman and the Poet in Our Time* by Eavan Boland. Copyright © 1995 by Eavan Boland. Used by permission of W. W. Norton & Company, Inc. and Carcanet Press.

Eavan Boland, 'Quarantine'. Copyright © 2005, 2001 by Eavan Boland, from *New Collected Poems* by Eavan Boland. Used by permission of W. W. Norton & Company, Inc. and Carcanet Press.

Eavan Boland, 'The Singers' from *In a Time of Violence* by Eavan Boland. Copyright © 1994 by Eavan Boland. Used by permission of W. W. Norton & Company, Inc. and Carcanet Press.

Eddie Brannigan, *Rebel Rabble Rubble* (1991). Reprinted by permission of the author and RTÉ Archives.

Maeve Brennan, 'A Daydream' from *The Long-Winded Lady: Notes from The New Yorker* (Counterpoint, 1997), pp. 264–5. Reprinted by permission of the Maeve Brennan estate.

Maeve Brennan, 'The Children Are Very Quiet When They Are Away' from *The Rose Garden* (Counterpoint, 2000), pp. 279–82. Reprinted by permission of the Maeve Brennan estate.

Robert Brennan, from *Ireland Standing Firm: My Wartime Mission in Washington* (University College Dublin Press, 2002), pp. 44–7. Reprinted by permission of UCD Press.

John Campbell, 'Finnish Winter' from *Mountain Troubadour* (Poetry Society of Vermont, 2008). Reprinted by permission of the author.

John Campbell, 'Harmony' and 'Snow' from *Mountain Troubadour* (Poetry Society of Vermont, 2012). Reprinted by permission of the author.

Siobhán Campbell, 'Call of the Corncrake' and 'Why Islanders Don't Kiss Hello' from *Heat Signature* (Seren, 2016). Reprinted by permission of the author and Seren.

Siobhán Campbell, 'When All This Is Over' from *Cross-Talk* (Seren, 2009). Reprinted by permission of the author and Seren.

Kevin Conmy, 'Caribbean' and 'First Dance' from *Between the Circus and the Sewer* (Dublin Writers' Workshop, 1988). Reprinted by permission of the author.

Ragnar Deeney Almqvist, 'The Statue Artist' from *The Stinging Fly*, 11:2 (Winter 2008–09). Reprinted by permission of the author.

Eamon Delaney, from *The Casting of Mr O'Shaughnessy* (New Island, 1995), pp. 101–09. Reprinted by permission of the author and New Island.

Denis Devlin, from *Lough Derg and Other Poems* (Reynall & Hitchcock, 1946). Reprinted by permission of The Dedalus

Press (www.dedaluspress.com), acting in good faith on behalf of the poet's estate.

Noel Dorr, from *Ireland at the United Nations: Memories of the Early Years* (Institute of Public Administration, 2010), pp. 62–87. Reprinted by permission of the author and the IPA.

Brian Earls, from 'The Sea of Anecdotes' in *Dublin Review of Books*, December 2010 (http://www.drb.ie/essays/the-sea-of-anecdotes). Reprinted by permission of *DRB*.

Joe Hayes, 'Chernobyl' from *Sunday Miscellany*, RTÉ Radio 1, 28 April 2019. Reprinted by permission of the author and RTÉ Archives.

Valentin Iremonger, from *Horan's Field: And Other Reservations* (The Dolmen Press, 1972). Reprinted by permission of the Iremonger estate.

Biddy Jenkinson, 'I Múrascaill Saronikós Tólos' from *Sceilg na Scál* (Coiscéim, 2017). Reprinted by permission of the author.

Biddy Jenkinson, 'Iníon Léinn i bPáras' from *Amhras Neimhe* (Coiscéim, 1997). Reprinted by permission of the author.

Biddy Jenkinson, 'Sráideanna Sarajevo' from *Oíche Bhealtaine* (Coiscéim, 2005). Reprinted by permission of the author.

Niall Keogh, from *Con Cremin: Ireland's Wartime Diplomat* (Mercier Press, 2006). Reprinted by permission of the author and Mercier Press.

Gerard Keown, from *First of the Small Nations: The Beginnings of Irish Foreign Policy in the Interwar Years, 1919–1932* (Oxford University Press, 2016), pp. 173–5 and pp. 186–9. Reprinted by permission of the author and Oxford University Press.

Michael Lillis, from 'Riddled with Light' in *Dublin Review of Books*, 2009 (https://www.drb.ie/essays/riddled-with-light). Reprinted by permission of the author and *DRB*.

P.D. Linín [Róisín O'Doherty, later McDonagh], from *Maidhc sa Danmhairg* (Sáirséal agus Dill, 1968), pp. 7–17. Reprinted by permission of the author's estate.

Irene Christina Lynch, *Beyond Faith and Adventure: Irish Missionaries in Nigeria Tell Their Extraordinary Story* (ICDL, 2006), pp. 123–31. Reprinted by permission of the author.

Irene Duffy Lynch, 'Réamhrá' *Titeann Rudaí as a Chéile le Chinua Achebe*, Irene Duffy Lynch a d'aistrigh (Coiscéim, 2018), pp. 7–11. Reprinted by permission of the author.

Joseph Lynch, from *Caherdaniel 2018* (Caherdaniel Parish, 2017). Reprinted by permission of the publisher and author.

Piaras Mac Éinrí, from *Britain and Ireland: Lives Entwined*, vol. 1 (British Council Ireland, 2005). Reprinted by permission of the author and British Council Ireland.

Eóin Mac White, 'Thomas Moore and Poland' from *Proceedings of the Royal Irish Academy*, 72C (1972), pp. 49–62. Reprinted by permission of the Royal Irish Academy.

Aoife Mannix, 'A Night Out in Taipei' from *Turn The Clocks Upside Down* (Tall Lighthouse, 2008). Reprinted by permission of the author.

Aoife Mannix, 'Halloween in Stockholm' from *The Elephant in the Corner* (Tall Lighthouse, 2005). Reprinted by permission of the author.

Aoife Mannix, 'The Last Borrower', 'Searched' from *Cocktails from the Ceiling* (Tall Lighthouse, 2013). Reprinted by permission of the author.

Bobby McDonagh, from *Original Sin in a Brave New World: An Account of the Negotiation of the Treaty of Amsterdam* (Institute of International and European Affairs, 1998), pp. 45–50. Reprinted by permission of the author and IIEA.

Philip McDonagh, 'A Visit to Loker Hospice Cemetery' from *Carraroe in Saxony* (The Dedalus Press, 2003). Reprinted by permission of the author and The Dedalus Press, www.dedaluspress.com.

Philip McDonagh, 'The Mausoleum of the Samanids' from Mary O'Connor (ed.), *Head Over Heels: Central Asia Through the Eyes of Foreigners* (Dara Foundation, 2013). Reprinted by permission of the author and Dara Foundation.

Peter McIvor, from *Studies: An Irish Quarterly Review*, 98:390 (2009), p. 196. Reprinted by permission of the author and *Studies: An Irish Quarterly Review*.

Josephine McNeill, 'Mochí Lal 's Mochí Rája' from *Finnsgéalta ó India* (Comhlucht Oideachas na hÉireann, 1932), pp. 33–6.

Máire Mhac an tSaoi, 'A Fhir Dar Fhulaingeas', 'Jack', 'Slán', 'Suantraí Ghráinne' from *Margadh na Saoire* (Sáirséal agus Dill, 1956). Reprinted by permission of the author.

Máire Mhac an tSaoi, 'Ar Thriall do Dhuine Áirithe Chun na hAifrice', 'Codladh an Ghaiscígh', 'Sea Never Dry' from *Codladh an Ghaiscígh* (Sáirséal agus Dill, 1973). Reprinted by permission of the author.

Máire Cruise O'Brien, from *The Same Age as the State* (The O'Brien Press, 2003), pp. 214–16. Reprinted by permission of the author.

Daniel Mulhall, from *A New Day Dawning: A Portrait of Ireland in 1900* (The Collins Press, 1999), pp. 18–23. Reprinted by permission of the author.

Daniel Murray, from *Electric Full Stops: Award-Winning Entries from the 1995 W.H. Smith Young Writers' Competition* (Macmillan Children's Books, 1996). Reprinted by permission of the author.

Paul Murray, from *From the Shadow of Dracula: A Life of Bram Stoker* (Jonathan Cape, 2004), pp. 177–9. Reprinted by permission of the author.

Sinéad Nic Coitir, from *The Sunday Tribune*, May 2003. Reprinted by permission of the author.

Helena Nolan, 'At First Sight' from *The Irish Times*, 12 April 2014. Reprinted by permission of the author and *The Irish Times*.

Helena Nolan, 'The Bone House' from *The Stinging Fly*, 20:2 (Winter 2011–12). Reprinted by permission of the author.

Helena Nolan, 'Making the Bed' and 'Things You Learned in the Ice Hotel' from Ruth Bolger (ed.), *Anthology, Baby* (University College Dublin, 2008). Reprinted by permission of the author.

Helena Nolan, 'Platform' from *The Stinging Fly*, 8:2 (Winter 2007–08). Reprinted by permission of the author.

Conor Cruise O'Brien, 'Carey Bloom' from *Atlantic* 202 (November 1958), pp. 142–6, 148. Reprinted by permission of the Cruise O'Brien estate.

Conor Cruise O'Brien, 'King Herod Explains' from *Herod: Reflections on Political Violence* (Hutchinson and Co., 1978), p. 187. Reprinted by permission of the Cruise O'Brien estate.

Kate Cruise O'Brien, from *A Gift Horse and Other Stories* (Poolbeg, 1978), pp. 10–14. Reprinted by permission of the author's estate.

Gearóid Ó Clérigh, from *Barra Trá: Clocha Cainteacha agus Glac Feamainne Filíochta* (Coiscéim, 2015), pp. 137–42. Reprinted by permission of the author.

Eimar O'Duffy, from *King Goshawk and the Birds* (Macmillan and Co., 1926), pp. 137–8, 139, 141, 146, 148–50, 239–41.

Eimar O'Duffy, from *Asses in Clover* (Puntam, 1933), pp. 251–3.

Una O'Dwyer, translation of J.L. de Belder, *Ship's Diary* (J.L. de Belder Stichting, 1986). Reprinted by permission of the translator.

Jacqueline O'Halloran Bernstein, from *Histopía Magazine* (Buenos Aires, April 2020). English translation provided by the author. Reprinted by permission of *Histopía Magazine*.

Seán Ó Riain, from *Feasta* (March 2001), p. 4. Reprinted by permission of *Feasta* and the author.

T.F. O'Sullivan, from *Goodly Barrow: A Voyage on an Irish River* (Ward River Press, 1983; reprinted The Lilliput Press, 2001), pp. 22–4. Reprinted by permission of The Lilliput Press.

Sean G. Ronan, from *Irish Writing on Lafcadio Hearn and Japan: Writer, Journalist and Teacher* (Global Oriental, 1997), pp. 140–53. Reprinted by permission of Brill.

Richard Ryan, 'Ireland', 'The Lake of the Woods', 'Midnight', 'Winter in Minneapolis' from *Ravenswood* (The Dolmen Press, 1973). Reprinted by permission of the author.

Richard Ryan, 'Master Plan' from *The London Magazine* (April–May 2016). Reprinted by permission of *The London Magazine* and the author.

Kate Slattery, 'Marmalade' from Malcolm Bradbury and

1920s
Eimar O'Duffy, *King Goshawk and the Birds* (1926)

1930s
Josephine McNeill, *Finnsgéalta ó India* (1932)
Daniel Binchy, 'Adolf Hitler' (1933)
Eimar O'Duffy, *Asses in Clover* (1933)

1940s
Denis Devlin, *Lough Derg and Other Poems* (1946)

1950s
Robert Brennan, *Ireland Standing Firm* (1958)
Máire Mhac an tSaoi, *Margadh na Saoire* (1956)
Conor Cruise O'Brien, 'Carey Bloom' (1958)

1960s
P.D. Linín [Róisín O'Doherty, later McDonagh] *Maidhc sa Danmhairg*
(1968)

1970s
Valentin Iremonger, *Horan's Field and Other Reservations* (1972)
Eóin Mac White, 'Thomas Moore and Poland' (1972)
Máire Mhac an tSaoi, *Codladh an Ghaiscígh* (1973)
Richard Ryan, *Ravenswood* (1973)
Maeve Brennan, 'A Daydream' (1976)
Conor Cruise O'Brien, *Herod: Reflections on Political Violence* (1978)
Kate Cruise O'Brien, *A Gift Horse and Other Stories* (1978)
Kate Slattery, 'Moving' (1979)

1980s
Tadhg O'Sullivan, *Goodly Barrow: A Voyage on an Irish River* (1983)
Una O'Dwyer, translation of J.L. de Belder, *Ship's Diary* (1986)
Kevin Conmy, 'Caribbean' and 'First Dance' (1988)

1990s
Mícheál Tierney, 'Cherry Time' (1991)
Eddie Brannigan, *Rebel Rabble Rubble* (1993)
Kate Slattery, 'Marmalade' (1993)

Eavan Boland, *In a Time of Violence* (1994)

Eavan Boland, *Object Lessons: The Life of the Woman and the Poet in Our Time* (1995)

Eamon Delaney, *The Casting of Mr O'Shaughnessy* (1995)

Daniel Murray, 'Sloane Square' (1996)

Biddy Jenkinson, *Amhras Neimhe* (1997)

Sean G. Ronan (ed.), *Irish Writing on Lafcadio Hearn and Japan: Writer, Journalist and Teacher* (1997)

Bobby McDonagh, *Original Sin in a Brave New World: An Account of the Negotiation of the Treaty of Amsterdam* (1998)

Daniel Mulhall, *A New Day Dawning: A Portrait of Ireland in 1900* (1999)


2000s

Seán Ó Riain, 'Don Ghiúdach a d'Imigh' (2001)

Mary Whelan, 'Ireland's Campaign for Election in 2000 to the United Nations Security Council' (2002)

Philip McDonagh, *Carraroe in Saxony* (2003)

Máire Cruise O'Brien, *The Same Age as the State* (2003)

Sinéad Nic Coitir, 'Flick' (2003)

Paul Murray, *From the Shadow of Dracula: A Life of Bram Stoker* (2004)

Biddy Jenkinson, *Oíche Bhealtaine* (2005)

Piaras Mac Éinrí, 'Britain and Ireland – Lives Entwined' (2005)

Aoife Mannix, *The Elephant in the Corner* (2005)

Niall Keogh, *Con Cremin: Ireland's Wartime Diplomat* (2006)

Irene Christina Lynch [Irene Duffy Lynch], *Beyond Faith and Adventure: Irish Missionaries in Nigeria Tell Their Extraordinary Story* (2006)

Helena Nolan, 'Platform' (2007)

Ragnar Deeney Almqvist, 'The Statue Artist' (2008)

John Campbell, 'Finnish Winter' (2008)

Aoife Mannix, *Turn The Clocks Upside Down* (2008)

Helena Nolan, 'Making the Bed' and 'Things You Learned in the Ice Hotel' (2008)

Siobhán Campbell, *Cross-Talk* (2009)

Michael Lillis, 'Riddled with Light' (2009)

Peter McIvor, 'St. Stephen's Day, 20th August 2006' and 'The Most of It' (2009)


2010s

Eavan Boland, *Code* (2001)

Noel Dorr, *Ireland at the United Nations: Memories of the Early Years* (2010)

Brian Earls, 'The Sea of Anecdotes' (2010)

Helena Nolan, 'The Bone House' (2011)

John Swift, 'Crisp' (2011)

John Campbell, 'Harmony' and 'Snow' (2012)

Aoife Mannix, *Cocktails from the Ceiling* (2013)

Philip McDonagh, 'The Mausoleum of the Samanids' (2013)

Helena Nolan, 'At First Sight' (2014)

Gearóid Ó Clérigh, *Barra Trá: Clocha Cainteacha agus Glac Feamainne Filíochta* (2015)

Siobhán Campbell, *Heat Signature* (2016)

Gerard Keown, *First of the Small Nations: The Beginnings of Irish Foreign Policy in the Interwar Years, 1919–1932* (2016)

Richard Ryan, 'Master Plan' (2016)

Denyse Woods, 'Wallpaper' (2016)

Biddy Jenkinson, *Sceilg na Scál* (2017)

Joseph Lynch, 'Skelligs' (2017)

Irene Duffy Lynch, *Titeann Rudaí as a Chéile* le Chinua Achebe, Irene Duffy Lynch a d'aistrigh (2018)

Sinead Walsh [with Oliver Johnson], *Getting to Zero: A Doctor and a Diplomat on the Ebola Frontline* (2018)

Joe Hayes, 'Chernobyl' (2019)

David Toms, *Northly* (2019)


2020

Anne Anderson, *Thinking With My Pen* (2020)

Eavan Boland, *The Historians* (2020)

Jacqueline O'Halloran Bernstein, 'Eliza Lynch in Context' (2020)

NOTE: *The following select bibliography is intended to indicate the range of writing published by Irish diplomats and their families since the Department's foundation in 1919. It is not intended to be exhaustive.*

*Conor Cruise O'Brien was particularly prolific and for that reason, his publications are not listed here. The editors refer the reader to the comprehensive bibliography in Donald Harman Akenson,* Conor: A Biography of Conor Cruise O'Brien. Volume II Anthology *(McGill-Queen's University Press, 1994), pp. 311–51.*

ANNE ANDERSON
*Thinking With My Pen* (2020).
'1916 to 2016: Reflections' in *American Journal of Irish Studies*, 14 (2017), pp. 165–76.
'UN Elections: Power, Influence, Reputation' in Sam Daws and Natalie Samarsinghe (eds), *The United Nations*, Vol. 3 (Sage, 2015, 8 Vols).

DANIEL BINCHY
*Corpus Iuris Hibernici* (Dublin Institute for Advanced Studies, 1978).
(ed.), *Scéla Cano Meic Gartnáin* (Dublin Institute for Advanced Studies, 1963).
(ed.), *Críth Gablach* (Dublin Institute for Advanced Studies, 1941).
'Adolf Hitler' in *Studies: An Irish Quarterly Review*, 22:85 (1933), pp 29–47.

EAVAN BOLAND
*The Historians* (W.W. Norton/Carcanet Press, 2020).
*Domestic Violence* (W.W. Norton/Carcanet Press, 2007).
*Code* (W.W. Norton/Carcanet Press, 2001).
*Object Lessons: The Life of the Woman and the Poet in Our Time* (W.W. Norton/Carcanet Press, 1995).
*In a Time of Violence* (W.W. Norton/Carcanet Press, 1994).
*Outside History* (W.W. Norton/Carcanet Press, 1990).

EDDIE BRANNIGAN
*Rebel Rabble Rubble*, RTÉ Radio 1 (1993).

MAEVE BRENNAN
*The Rose Garden: Short Stories* (Counterpoint, 2000).

*The Visitor* (Counterpoint, 2000).

*The Springs of Affection: Stories of Dublin* (Houghton Mifflin, 1997).

*Christmas Eve* (Scribner, 1974).

*In and Out of Never-Never Land* (Scribner, 1969).

*The Long-Winded Lady: Notes from the New Yorker* (Morrow, 1969).


ROBERT BRENNAN

*Ireland Standing Firm: My Wartime Mission in Washington* (University College Dublin Press, 2002).

*Goodnight, Mr O'Donnell: A Play in Three Acts* (James Duffy, 1951).

*The Man Who Walked Like a Dancer* (Rich and Cowan, 1951).

*Allegiance* (Browne and Nolan, 1950).

*The Toledo Dagger* (John Hamilton Ltd, 1926).

[as R. Selskar Kearney], *The False Fingertip* (Maunsel and Roberts, 1921).


JOHN CAMPBELL

'Harmony' and 'Snow' in *Mountain Troubadour* (Poetry Society of Vermont, 2012).

'Finnish Winter' in *Mountain Troubadour* (Poetry Society of Vermont, 2008).


SIOBHÁN CAMPBELL

and Nessa O'Mahony (eds), *Eavan Boland: Inside History* (Arlen House, 2017).

*Heat Signature* (Seren, 2016).

*Cross-Talk* (Seren, 2009).

*Darwin Among the Machines* (Rack Press, 2009).

*That Water Speaks in Tongues* (Templar, 2008).

*The Cold that Burns* (Blackstaff Press, 2000).


KEVIN CONMY

'First Dance' and 'Caribbean' in *Between the Circus and the Sewer* (Dublin Writers' Workshop, 1988).


RAGNAR DEENEY ALMQVIST

'The Statue Artist' in *The Stinging Fly*, 11:2 (Winter 2008–09), pp. 59–64.

'The Dog's Life' in Declan Meade (ed.), *Let's Be Alone Together: An Anthology of New Short Stories* (The Stinging Fly Press, 2008).

'Dents' in *Incorrigibly Plural* (Lemon Soap Press, 2006).

EAMON DELANEY
*The Casting of Mr O'Shaughnessy* (New Island, 1995).

DENIS DEVLIN
*Collected Poems* (Dolmen Press, 1964).
*Selected Poems* (Holt, Rinehart and Winston, [1963]).
*Memoirs of a Turcoman Diplomat* (Botteghe Oscure, [1959]).
*The Heavenly Foreigner: A Poem* (Dolmen Press, 1950).
*Lough Derg and Other Poems* (Reynal and Hitchcock, 1946).
*Intercessions: Poems* (Europa, 1937).

NOEL DORR
'Fermenting the Irish Dimension – Sunningdale to the Anglo-Irish Agreement' in *Inside Accounts, Volume I: The Irish Government and Peace in Northern Ireland, from Sunningdale to the Good Friday Agreement: Interviews by Graham Spencer* (Manchester University Press, 2020).
'The Years Before Good Friday: Some Personal Memories' in Mary Daly (ed.), *Brokering the Good Friday Agreement: The Untold Story* (Royal Irish Academy, 2019).
'A Year in the Life: Behind the Scenes in Irish Foreign Affairs 1972' in *Irish Studies in International Affairs*, 28 (2017), pp. 133–45.
*Sunningdale: The Search for Peace in Northern Ireland* (Royal Irish Academy, 2017).
*A Small State at the Top Table: Memories of Ireland on the UN Security Council, 1981–82* (Institute of Public Administration, 2011).
*Ireland at the United Nations: Memories of the Early Years* (Institute of Public Administration, 2010).

BRIAN EARLS
'"The Mother in Hoors and Robbers": Bram Stoker as Urban Folklorist' in *Béaloideas*, 80 (2012), pp. 205–19.
'Sea of Anecdotes' in *Dublin Review of Books*, December 2010 (http://www.drb.ie/essays/ the-sea-of-anecdotes).
'Supernatural Legends in Nineteenth-Century Irish Writing' in *Béaloideas*, 60/61 (1992/1993), pp. 93–144.
'Bulls, Blunders and Bloothers: An Examination of the Irish Bull' in *Béaloideas*, 56 (1988), pp. 1–92.
'A Note on Seanachas Amhlaoibh í Luínse' in *Béaloideas*, 52 (1984), pp. 9–34.

JOE HAYES

'Chernobyl', *Sunday Miscellany*, RTÉ Radio 1 (28 April 2019).

VALENTIN IREMONGER
*Sandymount, Dublin: New and Selected Poems* (Dedalus Press, 1988).
*Horan's Field: And Other Reservations* (Dolmen Press, 1972).
*Irish Short Stories* (Faber and Faber, 1960).
*Poems* (Envoy, 1950).
*Reservations* (Envoy, 1950).

BIDDY JENKINSON
*Táinrith* (Coiscéim, 2013).
*Duinnín ar an Sceilg* (Coiscéim, 2011).
*Bleachtaire* (Coiscéim, 2008).
*Gussaí Gaimbín* (Coiscéim, 2007).
*Oíche Bhealtaine* (Coiscém, 2005).
*Mis* (Coiscéim, 2001).
*Amhras Neimhe* (Coiscéim, 1997).
*Dán an hUidhre* (Coiscéim, 1991).
*Uiscí Beatha* (Coiscéim, 1988).
*Baisteadh Gintlí* (Coiscéim, 1987).

NIALL KEOGH
*Con Cremin: Ireland's Wartime Diplomat* (Mercier Press, 2006).

GERARD KEOWN
'Knocking on the Door: The Irish Presence at the Paris Peace Conference of 1919' in *Irish Studies in International Affairs*, 30 (2019), pp. 41–57.
'Global Horizons?' in Tommy Graham and Brian Hanley (eds), *The Irish Revolution 1919–21: A Global History* (Wordwell Books, 2019).
*First of the Small Nations: The Beginnings of Irish Foreign Policy in the Interwar Years, 1919–1932* (Oxford University Press, 2016).
'Creating the Template? Reflections on the First Decade of Irish Diplomacy and the United States' in *Irish Studies in International Affairs*, 26 (2015), pp. 137–45.
'Representing the Global Island: A Review of Ireland's Foreign Policy' in *Hague Journal of Diplomacy*, 10:4 (2015), pp. 430–39.
'Seán Lester: Journalist, Revolutionary, Diplomat, Statesman' in *Irish Studies in International Affairs*, 23 (2012), pp. 143–54.

Michael Lillis

'Riddled with Light' in *Dublin Review of Books*, 2009 (https://drb.ie/essays/riddled-with-light).

and Fanning, Ronan, *The Lives of Eliza Lynch: Scandal and Courage* (Gill and Macmillan, 2009).


Irene Duffy Lynch

(transl.), *Titeann Rudaí as a Chéile* [Chinua Achebe, *Things Fall Apart*] (Coiscéim, 2018).

(transl.), *Idir Mhná* [John McGahern, *Amongst Women*] (Coiscéim, 2015).


Irene Christina Lynch

*Beyond Faith and Adventure: Irish Missionaries in Nigeria tell their Extraordinary Story* (ICDL, 2006).

*Treasures of Our Elders: Words of Wisdom* (Academy Press, 2002).


Joseph Lynch

'Skelligs' in *Caherdaniel 2018* (Caherdaniel Parish, 2017).


Piaras Mac Éinrí

'Famine and the Irish Diaspora' in John Crowley, William J. Smyth, and Mike Murphy (eds), *Atlas of the Great Irish Famine* (Cork University Press, 2012).

'If I Wanted to Go There I Wouldn't Start from Here: Re-imagining a Multi-Ethnic Nation' in Michael G. Cronin, Peadar Kirby, and Debbie Ging (eds), *Transforming Ireland: Challenges, Critiques, Resources* (Manchester University Press, 2009).

and Coakley, Liam, 'Migration to Rural Ireland: A North Cork Case Study' in Birgit Jentsch (ed), *International Migration and Rural Areas* (Ashgate, 2009).

'Britain and Ireland – Lives Entwined' in *Britain and Ireland: Lives Entwined*, vol. 1 (British Council Ireland, 2005), pp. 33–45.


Eóin MacWhite

'Thomas Moore and Poland' in *Proceedings of the Royal Irish Academy*, 72C (1972), pp. 49–62.

'Vladimir Pecherin, 1807–1885: The First Chaplain of the Mater Hospital, Dublin, and the First Russian Political Émigré' in *Studies: An Irish Quarterly Reviews*, 60:236 (1971), pp. 295–310 and *Studies: An Irish Quarterly Review*, 61: 241 (1972), pp. 23–40.

'A Russian Pamphlet on Ireland by Count Markieviecz' in *Irish University Review*, 1:1 (1970), pp. 98–110.

'A New View on Irish Bronze Age Rock-Scribings' in *Journal of the Royal Society of Antiquaries of Ireland*, 76:2 (1946), pp. 59–80.


AOIFE MANNIX

*The Horizons of Doubt* (Peters Edition, 2019).

*The Walking Shadows* (Peters Edition, 2018).

*A Half Darkness* (Peters Edition, 2016).

*Cocktails from the Ceiling* (Tall Lighthouse, 2013).

*Turn the Clocks Upside Down* (Tall Lighthouse, 2008).

*The Elephant in the Corner* (Tall Lighthouse, 2005).


BOBBY MCDONAGH

*Irish Friends and Friends of Ireland: London Speeches 2009–2013* (Institute of International and European Affairs, 2014).

*Original Sin in a Brave New World: The Paradox of Europe: An Account of the Negotiation of the Treaty of Amsterdam* (Institute of International and European Affairs, 1998).


PHILIP MCDONAGH

*Crime and Punishment* (Arlen House, 2017).

*Gondla, or the Salvation of the Wolves* (Arlen House, 2016).

'Mausoleum of the Samanids' in Mary O'Connor (ed.), *Head Over Heels: Central Asia Through the Eyes of Foreigners* (Dara Foundation, 2013).

*Pesnya, Kotoruyu Pela Ivolga* (Rudomino, 2011).

*The Song the Oriole Sang* (Dedalus Press, 2010).

*Memories of an Ionian Diplomat* (Ravi Dayal, 2004).

*Carraroe in Saxony* (Dedalus Press, 2003).


RÓISÍN MCDONAGH (*née* O'DOHERTY)

[as P.D. Linín], *Maidhc sa Danmhairg* (Sáirséal agus Dill, 1968).

*Maidhc Bleachtaire* (Sáirséal agus Dill, 1961).

*Maidhc Abú* (Sáirséal agus Dill, 1960).


PETER MCIVOR

'St. Stephen's Day, 20 August 2006' and 'The Most of It' in *Studies: An Irish Quarterly Review*, 98:390 (2009), p. 196.

'Floating Lanterns' in *Life and Learning*, supplement to *Transactions of the Asiatic Society of Japan*, 20 (2006), pp. 6–9.

'"The Real Birthday of New Japan": Lafcadio Hearn's 'After the War" in *Transactions of the Asiatic Society of Japan*, 19 (2005), pp. 11–20.

'"Love and Loyalty of a Nation": Lafcadio Hearn's "Yuko: A Reminiscence"' in *Transactions of the Asiatic Society of Japan*, 17 (2002–3), pp. 59–68.

'"Feeling Not Reason": Lafcadio Hearn Considers Percival Lowell' in *Transactions of the Asiatic Society of Japan*, 15 (2000), pp 47–58.

JOSEPHINE MCNEILL

*Finnsgéalta ó India* (Comhlucht Oideachais na hEireann, 1932).

MÁIRE MHAC AN TSAOI

*Scéal Ghearóid Iarla* (Leabhar Breac, 2012).

*An Paróiste Míorúilteach: Rogha Dánta* (O'Brien, 2011).

[as Máire Cruise O'Brien], *The Same Age as the State: The Autobiography of Máire Cruise O'Brien* (O'Brien, 2003).

*An Galar Dubhach* (Sáirséal Ó Marcaigh, 1980).

*Codladh an Ghaiscígh: agus Véarsaí Eile* (Sáirséal agus Dill, 1973).

*Margadh na Saoire: Bailiúchán Véarsaí* (Sáirséal agus Dill, 1956).

DANIEL MULHALL

'An Enduring Connection: Ties that Bind Will Survive the Digital Age' in Terry Golway (ed.), *Being New York, Being Irish: Reflections on Twenty-Five Years of Irish America and New York University's Glucksman Ireland House* (Irish Academic Press, 2018).

and Biagini, Eugenio (eds.), *The Shaping of Modern Ireland: A Centenary Assessment* (Irish Academic Press, 2016).

'Yeats, Swift, and Ireland's Contested Eighteenth Century' in Kirsten Juhas, Patrick Müller and Mascha Hansen (eds), *'The First Wit of his Age': Essays on Swift and his Contemporaries* (Peter Lang, 2013).

'The Passing of a Millennium' in Eoin Brady (ed.), *The Quiet Quarter: An Anthology of Irish Writing* (New Island, 2004).

*A New Day Dawning: A Portrait of Ireland in 1900* (Collins Press, 1999).

DANIEL MURRAY

'In the Presence of His Enemies: The Controversy of James Dalton, May 1920' in *History Studies*, 16 (2015), pp. 51–60.

Binchy, Aaron, Quigley, Amye, and Maguire, Betty, 'Blood, Sweat and Books: Putting One of Ireland's Little Known Literary Collections On-Line' in *An Leabharlann: The Irish Library*, 21:2 (2012), pp. 15–19.

'Sloane Square' and 'Deadly Fans' in *Electric Full Stops: Award Winning Entries from the 1995 W.H. Smith Young Writers' Competition* (Macmillan Children's Books, 1996).


PAUL MURRAY

(ed.), *Lafcadio Hearn: Japanese Ghost Stories* (Penguin Classics, 2019).

*From the Shadow of Dracula: A Life of Bram Stoker* (Jonathan Cape, 2004).

'Lafcadio Hearn's Interpretation of Japan' and 'Lafcadio Hearn and the Irish Tradition' in Sean G. Ronan (ed.), *Irish Writing on Lafcadio Hearn and Japan* (Global Oriental, 1997).

*A Fantastic Journey: The Life and Literature of Lafcadio Hearn* (Japan Library, 1993).


SINÉAD NIC COITIR

'After Persephone' in *The Lion Tamer Dreams of Office Work: An Anthology of Poetry by the Hibernian Writers* (Alba Publishing, 2015).

'On Reading the Glossary on the *Lichens of Ireland* Website' in *Crannóg*, Feb. 2014.

[as Sinead Cotter] 'Funfair Washed out to Sea in Hurricane Sandy', Poetry24 website, 3 Nov. 2012.

'The Same Sea', 'Not an Arrow, but an Axe' and 'The Heart Can't Bear Lying', *Irish Independent*, 5 May 2012.

'Flick', *Sunday Tribune*, May 2003.


HELENA NOLAN

'Benediction' in *Abridged 0_40 Take Me Home* (2015); 'Shades' in *Abridged 0_13 Mara* (2014); 'The Glass-Blower's Apprentice' in *Abridged 0_23 Desire and Dust* (2012); 'A Question of Colour' in *Abridged 0_21 Magnolia* (2010), available at abridged.one.

'The Man Who Fell to Earth' (18 Oct. 2012),'The Real Meeting on the Turret Stairs' (26 May 2012), 'Leaving for Gliese' (3 May 2012), Poetry 24 website.

[as Hannah Nolan], 'The Kissing Bubble', *Irish Times*, 29 Dec. 2011.

'1984 Revisited' (2010), 'oranges, window, snow' (2009), 'First Kiss' (2008) in *The Stinging Fly*.

'Shaping' in *The Moth*, 4 (Spring 2011).

'Men and Monsters', *The Guardian*, 24 May 2010.

'A Hare's Nest' in Declan Meade (ed.), *Let's Be Alone Together: An Anthology of New Short Stories* (The Stinging Fly Press, 2008), pp. 139–44.

'Second Hand Evening' and 'Split Ends' in Yvonne Cullen (ed.), *All Good Things Begin: New Irish Writing* (Off Centre Publishing, 2006).

KATE CRUISE O'BRIEN
*The Homesick Garden* (Poolbeg, 1991).
*A Gift Horse* (Poolbeg, 1978).

GEARÓID Ó CLÉRIGH
*Barra Trá: Clocha Cainteacha agus Glac Feamainne Filíochta* (Coiscéim, 2015).
*Duilleoga le Gaoith: Aon agus Leathchéad Soinéad Gaelach agus Aguisíní* (Coiscéim, 2014).
*Seán-Anna agus Shenanigans na Staire: Turas Feasa i gCéin is i gCóngar ar Lorg Aigne na mBan is na Bhfilí* (Coiscéim, 2012).
*Dingle-Y-Whoosh!: Nó, Cad a Dhéanfa Muid Feasta Gan Gaeltacht?* (Coiscéim, 2008).
*An Ghaeilge: A Feidhm Feasta agus i gCónaí* (Coiscéim, 2004).
*Creach Coigríche agus Cnuas Cois Trá* (Coiscéim, 2003).

EIMAR O'DUFFY
*Asses in Clover* (Putnam's, 1933).
*Life and Money: Being a Critical Examination of the Principles and Practice of Orthodox Economics* (Putnam's, 1932).
*The Bird Cage: A Mystery Novel* (Geoffrey Bles, 1932).
*The Secret Enemy* (Geoffrey Bles, 1932).
*The Spacious Adventures of the Man in the Street* (Macmillan, 1928).
*King Goshawk and the Birds* (Macmillan, 1926).

UNA O'DWYER
'La Dynamique Historique des Relations Interinstitutionelles' in *Revue du Droit de l'Union Européenne*, 3 (2010), pp. 487–526.
(transl.), *Ship's Diary* [by J.L. de Belder] (J.L. de Belder Stichting, 1986).

JACQUELINE O'HALLORAN BERNSTEIN
'Eliza Lynch in Context' in *Histopía Magazine*, April 2020.
'The NPT at 50' in *Arms Control Today*, April 2018.

SEÁN Ó RIAIN
'Don Ghiúdach a d'Imigh' in *Feasta* (March 2001), p. 4.

T ADHG O'S ULLIVAN
*Goodly Barrow: A Voyage on an Irish River* (Ward River Press, 1983).

S EAN G. R ONAN
ed., *Irish Writing on Lafcadio Hearn and Japan* (Global Oriental, 1997).
and Koizumi, Toki, *Lafcadio Hearn: (Koizumi Yakumo): His Life, Work
and Irish Background* (Ireland Japan Association, 1991).

R ICHARD R YAN
*Ravenswood* (Dolmen Press, 1973).
*Poetry Introductions: 2* (Faber & Faber, 1972).
*Ledges* (Dolmen Press, 1970).

K ATE S LATTERY
[as C.M. Rafferty], 'Marmalade' in Malcolm Bradbury and Andrew
Motion (eds), *New Writing Two* (Minerva, 1993), pp. 322–6.
[as C.M. Rafferty], 'Mary Cleary Ate My Orange' in *Leaves on the
Line: New Fiction* (University of East Anglia, 1992), pp. 198–202.
[as Catherine Slattery], 'Crochet', *The Irish Press*, 17 Nov. 1979.
[as Catherine Slattery], 'Moving' in *The Wall Reader and Other Stories*
(Arlen House, 1979), pp. 46–53.

J OHN S WIFT
'Crisp' in *Studies: An Irish Quarterly Review*, 100:398 (2011), p. 192.
'Human Rights 1948–1998' in *Studies: An Irish Quarterly Review*,
87:348 (1998), pp. 406–14.

M ÍCHEÁL T IERNEY
'Cherry Time', *Criterion* (NUI Galway, 1991).

D AVID T OMS
*Northly* (Turas Press, 2019).
and Curran, Conor (eds), *New Perspectives on Association Football in
Irish History* (Routledge, 2018).
and Nygård, Maren, *dikt / actions osl / ondon* (Smithereens Press,
2017).
*Soccer in Munster: A Social History, 1877–1937* (Cork University Press,
2015).

ANNIE VIVANTI

*Fosca, Sorella di Messalina* (A. Mondadori, 1922).

*Naja Tripudians* (R. Bemporad, 1920).

*Zingaresca* (R. Quintieri, 1918).

*Vae Victis!* (R. Quintieri, 1917).

*Marie Tarnowska* (W. Heinemann/Century Co., 1915).

*The Devourers* (W. Heinemann/Putnam, 1910).


SINEAD WALSH [with Oliver Johnston]

*Getting to Zero: A Doctor and a Diplomat on the Ebola Frontline* (Zed Books, 2018).

and Mulhern, Emma, 'A Step in the Rights' Direction: Advocacy, Negotiation, and Money as Tools for Realising the Right to Education for Pregnant Girls in Sierra Leone during Ebola' in David A. Schwartz, Julienne Ngoundoung Anoko, and Sharon A. Abramowitz (eds), *Pregnant in the Time of Ebola: Women and their Children in the 2013–2015 West African Epidemic* (Springer Nature, 2018), pp. 319–416.

'Obstacles to NGOs' Accountability to Intended Beneficiaries: The Case of ActionAid' in *Development in Practice*, 26:6 (2016), pp. 706–18.


MARY WHELAN

*Negotiating the International Health Regulations: Global Health Programme Working Paper no. 1* (Geneva: The Graduate Institute Global Health Programme, 2008).

'Ireland's Campaign for Election in 2000 to the United Nations Security Council' in *Administration*, 50:1 (2002), pp. 3–40.


DENYSE WOODS

*Of Sea and Sand* (Hoopoe, 2018).

[as Denyse Devlin] *If Not Now …* (Penguin Ireland, 2008).

[as Denyse Devlin] *Hopscotch* (Penguin Ireland, 2006).

*Like Nowhere Else* (Penguin Ireland, 2005).

[as Denyse Devlin] *The Catalpa Tree* (Penguin Ireland, 2004).

*Overnight to Innsbruck* (Lilliput Press, 2002).